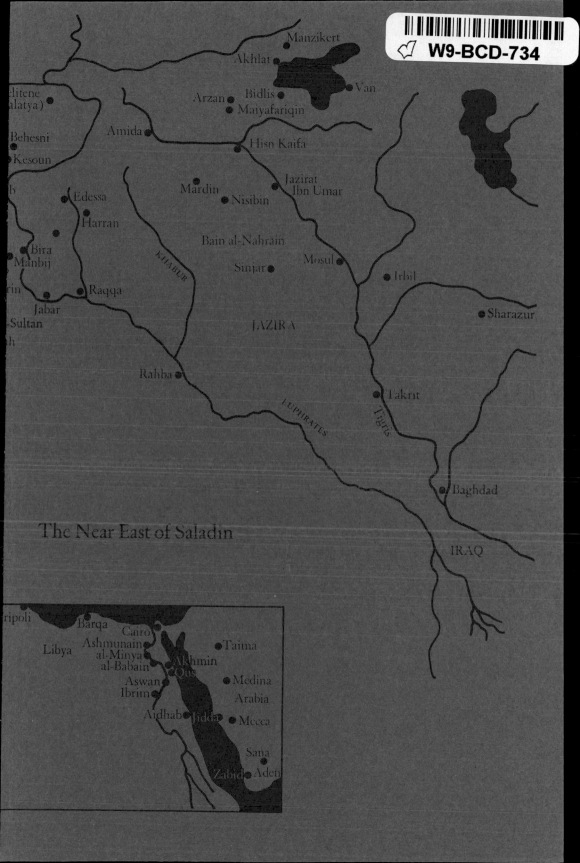

Manzikert

Akhlat

Van

elitene
(alatya)

Arzan

Bidlis

Maiyafariqin

Behesni

Amida

Hisn Kaifa

Kesoun

Mardin

Jazirat
Ibn Umar

b

Edessa

Nisibin

Harran

Bain al-Nahrain

Bira

Mosul

Irbil

Manbij

Sinjar

rin

Raqqa

KHABUR

Jabar

JAZIRA

Sharazur

-Sultan

h

Rahba

EUPHRATES

Tikrit

Tigris

Baghdad

The Near East of Saladin

IRAQ

ripoli

Barqa

Cairo

Taima

Libya

Ashmunain

al-Minya

Akhmin

al-Babain

Qus

Aswan

Medina

Ibrim

Arabia

Aidhab

Jidda

Mecca

Sana

Zabid

Aden

Saladin

Saladin

Andrew S. Ehrenkreutz

State University of New York Press Albany 1972

Andrew S. Ehrenkreutz is Professor of

Near Eastern History at The University of Michigan

SALADIN

FIRST EDITION

PUBLISHED BY STATE UNIVERSITY OF NEW YORK PRESS

99 WASHINGTON AVENUE, ALBANY, NEW YORK 12201

PRINTED IN THE UNITED STATES OF AMERICA

Library of Congress Cataloging in Publication Data
Ehrenkreutz, Andrew S
Saladin.
Bibliography: p.
1. Saladin, Sultan of Egypt and Syria, 1137–1193.
DS38.4.S24E34   962'.02'0924 [B]   78-161443
ISBN 0-87395-095-X

TO BLANCHE & STEFAN

Contents

Acknowledgments

In producing this book I was fortunate enough to obtain in 1967–68 a Fulbright-Hays grant from the U.S. Department of Health, Education and Welfare, which enabled me to get away from the troubled atmosphere of my university campus, to write the first draft of the manuscript in the shadows of the equally noisy but functionally healthy bazaars of Istanbul.

That this manuscript ultimately reached a publishable form is the contribution of my friends: Professor Carlton F. Wells of The University of Michigan, Norman Mangouni, Director of the State University of New York Press, and Mrs. Margaret Mirabelli who served as copy editor.

To them as well as to the anonymous readers and critical evaluators— *shukrān kathīran lakum!*

My wife, Blanche, deserves special thanks for putting up patiently with the long years of the "don't-disturb-me" refrain. It should further be acknowledged that without a steady exchange of ideas and without encouraging contacts with my colleagues, students, and my son Stefan, this book would not have come into existence at all.

In closing these acknowledgments, I wish to invoke the memory of my late parents, Professor Cezaria Baudouin de Courtenay Jedrzejewicz and Professor Stefan L. Ehrenkreutz, whose distinguished academic careers were tragically terminated in 1939, by the joint Nazi and Communist invasion of Poland.

Andrew S. Ehrenkreutz

NUR AL-DIN'S FAMILY (THE ZANGIDS)
Imad Al-Din Zangi, d. 1146

Sayf Al-Din Ghazi I
d. 1149

Qutb Al-Din Mawdud
d. 1169

Nur Al-Din Mahmud
d. 1174

Al-Malik Al-Salih
d. 1181

Sayf Al-Din Ghazi II
d. 1176

Izz Al-Din Masud I
d. 1193

Imad Al-Din Zangi II
d. 1198

THE FAMILY OF SALADIN
Shadhi Ibn Marwan

Najm Al-Din Ayyub
d. 1173

Asad Al-Din Shirkuh
d. 1169

Nur Al-Dawlah
Shahan Shah
d. 1148

Shams Al-Dawlah
Turan Shah
d. 1180

Salah Al-Din (Saladin)
Yusuf, Al-Nasir
d. 1193

Sayf Al-Dawlah
Tughtigin
d. 1197

Sitt Al-Sham
d. 1220

Sayf Al-Din
Al-Adil
d. 1218

Taj Al-Muluk
Buri
d. 1183

Rabiah
Khatun
d. 1245

Nasir Al-Din Muhammad
d. 1185

Asad Al-Din
Shirkuh II
d. 1240

KINGS OF JERUSALEM (1162–1197)

Amalric I (1162–1174)
Baldwin IV (1174–1185)
Baldwin V (1185)
Guy of Lusignan (1186–1192)
Conrad of Montferrat (1191–1192)
Henry of Champagne (1192–1197)

Introduction

"I have become so great as I am because I have won men's hearts by gentleness and kindness."
—Saladin to his son Zahir

With the death of Saladin, on 4 March 1193, there disappeared an outstanding Muslim leader whose career decisively affected the history of Islam and its relations with Christendom. It was Saladin who administered the coup de grace to the Fatimid caliphate in Cairo. It was Saladin who established the Ayyubid regime in Egypt, Syria, and the Yemen. Above all, it was Saladin who recovered Jerusalem from the infidels and successfully resisted the onslaught of Christian armies from Europe.

Actually, news about Saladin's death evoked mixed reaction from the people of Islam. There was immediate grief and mourning in Damascus and Cairo, but a feeling of relief in Mosul, and outright rejoicing in Akhlat. Nor did the record of his achievements appear to inspire his political successors with any idealistic policies, for Saladin's death was followed by political disintegration, internal struggle for power, and abortive efforts at restoring unity.

Hardly thirty-six years had passed when Saladin's nephew surrendered Jerusalem to a Christian emperor (1229). Thereafter, following the rise of the Mongols, Mamluks, and the Ottomans, the traditional Islamic political superstructure vanished from the lands of the Near East. And yet the memory of Saladin continued unabated. To this day his tomb in Damascus attracts many pilgrims and tourists. Over the city of Cairo his mountain citadel dominates. And the Kurds all over the Near East speak with proud reverence the name of the "international" hero whom their people produced.

The best measure of Saladin's lasting attractiveness is the fact that seven centuries later, authors in historical and literary fields still find it rewarding to write about the great sultan. During the last twenty-five years there has appeared an impressive number of new books and articles dealing with his career,[1] as well as new editions and reeditions of Arabic medieval sources whose appearance on scholarly markets further attest the sustained interest in his history.[2]

The richness of preserved source materials has made historical studies of Saladin and his time particularly interesting. Saladin's life coincided with a prolific period of Islamic historiography, characterized by the writing of general chronicles, local histories, monographs, biographies, and autobiographies. Moreover, historians of that period recognized the value of diplomatic and administrative documents as corroborative elements in their accounts, and by integrating such documentation into their narratives they salvaged for posterity textual evidence of paramount historical significance. Some of the Muslim authors writing on Saladin were his contemporaries, others belonged to generations that immediately followed. Baha al-Din (d. 1234), the author of a biography of Saladin, Imad al-Din (d. 1201), another original chronicler, and al-Qadi al-Fadil (d. 1199), whose profuse correspondence has survived, were not only highly placed officials, but genuine friends of the great sultan. On the other hand, Ibn Khallikan (d. 1282), Abu Shamah (d. 1268), and Ibn Wasil (d. 1298), though not Saladin's contemporaries, knew people belonging to the preceding generation who could verify, supplement, or rectify their accounts.

The main merit of this body of information is that it was mostly gathered from people who were directly or indirectly involved in Saladin's career. Some of them witnessed or even participated in many of his activities, others depended on oral or written accounts of eyewitnesses, still others were personally affected by the successes and failures of the great sultan. Those twelfth- and early thirteenth-century authorities not only wrote about the history of Saladin; they were themselves part of that history. They recorded not only what they actually had seen, heard, or read about Saladin, but what their feelings toward him, consciously or subconsciously, dictated them to write. Not surprisingly, some of these accounts reflect local bias or religious prejudice. Thus, for instance, Ibn al-Athir (d. 1233), raised in Zangid Mosul, sided with Sultan Nur al-Din against the great hero, while Ibn Abi Tayy (d. 1232), holding a grudge against the Zangids of Aleppo, favored Saladin over Nur al-Din. Other authors indiscrimi-

nately recorded several versions of the same episodes in the life of
Saladin. Because of its rich inclusiveness, this heritage from the medieval Arab authors allows modern scholars to examine Saladin's career
from different angles, making possible a better understanding of its
historical significance.

On the other hand, the treatment of Saladin by those early biographers and historians suffered from a tendency to hero-worship and to
idealize their heroes in the tradition of moralistic historiography. Ibn
al-Athir wrote: "When the kings read in the history books about the
biographies of just rulers and how they were highly esteemed by their
subjects, they would try to follow their examples. And when they
knew, through history, of the tyrants and how much they were scorned
and hated, they would refrain from following their policy." [3] The no-
tion of this alleged "historiographical responsibility" was evident in
the contribution of Baha al-Din and of other medieval writers perpet-
uating the image of Saladin's personality. "Our Sultan," wrote Baha
al-Din, "was very noble of heart, kindness shone in his face, he was
very modest, and exquisitely courteous." [4]

In their pursuit of didactic effects, Saladin's biographers depicted
him as the ideal Muslim ruler understanding the principles of a good
rulership and conscious of the edifying nature of his career. Not long
before his death, when counselling a son about to take a provincial
government position, Saladin thus allegedly defined the source of his
own strength:

> "My son," he said, "I commend thee to the most high God, the
> fountain of all goodness. Do His will, for that way lieth peace.
> Abstain from the shedding of blood; trust not to that; for blood
> that is spilt never slumbers. Seeks to win the hearts of the people,
> and watch over their prosperity; for it is to secure their happiness
> that thou are appointed by God and by me. Try to gain the hearts
> of thy emirs and ministers and nobles. I have become great as I
> am because I have won men's hearts by gentleness and kindness." [5]

Arabic authors are not the only twelfth-century sources of information about Saladin. His dramatic activities against the Crusader establishments in the Near East, which finally provoked a great European
invasion generally known as the Third Crusade, were also recorded

3

and commented upon by non-Muslim chroniclers. The most important was William of Tyre (d. ca. 1183) who, notwithstanding his dedication to the Crusader cause, produced a relatively impartial account of the events between 1144 and 1183 that affected the Crusader kingdom. To his credit William's references to Saladin, if not always accurate, were not colored by religious prejudice or political bias. As for West European sources, historical objectivity could hardly be expected in their views of the Muslim hero. The "Poème contemporain sur Saladin," written shortly after the loss of Jerusalem in 1187, shows nothing but bitter hatred. Others, composed after the abortive Third Crusade, lack neither historical misrepresentation nor vilification of Saladin. And yet, in spite of their hostility toward the "inimicus crucis," many of these sources acknowledged Saladin's personal attributes such as "prudentia," "astutia," and generosity as well as his abilities as military commander.[6]

Although he early acquired the status of an internationally known political personality, Saladin long awaited serious biographical treatment from a European. In 1785 a French authority, Louis-François-Claude Marin, published a *Histoire de Saladin, Sulthan d'Egypte et de Syrie,* an admirable study based not only on the chronicles of the Crusades but on the Arabic materials contemporary with Saladin as well. In spite of its merits, however, the book remained almost unknown until it was "discovered" by the famous British orientalist and historian, Stanley Lane-Poole, who in 1898 published his *Saladin and the Fall of the Kingdom of Jerusalem,* still the best-known book on Saladin by a European.

The main professional significance of Lane-Poole's biography was his full use of all the then available Oriental and Occidental source materials—textual, archaeological, epigraphical, and numismatic. The most impressive feature of his book is its enthusiastic and persuasive admiration for the personality of Saladin. "Gentleness was the dominant note of his character," wrote Lane-Poole about his hero.

We search the contemporary descriptions in vain for the common attributes of Kings. Majesty? It is not mentioned, for the respect he inspired sprang from love, which "casteth out fear." State? Far from adopting an imposing mien and punctilious forms, no sovercign was ever more genial and easy of approach. He loved to surround himself with clever talkers, and was himself "delightful to talk to." He knew all the traditions of the Arabs, the "Days" of their ancient heroes, the pedigrees of their famous mares. His sympathy and unaffected interest set every one at his ease, and instead of repressing freedom of conversation, he let the talk flow at such a pace that sometimes a man could not hear his own voice. . . . At Saladin's court all was eager conversation—a most unkingly buzz. Yet there were limits which no one dared to transgress in the Sultan's presence. He suffered no unseemly talk, nor was any flippant irreverence or disrespect of persons permitted. He never used or allowed scurrilous language. He kept his own tongue, even in great provocation, under rigid control, and his pen was no less disciplined: he was never known to write a bitter word to a Muslim.[7]

The range of primary evidence consulted by Lane-Poole was so wide and its historical and philological handling so professional that his book has become a standard biography serving many authors who have since produced scholarly and popular works telling the story of the chivalrous Saladin. As a rule, all of these authors, persuaded by the enthusiasm of Lane-Poole or his Muslim medieval predecessors, have perpetuated an untarnished image of the sultan. Even the great British Orientalist, H. A. R. Gibb, appeared under the spell of Saladin (or of Lane-Poole, rather), when he eulogized the "very perfect" Saladin.

Neither warrior nor governor by training or inclination, he it was who inspired and gathered round himself all the elements and forces making for the unity of Islam against the invaders. And this he did, not so much by the example of his personal courage and resolution—which were undeniable—as by his unselfishness, his humility and generosity, his moral vindication of Islam against both its enemies and its professed adherents. He was no simpleton, but for all that an utterly simple and transparently honest man. He baffled his enemies, internal and external, because they expected to find him animated by the same motives as they were, and playing the political game as they played it. Guileless him-

5

self, he never expected and seldom understood guile in others—a weakness of which his own family and others took advantage, but only (as a general rule) to come up at the end against his singleminded devotion, which nobody and nothing could bend, to the service of his ideals.[8]

There have been deviations from the prevailing tendency toward worship. As early as 1930 Charles J. Rosebault questioned the traditional views regarding Saladin's adolescence.

Perhaps it is not so certain that young Saladin was the naive and retiring person he has been made out to be, and possibly there is another and quite different explanation for the fact that such rigid silence as to his growing years was maintained by the biographers of his day. Did they possibly withhold their pens because they wished, with true oriental reticence, to maintain before the world the ideal character of later years, untouched by any spot of youthful frivolity? Could it not even be that the idol of Beha ed-din and many of his confreres was given to pleasures in the heyday of his life which caused the graybeards to look askance, and to refrain from comment, out of regard for his family?[9]

About twenty years later, a famous Orientalist, V. F. Minorsky, presented a drastically revisionist account of the political background of Saladin's family: "Saladin's father and uncle did not come to Iraq and to Syria as semi-barbarous shepherds used to the daylong watching of flocks from some distant crag. They brought with them recollections of a whole system of politics and behaviour."[10]

In 1955, Gertrude Slaughter challenged earlier explanations of Saladin's promotion to the Fatimid vizirate:

It has been supposed that Saladin was chosen among many who seemed more deserving because of his docility. But he had not shown himself to be docile at Alexandria or in his treatment of Shawar. He had been his uncle's chief assistant; he was familiar with the practical affairs of government; he came of the Mountain Lions' sturdy stock, and he was a most agreeable companion. Moreover, the Caliph, to judge from what we know of his character, was not looking for a willing tool. He wanted someone who would take the troubles of government into his own hands. . . .[11]

A few years later, Claude Cahen contributed to the new edition of the *Encyclopaedia of Islam* a statement which somewhat darkened the hitherto untarnished image of Saladin: "Salah al-Din adopted the idea (of the holy war), though it is not possible to discern to what extent ambition was combined with undoubtedly sincere conviction."[12] In 1965, a fresh and utterly prosaic view of the career of the Muslim hero was offered by Zoe Oldenbourg in her major work on the Crusades: "Moslem courts were ruled by the law of the jungle, and at that moment Saladin merely happened to be the swiftest and most agile; but it cannot be said that his part in the affair was a glorious one. . . . Saladin was what would be called a self-made man.[13] First and foremost, Saladin was an ambitious man."[14]

If the competence of Rosebault, Slaughter, and Oldenbourg as historians of the Crusades raises skeptical objections about their opinions, such criticism could hardly apply to the contributions of Minorsky, Cahen, and Joshua Prawer. In the latter's magnum opus, *Histoire du Royaume Latin de Jérusalem*—a work awarded the Gustave Schlumberger prize by the Academie des Inscriptions et Belles-Lettres—one finds an explicit expression of dissatisfaction with the treatment Saladin has received at the hands of modern historians: "Modern historians, seduced by Arabic sources, have sometimes been misled by their tendentious character.[15] . . . There prevails among the historians a tendency to attribute a single, dominating idea (*une pensée directrice*) to all of Saladin's actions from the day he seized power in Egypt (1169) to his death, twenty-four years later (1193)."[16] Finally: "A critical biography of the hero of Islamic history is still lacking."[17]

Nearly three quarters of a century have passed since the appearance of Lane-Poole's *Saladin*. Some new important sources have since become available to historians; other earlier works have been reedited with fresh and searching thoroughness. Likewise, able historians have contributed a great many specialized articles on various aspects of Saladin's career. Has all this new professional literature been able to humanize the almost sanctified image of Saladin? Have the old twelfth-century sources yielded any new information when analyzed by modern historical methodology? Was Saladin really what his medieval and modern admirers have wanted us to believe? If not, then what was he really like?

One thing is rather obvious. The political, social, and economic climate prevailing in the Near East in the second half of the twelfth century was not conducive to seeking power through the exercise of tolerance, magnanimity, chivalry, or any altruistic behavior. Besides suffering from the intrusion of the Crusaders, the Byzantines, and the Turkomans, Near Eastern society was torn asunder by factional in-fighting at all levels of the political hierarchy. In the merciless struggle —whether between the Sunni caliphate of the Abbasids and the Shiite caliphate of the Fatimids, the Saljuqid sultans and the Arab amirs, or between local dynasts and ambitious atabegs—all means were em-ployed to achieve victory. Ideological or religious principles were read-ily compromised; the presence of the Crusaders primarily furnished an opportunity for expanding diplomatic intrigues, or for promoting sel-fish propaganda, rather than uniting the leaders in a sincere effort to defend Islam. Hence one finds Sunni viziers and jurists in the service of the Shiite Fatimids, military assistance rendered by Arab tribes to the Crusaders, or an alliance between Muslim Damascus and the Latin Kingdom of Jerusalem. In this dangerous political game there was no place for people lacking ambition or leadership qualities. To become a contender one needed the support of family or a faction; to overcome other contenders one required proper military training, political and diplomatic skills, as well as a natural talent of charismatic leadership. Above all, one needed a lot of luck!

Saladin abounded in all those attributes. Indeed, the significance of his spectacular accomplishments lies not in the alleged romantic or chivalrous aspects of his career, but in the degree to which he fulfilled a political mission to which he had been destined by his ambitious family background, by his personal talents and inclinations, by his po-litical sagacity, governmental education, and military training, as well as by his outstanding leadership qualities.

The purpose of this study is to take a fresh look at both Saladin's outstanding personality and his political accomplishments in the in-tricate setting of Syro-Egyptian relations. It also interprets Saladin's involvement with the Crusaders, without rehashing all the well-known details of the Third Crusade, but explaining the real significance of his military contributions and failures in the struggle for the cause of Islam. Responsible methodology has salvaged many a hero from the realm of mythology. I hope that by furnishing new information derived from original sources and by using more realistic perspectives, this study will serve to revise and clarify our knowledge of Saladin and his well-deserved place in history. Perhaps, also, this interpretative dissent will help to discourage the authorship of monotonous pastiches presenting "a noble portrait of the Sultan whose chivalry and generosity excited the admiration of the Crusaders." [18]

1 Egypt before Saladin

"Egypt is the gift of the river."
—*Herodotus*

Preliminary remarks

Although Syria and Egypt served as the main scene of Saladin's career they did not perform similar functions in the history of the great Muslim hero. In Syria Saladin spent his childhood and adolescence. There he received his military training, and it was at the court of the Syrian sultan, Nur al-Din, that Saladin gained experience and reputation as staff-officer. It was in Syria—in its broader historical sense including Palestine and Jordan—that Saladin achieved his splendid victories over the Crusaders, and in its capital, Damascus, he died and was laid to rest.

But the country where Saladin rose to prominence and which made his triumphs in Syria possible was Egypt. In Egypt he emerged as the most outstanding military leader in the Syrian expeditionary army sent by Sultan Nur al-Din, and there Saladin succeeded in establishing his own power base which supplanted the decadent regime of the Fatimid caliphate. By strengthening his military position through the economic resources of Egypt, Saladin not only resisted pressure from Nur al-Din, but also embarked on an expansionist policy which ultimately extended his authority over Syria and parts of Mesopotamia. Finally, without the support of Egyptian land and naval forces Saladin could not have sustained his dramatic military effort against the Crusaders.

Spectacular though they were, the accomplishments of Saladin did not produce any drastic changes in Syria. It is true that Saladin recovered for Islam many Crusader territories, including the holy city of Jerusalem; furthermore, he substituted the rule of his Kurdish family for the Turkish regime of the Zangids. Otherwise, however, political, religious, social, and economic conditions in Syria at the time of Saladin's death or shortly thereafter hardly differed from the situation prevailing prior to his bid for power. Muslim Syria continued to be ruled by a feudalistic military hierarchy whose leading members exploited the country's overstrained resources to finance military campaigns against the Crusaders, against Muslim rivals in Asia Minor and Mesopotamia, as well as against each other. The Crusaders controlled nearly all of the strategic coastal area, and the dangerous Assassins remained in possession of numerous strongholds in northern Syria.

On the other hand, Saladin profoundly affected the course of Egyptian history, but this aspect of his career has never been properly analyzed. It was largely through his efforts that the Crusaders of King Amalric failed to conquer the country of the Nile in the last quarter of the twelfth century. It was Saladin who suppressed the Fatimid caliphate and founded the Ayyubid dynasty which paved the way for the installation of the nefarious Mamluk regime in Egypt. Finally, it was Saladin's expansionist policy and its attendant large-scale mobilization of the resources and of the productive forces of Egypt, which eventually precipitated a far-reaching feudalization of her economy.

In order to understand the part Egypt played in Saladin's career and, conversely, to appreciate the effects of Saladin's achievements on the history of Egypt, it is necessary to survey the situation prevailing in that country just prior to his appearance.

The Egyptian raisons d'etat

Specific geographic conditions have predetermined the main course of policy to be followed by any regime genuinely concerned to promote the vital interests of Egypt. The pivotal axioms of such a policy must be both a proper utilization of the Nile for intensive agricultural production and a maximum exploitation of Egypt's land and sea connections to further export, import, and transit trade activities. These economic imperatives could not be implemented without political and administrative stability based on internal and external security. With the bulk of the Egyptian population concentrated in the valley and delta of the Nile, no large military or police units were needed to maintain internal security, while the extensive coastal and desert regions serving as Egypt's borders allowed moderate naval and land forces to guard the external security of the country.

As long as the ruling institutions provided conditions propitious for unhampered economic activities and as long as the Egyptian economy was capable of financing the political and administrative structure, the country advanced in societal improvements. But any regime which failed to safeguard these economic and military factors, either through simple indolence, impotence, or extraneous commitments incompatible with the Egyptian raisons d'etat, was bound to generate regressive, repressive, and even destructive trends.

The Fatimid dynasty during its early Egyptian period was a good example of a constructive Nilocentric regime. The Fatimid caliphate, established in 909 in North Africa by the extremist Ismaili sect of the Shiite movement, was ideologically committed to supplanting the Sunni caliphate of the Abbasids in Baghdad. And yet despite their initial eastward expansion, the *Drang nach Osten* of the Fatimids was virtually suspended following their acquisition of Egypt in 969. Once in control of the country of the Nile, the Fatimids surrendered their policy of costly anti-Abbasid expansion to a policy dictated by the Egyptian reasons of state. Ruling from their newly established capital of Cairo, the Ismaili caliphs created a zone of security in and around Egypt and promoted economic developments which resulted in what by medieval Mediterranean standards amounted to economic and political prosperity.

The Fatimid caliphate in the middle of the twelfth century

By the middle of the twelfth century the Fatimid dynasty was headed toward total extinction; several decades of gradual decline had sapped the vitality of Egypt at different levels of her political and economic organization. Fatimid caliphs reigning during that century no longer enjoyed the religious and political authority of their great predecessors. When they abandoned claims to the imamate, or spiritual leadership, they lost their supremacy over the religious movement which once had constituted a powerful force behind the rise, unity, and dynamic expansion of the Fatimid empire. Violent conflicts in 1094 and 1130 arising from irregularities in the succession to the caliphate not only alienated many Ismaili followers inside and outside of Egypt,[1] but also led to the emergence of secessionist sects of which the Nizaris, or Assassins, were to give deadly proofs of their hostility to the Fatimids. Although on each occasion Ismaili unity in Egypt was restored by drastic military measures, such developments did not enhance the religious prestige of the caliphs. Their popularity was not helped either by the appointment of Bahram, a Christian Armenian, and of Ibn al-Sallar, a Sunni Muslim of Kurdish origin, to the vizirate (1135–37 and 1150–53, respectively). The former, because of his unscrupulous pro-Christian and pro-Armenian favoritism, provoked serious criticism and general resentment among the Shiites and Sunnis alike.[2] The second antagonized the Shiites by reestablishing officially a Sunni juridical school of the Shafite rite in Cairo.[3] That the Ismaili creed had ceased to be unchallenged as the official religion of the Fatimid establishment was demonstrated in the admission, beginning 1131, of Sunni jurists to the supreme judicial college in Egypt.[4]

If the religious prestige of the twelfth century Fatimid caliphs was thus compromised, their political status was completely stripped of executive powers. Ever since the vizirate of Badr al-Jamali (1074–94) and that of his son al-Afdal (1094–1121), who had established themselves as virtual rulers of the Fatimid empire, the caliphs were politically dominated by their vizirs. Although some of the caliphs, such as al-Amir (1101–30) and al-Hafiz (1130–49), attempted to uphold the status of the caliphate by drastically disposing of their vizirs and appointing men of their own choice, or even by trying to rule without the vizirs, they ultimately failed to recover the executive attributes once held by Fatimid sovereigns. It is true that they continued to preside solemnly over various court, state, and popular festivities, that they officially represented Egypt in diplomatic *pourparlers* and correspondence, and that they indulged in political intrigues of their own. But in reality, the Fatimid caliphs of that period were reduced to official figureheads, with no decisive say in matters of government, which were left in the hands of the vizirs. At least until 1150 the vizirs had been appointed by the caliphs. Beginning that year, however, succession to the vizirate was determined by often violent contests among ruthless military commanders or ambitious politicians, the caliphs passively accepting and confirming the successful usurpers.[5]

In fact, neither the loss of political authority by the caliphs, nor the usurpation of the supreme executive powers by the vizirs was as pernicious as the rivalry between the various factions. The main objective of this factional struggle was control—or at least influence over—the court establishment whose main assets were the institutional prestige of the caliphate and the treasury located within the fortified precincts of the palace area. Despite the caliphs' loss of effective authority over the armed forces of Egypt, their court establishment was well protected by a special regiment of Sudanese and Armenian guards.[6] Various people—the vizirs and aspirants to the vizirate, religious and judicial dignitaries, military commanders and chancellery officials, the eunuchs, and even poets—all were taking part in intrigues and plots focussed on the institution of the Fatimid caliphate. It must be emphasized that since they were trying to promote their own cause within the political framework of the court establishment, the rival factions or contestants did not attack the institution of the caliphate itself. It is true that individual caliphs fell victim to the struggle for power, but they were immediately replaced by other members of the dynasty. Under those circumstances there remained an outside chance that the caliphs themselves might, by exploiting the factional rivalries, emancipate their office from the control of the vizirs.

The office of the vizirate itself was another prize in the struggle for power. Whether attained by pressure tactics or naked force, the accession to the vizirate was not officially confirmed without a formal investiture on the part of the caliph, which the latter could hardly afford to refuse. Operating amid different pressure groups and exposed to various political and military factions, the vizir was held responsible for the conduct of domestic and foreign policy. It is obvious that even competent vizirs were in danger of assassination.

In this internal struggle the people of Alexandria or their leaders held an interesting position. The city's prosperity, if not her very existence as the major Egyptian city, depended on the freight and passenger traffic flowing to and from her harbour. Commerce was the life blood of that coastal city. However, the interests of her merchants were hurt when in the eleventh century the caliphs of Cairo began to concede trade privileges to European merchants, mostly of Italian origin.[7] Alexandria's situation deteriorated further in the first half of the twelfth century, when the Crusaders captured the Syrian littoral, with obvious advantages for European maritime trade. However, in spite of the Crusader monopoly of Syrian ports and their interference with the flow of land traffic between Egypt and Syria, the Crusaders did not cut off the port of Alexandria. Indeed, Alexandria continued to serve as the main port for that part of the Egyptian export, import, and transit trade mainly intended for European markets. The North Italian textile industry depended on the supply of alum and natron, two minerals located in Egypt, and for that very reason Italian importers were interested in keeping Alexandria open. The people of Alexandria were assured of economic advantages derived from diverse commercial operations as long as their harbour and its connections with the Nile and the Red Sea remained open and even if the Christian pilgrims preferred to proceed directly to the Holy Land, Muslim pilgrims traveling from the Western Mediterranean to Mecca continued to pass through Alexandria.

These factors necessarily conditioned the attitude of the commercial capital of Egypt toward Cairo and the Crusaders. The Alexandrians had to be very critical of any administration which failed to protect the coast of Egypt from foreign attacks; they necessarily opposed any negotiations which would compromise Egyptian fiscal and political sovereignty; they were also ready to support a leader who could rid Egyptian trade of the threat created by the pressure of the Crusaders.

The serious internal instability of Egypt may easily be grasped from the following events. In 1149 al-Zafir, age 17, was enthroned as caliph. In 1150 Ibn al-Sallar seized the vizirate by chasing out and executing Ibn Massal. He in turn was assassinated and succeeded by Abbas in 1153. The following year Abbas liquidated Caliph al-Zafir and replaced him with his son al-Faiz, age 5. Still in that same year Talai drove Abbas from Cairo and he was killed by the Crusaders. Talai took over the vizirate. In 1159 Alexandria and Upper Egypt revolted against the vizir. The following year Caliph al-Faiz died and was succeeded by al-Adid, age 11. In 1161 Vizir Talai was assassinated; his son Ruzzayk succeeded. By February 1163, Ruzzayk was deposed and later executed; Shawar became the new vizir. But by August Dirgham had ousted and succeeded Vizir Shawar. Alexandria opposed the new vizir. We can see that the fifteen-year period between 1149 and 1163 witnessed a succession of three juvenile caliphs and seven vizirs, most of these disruptive events being produced by violent coups.

Economic situation

It is obvious that such frequent political convulsions gravely weakened Egyptian economic activities. Savage street fighting in Cairo (1149, 1154) [8] and Alexandria (1159),[9] in addition to Norman naval attacks against the latter,[10] as well as against Tinnis (1154, 1155),[11] Damietta (1155),[12] and Rosetta (1155),[13] must have interfered with normal productive operations at all these important manufacturing and trading centers. Military campaigns in Lower and Upper Egypt (1150, 1159, 1162, 1163) [14] obstructed agricultural production. Heavy losses in urban population, caused by outbreaks of plague in Alexandria (1142) [15] and Damietta (1150–51),[16] and a dangerous—though temporary—food shortage caused by the low Nile (1159),[17] constituted natural factors adversely affecting Egyptian economy in that period.

Certain disturbing fiscal trends were taking place. In 1145, the land tax still yielded 1,200,000 dinars of net income; [18] thereafter this state revenue declined, and tax collecting was not functioning correctly. Vizir Ruzzayk, for instance, had to forego a substantial amount of tax arrears and outstanding liabilities owed to the treasury.[19] This was particularly true of the *mukus* or the noncanonical taxes, whose range was greatly expanded in the late Fatimid period. And yet, by 1168, the cash arrears in that branch of revenue amounted to over 1,000,000 dinars, in addition to the long overdue deliveries in kind.[20] The practice of selling government positions to highest bidders on a semi-annual basis, to which Vizir Talai resorted (1154–61),[21] indicated the increasing pecuniary complications of Fatimid government. Finally, the prestige of Fatimid gold coinage, which had earlier enjoyed the status of international currency, was undermined in the twelfth century when greatly debased pseudo-Fatimid dinars struck by the Crusaders flooded Mediterranean markets.[22]

It should be emphasized, however, that the scope of these economic difficulties did not compare with the tragic political decline. On the contrary, available textual, archaeological, and numismatic data indicate that Egypt in the middle of the twelfth century was far from poor. Except in 1159, Egypt's agricultural production—always the backbone of her economy—supplied enough food to preserve a remarkable price stability. Manufacturing activities continued despite frequent military upheavals or outbreaks of plague. And commerce—the main factor contributing to the earlier Fatimid prosperity—continued to flourish both locally and internationally by handling Egyptian imports and exports and transit trade.

Thus, in spite of the reported drop in revenue and other pecuniary troubles, there are no indications that the Fatimids actually experienced budget crises or shortages of cash during this period. Their treasury was full and their gold coinage continued to be of superb quality and stability. In short, Egypt was still a rich country, abounding in economic opportunities and resources. It was nevertheless obvious that her decadent political regime could not properly employ these resources to cope with grave perils arising from an ever-increasing external pressure.

Egypt and the Crusaders

During the very period of her domestic political embroilment, Fatimid Egypt became the prime target of foreign invasions. Already during the eleventh century Fatimid defensive potentials were greatly curtailed by the loss of North African provinces, by the Norman conquest of Sicily, and by the Saljuqid penetration of Syria. The establishment of the Crusaders in Syria toward the end of that century further reduced Fatimid territories which were thus limited to Egypt and her southern and western approaches. In fact, the failure of the

Fatimids to nip this new danger in the bud decisively contributed to the ultimate downfall of their regime. For unlike the earlier Fatimid enemies in Syria, the Crusaders not only depended on effective military land organization but enjoyed substantial naval support periodically received from Europe.

And yet, during the first half of the twelfth century the Crusaders neither attempted nor indeed were in a strategic position to launch a large-scale invasion of Egypt. Involved in complicated warfare along their northeastern borders, they were content to consolidate their holdings in Palestine and safeguard them from Egyptian attacks. Limited though it seemed, the early strategy of the crusading Franks slowly sapped Egypt's defensive potentials. The loss of Syrian coastal towns (Ascalon being the only exception) disrupted the naval alert system which was indispensable for the security of Egyptian shores. It also deprived the Egyptian fleet of convenient supply bases, such as Acre and Tyre (captured by the Crusaders in 1104 and 1124, respectively), thus reducing the operational perimeter of the vessels sailing from Egypt. The erection by the Crusaders of a number of fortresses, such as Bait Jibrin (1137), Yibna (1141), Tall al-Safiya (1142), and Gaza (1149–50), around Ascalon drastically reduced the power of resistance of that crucial strategic base in the system of Egyptian outer defences. Apart from helping to blockade Ascalon, these Christian fortresses controlled coastal connections between Syria and Egypt. Others, such as Shaubak (1115), Ailah on the Gulf of Aqabah (1116), and Kerak (1142), impeded civilian and military traffic along Jordanian transit routes, with obvious military and economic disadvantages to the Muslims.[23]

The second half of the twelfth century witnessed a change in the Crusaders' Egyptian strategy. The activities of Zangi, the powerful atabeg of Mosul (1127–46), and those of his son, the famous Nur al-Din (1118–74) of Aleppo, resulted not only in recovery of a number of Frankish territories, such as the county of Edessa and most of the county of Antioch, but led to a considerable degree of political and military integration of Muslim Syria under their command. Reacting to this renascent Muslim power in Syria, the Franks turned their aggressive attention toward Egypt, hoping to compensate for their losses in Syria at the expense of the Fatimids. A decisive step towards the realization of the new strategy was the seizure of Ascalon in 1153. With the fall of that coastal fortress there vanished the last external bastion against a large-scale invasion of Egypt by the Crusaders. The Egyptian naval and coastal defense system lost its last interception and observation outpost, while the Franks gained an important base which would permit them to launch unflanked naval and land drives into the heart of the Fatimid state.

It was obvious that Egypt's debilitated political regime could not sustain the enemy pressure for long. Already in 1154, only one year after the fall of Ascalon, a Norman fleet sacked Tinnis.[24] In 1155, the Normans raided Damietta and again sacked Tinnis, in addition to Rosetta and Alexandria.[25] On land, however, a temporary respite was gained by further successes of Nur al-Din, culminating in his annexation of Damascus in 1154. Exploiting the involvement of the Crusaders against the Syrian sultan, the Egyptian vizir, Talai ibn Ruzzayk—notwithstanding the crumbling foundations of his own position—successfully risked a number of limited naval and land counteroperations against the Christian enemy.[26] He also tried to make up for the loss of Ascalon, by constructing a fortress at Bilbais,[27] which was destined to play a major role in Saladin's rise. On the other hand, ibn Ruzzayk was not successful in his appeal for help from Nur al-Din. In 1160, a *khilah* or a robe of honor was sent in the name of caliph al-Adid to Nur al-Din. The Syrian sultan accepted the *khilah*—a diplomatic gesture symbolizing mutual recognition between the two parties—but despite the economic advantages promised by the Fatimid government, he did not furnish military assistance to Egypt.[28] Consequently, when in 1161 the Crusaders entered Egyptian territory, Talai decided to negotiate. Having previously spent 200,000 dinars on his abortive offensive operations, he secured the Frankish withdrawal by promising them 160,000 dinars annually. In that very same year the vizir was assassinated and succeeded by his son Ruzzayk.[29] To protect Egyptian frontiers the new chief executive had at his disposal only 40,000 cavalry and 36,000 infantrymen most of whom had been drawn into the whirlpool of Egyptian internal intrigues. Indeed, during the two years 1162–64 there occurred four coups d'etat directed against the persons successively holding the vizirate.[30] This story deserves closer attention because it both reveals the ruthless and pervasive character of political intrigues in the Fatimid state and because it immediately precedes Saladin's arrival in Egypt.

Political crisis in Egypt

Ruzzayk, influenced by his cousins, especially by Izz al-Din Husam, decided to dismiss Shawar, an Arab governor of Upper Egypt. Shawar, securing the support of local forces and of the Bedouins, set out to get control over the capital. He had previously been in correspondence with some military commanders who joined him as he was approaching Cairo. Ruzzayk tried to escape but was captured by the Bedouins and delivered to the leader of the victorious rebel army. Shawar entered the capital and was invested by al-Adid with the office of the vizirate. There followed a purge of Ruzzayk's supporters. Some were crucified, others sought refuge in the countryside. Ruzzayk himself was cast into prison.[31] As for Izz al-Din Husam, the principal cause of the clash, he managed to slip out of Egypt to Syria where he acquired landed estates with the help of 70,000 dinars, which during his perilous escape had been safely deposited with the Crusaders.[32]

In performing the function of vizir, Shawar depended on his sons, particularly on Tayy and al-Kamil, on Yahya ibn al-Khayyat, who served as his chief military commander, and finally, on the advice of a prominent Egyptian politician, Shams al-Khilafah.[33] Another influential member of Shawar's entourage was the head of the army, Abd al-Rahman al-Baysani. It is relevant to observe here that this former scribe of Palestinian origin must have had contacts with the people of Alexandria since he had earlier distinguished himself as a governmental employee in that city.[34]

Even with such backing, Shawar was not secure in his position. A certain Dirgham, then holding the post of the Warden of the Gate, and his brother Mulham conspired to restore the imprisoned Ruzzayk. Tayy learned about their plans and urged his father to put Ruzzayk to death. When Shawar refused, Tayy took the matter into his own hands, went to the jail, and personally executed the helpless prisoner. The news of this cold-blooded act spurred Dirgham and Mulham to immediate action. Their troops routed the supporters of Shawar and he himself was forced to flee for his life in the direction of Syria. His sons, Tayy and Sulayman, were executed by Dirgham's order; al-Kamil would probably have shared their fate had it not been for an intercession of Mulham. He was thrown into prison instead, where he was joined by Abd al-Rahman al-Baysani.[35]

Thus in August 1163, about a half year after the overthrow of Ruzzayk and the installation of Shawar, Dirgham was himself invested with the dignity of the vizirate by Caliph al-Adid.[36] However a group of military commanders hostile to the new vizir began to plot against him; contacts were established with Shawar, who had successfully reached Damascus.[37] To crush the new conspiracy, Dirgham resorted to wholesale massacre. Prominent generals, some seventy of them, were invited to a banquet. There, the henchmen of Dirgham slaughtered them, one after another, "without regard to the rank or wealth of the victims." [38] The bloody purge may have provided a short-term satisfaction to the vizir; in the long run, however, it fatally crippled the Egyptian armed forces. Weakened as it had been by earlier external and internal difficulties, the Fatimid army was now deprived of professional leadership and could no longer be relied upon as a political and diplomatic deterrent, still less as protection against foreign invaders.

This became evident when in the autumn of 1163 an army of Crusaders under King Amalric invaded Egypt. The country was on that occasion saved only by flooding the area of the Crusaders' offensive operations.[39] Arab chroniclers well understood the historical significance of Dirgham's fatal action against his military staff. To quote Abu Shamah: "That was the main cause of his own destruction and of the demise of the Fatimid dynasty, for by killing the commanders, Dirgham reduced the power of the army of Egypt." [40]

Shawar, Shirkuh, and Saladin

In the meantime Shawar reached the court of Nur al-Din in Damascus, where he lost no time in displaying his talents in diplomatic negotiations. He was convinced that with the help of a Syrian contingent furnished by the sultan of Damascus, he could easily retrieve the vizirate of Egypt. The possible risk which direct Syrian involvement might produce, especially considering Fatimid military impotence, did not seem to trouble Shawar. After all, he had nothing to lose, and in any event he could always try neutralizing hostile pressure from Syrian troops by appealing to the Crusaders. However, Nur al-Din was not easily persuaded.[41] On earlier occasions he had turned down Egyptian appeals for military assistance against the Franks,[42] and this time it would mean marching against the "legitimate" government of Egypt. Concerned primarily about Syria, the sultan was afraid lest he overextend his military commitments. Nor was he eager to risk his troops in an operation which involved crossing territory dominated by Crusader castles.

On the other hand, the prospect of Syrian troops installing a government in Egypt did present political and strategic advantages, particularly in the light of Amalric's ominous attack. Dirgham attempted to foil this scheme of Shawar by sending Ilm al-Mulk ibn al-Nahhas, a prominent figure in the Fatimid establishment, with a letter to the ruler of Damascus. The letter reiterated Egypt's respect for Nur al-Din and asked for repudiation of Shawar. The sultan ostensibly showed sympathy for Dirgham's position and the envoy was sent back with an appropriate reply;[43] but in reality Nur al-Din proceeded with preparations for military intervention in Egypt. His decision in favor of such involvement may have been swayed by the prospects of political cooperation and of huge financial compensations which Shawar promised.[44]

Considering all the political, military, and logistic risks of such an intervention, the question of leadership was of utmost importance. Since his presence was required in Syria, Nur al-Din had to entrust one of his top military personnel with command over the expeditionary forces. Shawar, of course, was hoping to be given the command himself. When he was informed that Asad al-Din Shirkuh was leader, the information pleased him not at all.[45]

Not only was Shawar disappointed that he was not leader, he also knew that Shirkuh's reputation and military status were too great for Shawar to cherish hopes of imposing his authority over the Syrian troops. At any rate, powerless as he was, Shawar had no choice but to comply; after all, these troops were being dispatched to restore him to the vizirate in Cairo.

And so, in the spring of 1164, a Syrian army set out on the strenuous march to Egypt. Its intervention on behalf of Shawar started a chain reaction of momentous events which were to transform an internal struggle for power into a major international conflict, upon whose outcome hinged the destiny of Egypt if not of the entire Near East. And among Shirkuh's outstanding and trustworthy officers was his nephew, Salah al-Din or Saladin, whose ability and ambition were to find full scope in this opportunity.

2 Saladin before the Egyptian expedition

". . . far from exhibiting any symptoms of future greatness, he was evidently a shining example of that tranquil virtue which shuns 'the last infirmity of noble minds.'"
—Lane-Poole

Misconceptions about Saladin's upbringing

The selection of Saladin to serve on the officer staff of the Syrian expedition to Egypt calls for discussion. His appearance there was unsurprising to Nur al-Din's followers; by that time Saladin's credentials must have been well known in Damascus. Nor did medieval biographers, commenting on that event, bother to specify Saladin's qualifications. They were too impressed by Saladin's later triumphs to record details from his pre-Egyptian career, which seemed unimportant, perhaps even incompatible with the idealized hero they presented for posterity to emulate. More perplexing is the fact that modern writers, having uncritically accepted the reticence of medieval biographers, indulge in ridiculous hypotheses about Saladin's character formation and upbringing. The result is a myth that Saladin suddenly turned from a withdrawn and contemplative Muslim youngster into a prominent public figure. Even so distinguished an authority as Sir Hamilton Gibb was not free from this distortion, when in his article "The Achievement of Saladin" he asserted that Saladin has been "neither warrior nor governor by training or inclination." [1]

A colorful story of Saladin's pre-Egyptian career, based on imagination rather than on historical evidence, was contributed by Lane-Poole. After stating that absolutely nothing is known of the family of Ayyub (the father of Saladin) between 1139 and 1146, the period of their residence at Baalbek,[2] Lane-Poole offered a rather lengthy conjectural version of Saladin's adolescence.

> From 1154 to 1164, Saladin lived at Damascus, at the court of Nur al-Din, with the consideration that belonged to the son of the

commandant. As to what he did, what he studied, how he passed his time, and with whom, the Arab chroniclers maintain exasperating silence. We are informed that he learned from Nur al-Din how "to walk in the path of righteousness, to act virtuously, and to be zealous in fighting the infidels." . . . This is all we are told of Saladin up to the age of twenty-five.[3] . . . It was not until Shirkuh made his memorable expedition to Egypt that the future "Sultan of the Moslems" emerged from his voluntary retirement and stepped boldly into his uncle's place as the true successor of Zengy in the role of the Champion of Islam.[4] . . . He was one of those who have greatness thrust upon them; and though, when once fairly launched, he missed no opportunity of extending his power, it may well be doubted whether he would ever have started at all but for the urgency of his friends. An uneventful youth might have gently passed into a tranquil old age, and Saladin might have remained plain Salah-ed-Din of Damascus with a name too obscure to be Europeanized.[5]

The myth about the background of Saladin's father and uncle

A similar imaginative approach characterized Lane-Poole's treatment of the background of Ayyub and Shirkuh, Saladin's father and uncle. They were Kurds "of the Rawadiya clan, born at their village of Ajdanakan near Dawin in Armenia. From time immemorial the Kurds have led the same wild pastoral life in the mountain tracts between Persia and Asia Minor. . . . They have ever been a gallant and warlike people, impervious as a rule to civilization and difficult for strangers to manage, but possessed of many rude virtues. At least, they gave birth to Saladin."[6]

This romantic view is no longer acceptable. V. F. Minorsky, in his *Studies in Caucasian History,* states that unquestionably, Ayyub and Shirkuh were Kurds, originating from Armenia, where their father Shadhi ibn Marwan had been in the service of the Shaddadid dynasty in Dvin. He notes, however, "in the light of the stormy history of

Dvin, the frame of the 'wild pastoral life' no longer suits the story of the Ayyubid origins. . . . To survive amid the clashes of local interests and foreign invasions one needed a perfect comprehension of the issues involved.[7] . . . In a word, Saladin's father and uncle did not come to Iraq and Syria as semibarbarous shepherds used to day-long watching of flocks from some distant crag. They brought with them recollections of a whole system of politics and behavior." [8]

The career of Ayyub and Shirkuh in Mesopotamia and Syria

Whatever their practical public initiation in Dvin, the character and political experience of Ayyub and Shirkuh were revealed during their career in Iraq and Syria. Their rise to political prominence began shortly after 1130, in the service of Bihruz, a longstanding Saljuqid official in Baghdad. He placed Ayyub in charge of his feudal appanage of Takrit, where apart from ordinary administrative aspects, Ayyub's duties entailed special strategic responsibilities, because the fortress of Takrit, in which he and Shirkuh established their residence, commanded an important crossing over the Tigris.

Not long after assuming that responsibility Ayyub had an opportunity to display his reliability. When the Saljuqid ruler, Mahmud, died in 1130, a serious military conflict arose over the succession, which involved the direct intervention of Zangi, the atabeg of Mosul and a longstanding enemy of Bihruz. In an attempt to strengthen his influence in Baghdad, Zangi led an army toward the capital of Mesopotamia, but was utterly defeated by his enemies. Barely escaping with his life, the atabeg showed up at Takrit desperately wanting to cross over the river. Thus, Zangi's escape from the pursuing enemy—very possibly a matter of life and death—depended on Ayyub's decision. And Ayyub—in sheer disloyalty toward his feudal overlord—offered assistance to the fleeing atabeg. Zangi and his followers were ferried across the Tigris and provided with shelter and supplies in Takrit. It is impossible to establish the motivation for Ayyub's decision. This much is certain, however; the obvious breach of trust was to pay off in Ayyub's later career. *"Li-kull shay sabab*—everything has its cause," Ibn Wasil remarked philosophically, concluding his version of the incident.[9]

Although severely reprimanded by Bihruz, Ayyub and Shirkuh continued their employment in Takrit. Shortly after that incident they disobeyed their overlord again. Al-Aziz, a prominent Mesopotamian political figure whose nephew Imad al-Din later became Saladin's secretary, was arrested and put in Ayyub's custody at Takrit. It was on that sad occasion that Imad al-Din met Ayyub and Shirkuh for the first time.[10] On specific instructions from Baghdad, Bihruz ordered execution of the political prisoner, an order which Ayyub refused to carry out. Although al-Aziz was ultimately executed, Ayyub appears not to have been party to the killing, for Imad al-Din's acquaintance with him was not upset by the tragic incident but instead the acquaintance turned later into a real friendship. As on the previous occasion Bihruz did not proceed with any drastic measures against his recalcitrant subordinates who stayed on in Takrit. It is possible that the bold attitude of Ayyub and Shirkuh and the leniency of Bihruz may have been caused by Bihruz's political insecurity with Baghdad. That changed in 1138, when Bihruz was appointed as the *shihnah* (military commander) of Baghdad. Somewhat later he learned that Shirkuh had killed a Christian scribe in an outburst of temper; the overlord of Takrit immediately dismissed Ayyub from his service fearing that any further license for the two brothers might endanger his own position. This inglorious termination in 1138 and the exodus of Ayyub from Takrit coincided with Saladin's birth.

Mindful of the vital assistance once given to Zangi, both Ayyub and Shirkuh tried their luck at Mosul. The atabeg did not disappoint them. The two brothers were readily accepted into his service where they quickly rose to positions of prominence.

In 1139 Zangi attacked and captured Baalbek. For the unification of Muslim forces against the Crusaders it was an important action. It must be stressed, however, that it was primarily directed against another Muslim ruler, Jamal al-Din Buri of Damascus. The hostility between Buri and Zangi was so bitter that the former preferred to cooperate with the Crusaders rather than to yield to his Muslim rival. Zangi's uncompromising stand toward Damascus was demonstrated by his vindictive treatment of Baalbek's heroic defenders. After promising them safe-conduct, the atabeg ordered a ruthless execution of the surrendered garrison, a crime which aroused popular indignation.[11] In charge of that city, stained with the blood of Zangi's victims, was placed Ayyub, the father of Saladin.

Thus, the childhood of Saladin was spent in Baalbek, where his father acted as local governor on behalf of the powerful atabeg of Mosul. In 1146 when Saladin must have been about eight years old, Zangi was assassinated and his military and political organization was temporarily paralyzed by problems of succession. The ruler of Damascus wasted no time in dispatching an army to recover Baalbek. After tenacious resistance, Ayyub succeeded in striking a deal with the enemy. He surrendered to the victors but only on condition that he continue to govern in Baalbek, this time on behalf of Damascus. Unlike Zangi's treachery, the pledge was respected. As an additional bonus for his switch of allegiance, Ayyub received a substantial money grant and a handsome fief consisting of a house in Damascus and ten villages near the capital.

Ayyub's new situation proved, at first, to be a source of embarrassment to his brother Shirkuh, who remained faithful to the house of Zangi, helping Nur al-Din, son of the late atabeg, get established as sultan of Aleppo. Nur al-Din understandably resented Ayyub's move and, fearful of its adverse effect on Shirkuh, cooled in his attitude toward the Kurdish commander. The misunderstanding between Nur al-Din and Shirkuh was partly responsible for a military reverse the Muslims suffered at the hands of the Crusaders in 1148, at Yaghra. Shortly after that battle Shirkuh was restored to Nur al-Din's confidence, and after distinguishing himself in many encounters against the Franks, he became Nur al-Din's top military commander.

Subsequent developments demonstrated that the Kurdish brothers knew how to profit from serving two masters. In July 1151 they were among representatives of the opposing camps negotiating the reaffirmation of Aleppo's nominal suzerainty over Damascus.[12] In 1152 Saladin was accepted in the service of Nur al-Din.[13] The final extinction of the dynasty in Damascus, which Ayyub served, and its integration into the realm of Nur al-Din, did not impede Ayyub's political advancement. Shirkuh, appointed military commandant of Damascus in 1154, interceded on behalf of his brother. Far from holding a grudge for the 1146 incident, Nur al-Din placed Ayyub in charge of the capital of Syria.[14] Before long, the two brothers occupied a prominent place in the military and political elite of Nur al-Din's state. Ayyub was even granted an exclusive privilege to remain seated in the presence of the sultan.

The staggering success of Ayyub and Shirkuh was more than military and political. While in Damascus they did not neglect to acquire real estate, nor did their sons. Their economic situation was prosperous enough for them to finance the establishment of a few pious foundations in Aleppo, Damascus, and Medina.[15] The quest of material gain was emulated by Shirkuh's subordinates in Damascus, indeed they did not shun extortionist practices. Their scandalous and rapacious behavior went so far that Nur al-Din had to set up a special board of inquiry.[16]

According to yet another story told by Ibn al-Athir and repeated by Lane-Poole,[17] Shirkuh in 1159 was on the brink of staging a coup d'etat in Damascus. As the story went, Sultan Nur al-Din fell ill during a campaign in northern Syria and his condition critically deteriorated after returning to Aleppo. Thereupon Shirkuh turned up in Damascus and discussed with his brother the possibility of taking over that city. Ayyub disapproved. "You will destroy us in this way," Ayyub is quoted by Ibn al-Athir, as if anyone could have been present at such a confidential conversation. "You should rather go back to Aleppo. If you find Nur al-Din alive, you would reassure him about your devotion to him in the difficult crisis. If, however, Nur al-Din is dead, then—after all—I am here in Damascus, and I'll do whatever you desire to get hold of the city." [18]

Interesting though it is, the alleged attempt to conspire against Nur al-Din should be regarded as an invention of Ibn al-Athir. Nur al-Din's predicament in 1159 occurred in Damascus, and on that occasion Shirkuh loyally defended the interests of his overlord against known conspirators.[19] On the other hand, Nur al-Din did suffer a critical illness in Aleppo in 1157-58. On that occasion Shirkuh did stay in Damascus, but he had been sent there on specific orders of the sultan to ward off possible Crusader attacks.[20] Having watched over the safety of Damascus, he returned to Aleppo only after his master showed signs of recovery. Needless to say, this loyal attitude of Shirkuh at a time of crisis further enhanced his status at the court of Nur al-Din.

The influence of Saladin's family on his early career

Ayyub and Shirkuh were not the only members of Saladin's family who displayed military ambitions and talents. Shihab al-Din al-Harimi, a brother of Saladin's Kurdish mother, became one of Nur al-Din's top commanders. Saladin's older brother Shahan Shah was killed in action against the Crusaders in 1148. Yet another brother, Turan Shah, was *shihnah* of Damascus around 1156. The best indication of the ambitions of Saladin's brothers is the impressive record of their eventual exalted status. Turan Shah ruled over the Yemen. He was succeeded by Sayf al-Din Tughtigin (whose son, incidentally, liked to boast that their family was descended from the Umayyad caliphs), who founded the dynasty of the Ayyubids in Yemen. Finally, Sayf al-Din al-Adil became the sultan of Egypt and Syria. In light of such achievements, small wonder that Ayyub, the father of Saladin, has been referred to by Arab historians as *Walid al-muluk* or the "Father of the Kings." [21]

But what about young Saladin himself? What was his upbringing amid that military family? How did he react to political pressures generated by the ambitions of his father, uncles, and brothers? Did their quest for power provoke a negative response, an attitude of introspective meditative self-withdrawal, or a reluctance to become involved in political, military, or administrative activities? Quite the contrary. Available evidence plainly suggests that from a tender age, Saladin was committed to a professional military career.

Whatever fundamental education Saladin might have achieved in Baalbek, his qualifications were adequate to get him a position in the military establishment of Nur al-Din. In 1152, at the age of fourteen, he joined his uncle at Aleppo in the service of his Syrian sultan, for which he was allotted a fief of his own. [22] His performance must have been meritorious, for in 1156, at the age of eighteen, he took over the responsible post of *shihnah* of Damascus from his older brother Turan Shah.[23] Age apparently did not hamper his administrative capacity. A few days after he assumed responsibility he detected some fraudulent procedure of the chief accountant. Resigning in protest over this incident, Saladin returned to Aleppo to resume his service in the army.[24] By then Nur al-Din must have been greatly impressed by the character and performance of the young officer because he named him aide-de-camp. Serving as liaison officer between Nur al-Din and his commanders, and "never leaving the Sultan whether on the march or at court," [25] Saladin there acquired a first-hand practical experience in the art of ruling a feudal military organization.

In 1157 the young commander had a close brush with death when he was trapped in Hamah during a devastating earthquake. Fortunately for students of history, less so for the Crusaders, amid all the houses turned into rubble by that catastrophe, the one sheltering Saladin remained intact.[26]

At twenty-six Saladin was established enough to own a house in Damascus.[27] He must have excelled in horsemanship because Nur al-Din regarded him as a favorite partner in the strenuous game of polo.[28] Considering that Saladin enjoyed hunting throughout his adult years,[29] it is fair to assume that his passion for that sport developed during his adolescence. He seems to have remained single—at least no marital involvements prior to 1164 are reported. According to his medieval biographers, early in 1169 Saladin "gave up drinking wine and turned away from the sources of pleasure." [30] On its face, this statement—if believed at all—suggests that until he turned thirty-one, Saladin had not always been averse to drinking and other worldly temptations. And it would indicate that the young officer was not too strongly influenced by the moral example of Nur al-Din, who was well known for his ardent attachment to religion and for his scrupulous observance of Islamic precepts. In any event, Saladin never performed a pilgrimage to Mecca, in spite of the fact that in 1157 Ayyub [31] and in 1160 Shirkuh,[32] each led a caravan of pilgrims from Damascus. In 1161 Shirkuh once again served as the leader of the pilgrim caravan which included the mighty Nur al-Din himself.[33] In spite of these examples set by his father, his uncle, and his influential superior, Saladin did not avail himself of those opportunities to fulfill the fundamental religious obligation incumbent on every Muslim.

In view of Saladin's intimate association with his immediate family it is difficult to imagine him unaffected by their military and political ambitions. Certainly he was benefiting from the successful career of his father and uncle. Witnessing the ascendancy of his father at Nur al-Din's court, knowing it followed an earlier post in the opposing camp, Saladin must have realized the practical virtues of political flexibility. Had he resented the atmosphere of political pressures and intrigues, he need not have entered military service in Aleppo. As it was, his meritorious performance attracted the eye of the stern sultan, who set him right on the same path taken by the other members of his family.

In organizing the expedition to Egypt Nur al-Din and Shirkuh were unlikely to select personnel with questionable loyalty or inadequate professional qualifications. The intervention in Egypt was not regarded as a minor operation but as a hazardous campaign with no place for novices or lukewarm participants. Only experienced officers and troops deserved the distinction of taking part in that expedition. Had Saladin shown any aversion to military and political activities, he need not have joined the expeditionary force. Had Saladin not been militarily and politically competent, he could hardly have been included in the officer staff. The selection of Ayyub's son to participate in that difficult and dangerous military operation suggests that at age twenty-six, Saladin enjoyed the reputation of a trustworthy and competent warrior.

3 Saladin and the campaigns of Shirkuh in Egypt

"The only error in my life was the sending of Asad al-Din to Egypt."
—*Nur al-Din during his fatal illness*

Modern biographers of Saladin have not shown much interest in the story of the Syrian intervention in Egypt. To dilate on that subject did not seem worthwhile to those who maintained that Saladin's spectacular career had begun after the victory of the Syrians and the death of their leader, Shirkuh. Difficulties in securing and interpreting relevant information from Arabic sources might have also accounted for this regrettable attitude. In my opinion, without studying Saladin's performance in the Syrian expeditionary corps it is hardly possible to understand the circumstances of his subsequent rise to prominence. Prior to going to Egypt, he had enjoyed the reputation of a promising staff officer, but the Egyptian campaigns revealed he was a trustworthy and inspiring leader of men, heroically discharging diverse combat responsibilities under hazardous conditions. A reconstruction of this phase in Saladin's life is presented below. Some of its details have never appeared in print, others were misinterpreted or simply ignored. All of them serve to show the leading role of Saladin in Shirkuh's army, as well as the volatile and explosive nature of Egypt's internal and external politics with which he was later to cope.

The 1164 expedition

What started out as an armed intervention on behalf of a deposed Egyptian vizir turned into a confrontation between the Syrian troops and a coalition of Egyptians and Crusaders. That the isolated Syrian contingent escaped total annihilation and eventually managed an orderly withdrawal from a military trap set up by Shawar was due to the cool-headed leadership of Shirkuh, bravely assisted by Saladin.

The beginning of the expedition threatened no such complications. An improvised, poorly commanded, ill-trained, and spiritless army sent out by Dirgham to engage the Syrian force was slaughtered at Bilbais. Shawar wasted no time in dispatching emissaries to Cairo to secure the cooperation of the palace establishment. When Dirgham attempted a stand in the capital, he found himself abandoned by the people, by remnants of his army, and by the caliph as well. By the end of May 1164 Shirkuh's expedition attained its primary objective. Dirgham and his brother Mulham were killed on 25 May, and on 29 May Caliph al-Adid officially reinstated Shawar as vizir of Egypt. Apart from the political triumph, Shawar also rejoiced, for his son al-Kamil emerged unharmed from his incarceration, together with his fellow prisoner, al-Qadi al-Asad. Moved by the joyful occasion, Shawar hailed the loyal official as al-Qadi al-Fadil, or Eminent Judge—the title by which he is commonly known in Muslim historiography.[1]

Shirkuh's victory eliminated the bloody regime of Dirgham, but it did not rid Cairo of pernicious intrigues. Immediately Shirkuh approached a group of theologians, notably al-Kizani, Ibn Hattiyah, Abu Amr ibn Marzuq, and Ibn Naja on the possibility of seizing the country and overthrowing the Ismaili dynasty of the Fatimids.[2] On the other hand, Shawar was eager to see the Syrian contingent evacuate Egyptian territory. He cynically refused to pay Shirkuh the money stipulated in the agreement with Nur al-Din, and after Shirkuh's refusal to accept a token amount of 30,000 dinars,[3] the Egyptian vizir realized that nothing short of a military action would make his former ally depart. While Shawar was mustering his forces behind the walls of the capital,[4] Shirkuh proceeded with tactical countermoves of his own. Preferring to engage Shawar's forces in an open battle he pulled back, establishing his camp in the immediate vicinity of the capital.[5] At the same time, Shirkuh decided to secure a suitable logistic base to which his army could retreat if necessary. His choice fell on the recently constructed fortress of Bilbais. To prepare this base the Syrian leader sent a military contingent to collect supplies from the countryside for storage in Bilbais. It was Saladin he entrusted with this responsible mission, his first independent field command. The mission was a dangerous one. Saladin had to struggle to seize al-Huf and he lost some of his Turkish soldiers in an encounter with the local army.[6] In spite of these difficulties Saladin successfully completed his task of stockpiling supplies in Bilbais.[7]

By the middle of July, Shawar decided that his troops were ready to tackle the Syrians. On 18 July there took place a major battle at Kawm al-Rish,[8] ending in a total rout of the Egyptians. Shawar had to flee for his life and was almost killed by the frustrated inhabitants of Cairo. The Syrians, reinforced by the Kinanah Bedouins and numerous Egyptian defectors, followed up their victory with a thrust against the capital. They penetrated the northern section of the city, but when Shirkuh was on the verge of a total success, the palace decided to intervene. It is said that Caliph al-Adid, who had followed events from the Golden Gate, threw his own men into the thick of the battle. As a result of their counterattack, the Turks and Kinanah warriors were thrown back and Shirkuh's army withdrew to its encampment.[9] The Syrians might have achieved a major triumph in Egypt, had it not been for the intervention of the palace troops, a circumstance Shirkuh's men were not likely to forget.

Shawar now appealed to Amalric, the king of the Crusaders, offering him huge monetary compensations and quickly persuading him that Nur al-Din's control of Egypt would drastically jeopardize the Frankish kingdom. The Crusaders, responding favorably, wasted no time in setting out. This new development forced Shirkuh to retreat to Bilbais, where he was in turn besieged, beginning 4 August, by a combined Crusader and Egyptian force.

How well Saladin had supplied Bilbais was demonstrated by the outnumbered garrison resisting relentless enemy pressure for over three months.[10] Unable to break down the spirit of the defenders, Amalric and Shawar finally began negotiations, and on 9 November an armistice agreement providing for a peaceful withdrawal of the Syrians and Crusaders was concluded. On the surface Shawar's policy seemed to have ended in success. He recovered and held his position as vizir; he also obtained the evacuation of foreign troops. He had not, however, succeeded in long diverting the covetous eyes from his country.

The aftermath of the first expedition

Shirkuh's expedition did not satisfy Nur al-Din's overall strategy, because it failed to secure Shawar's cooperation or any of Egypt's economic resources for support of the holy war against the Crusaders. On the other hand, the stay in Egypt had given Shirkuh first-hand knowledge of political and military conditions there. He had even established personal contacts with elements hostile to the Fatimid regime. Furthermore, his troops and officers—particularly Saladin—had gained valuable war-making experience in the operationally rather peculiar Egyptian terrain. Thus, Shirkuh urged Nur al-Din to press for mastery over Egypt, pointing out her military impotence while stressing at the same time her economic assets.

Whatever his appraisal of the expedition as a whole, Nur al-Din must have been pleased with Saladin, because in late 1164 the latter was appointed as the *shihnah* of Damascus,[11] an office he had previously held in 1156.[12] During the second term in that office Saladin showed less zeal in discharging his public responsibility. Indeed, Arab chroniclers maintain, without being specific, that his conduct incurred serious criticism and protracted enmity from the senior judge of Damascus, Kamal al-Din ibn al-Shahrazuri, to whose highly regarded legal and moral authority Saladin did not bother to bow.[13]

As we have seen, Shawar appeared to have attained all his basic objectives. He was restored as vizir; he had extricated himself from his commitment to pay one-third of the produce of Egypt to Nur al-Din; and, finally, he had managed to rid the country of all foreign troops, even though this last accomplishment was at some cost. However, Shawar felt far from secure from his internal enemies. Toward the end of 1164 he had dismissed Diya al-Din ibn Kamil al-Suri from the office of the supreme judge and appointed Judge al-Awris in his place;[14] early in January of 1165, he had to stamp out a rebellion,[15] which was followed by unrest among the Bedouin tribes whose pacification required several expeditions led by Shawar's sons and brother.[16]

In the capital itself, the supporters of Dirgham and those accused of communication with Shirkuh were persecuted and imprisoned. Some of them escaped to seek political asylum with the Crusaders or with Nur al-Din. The less fortunate were put to death.[17]

The 1167 expedition

In January 1167 Shirkuh led a fresh army, and once again, Saladin was included in the officers' staff. The Syrian invasion produced an immediate reaction from Amalric, who marched his army out to succor Shawar's precarious regime. As in 1164 Shirkuh faced a coalition of the fearsome Crusaders and the less combative Egyptians. Although Shirkuh once again secured an armistice providing for Syrian and Crusader evacuation of Egypt, the Christians scored the gain of a token garrison in Cairo, in addition to obtaining an annual monetary tribute for the king of Jerusalem.

Inconclusive though it was, this phase of the campaign for Egypt proved momentous for two of its participants. Shawar emerged from that conflict heading precipitously toward self-destruction. Saladin, however, by his heroic role in that dramatic year, became a celebrity, admired by friends, envied by rivals, and feared by enemies.

Shawar's moment of decision came early in the campaign, when the opposing armies were encamped near Cairo, the Syrians at Giza and their enemies at Fustat. The mood on the Frankish-Egyptian side left much to be desired. Frustrated by their failure to end the Syrian aggression through an immediate showdown, the Franks threatened to pull out unless Shawar met their ever-increasing monetary demands. Shawar realized that a Frankish withdrawal would leave him to confront the mighty Shirkuh alone. With the Egyptian army enervated, Shirkuh could assert not only military control but political as well. At stake was not the vizirate alone, but the fate of the Fatimid caliphate itself. Thus, Amalric's assistance appeared absolutely necessary, even if such an alliance should result in a dangerous ascendancy of the Crusaders. However, to secure Frankish cooperation Shawar had to comply immediately with their monetary demands, a condition he was then unable to fulfill, for he was suffering from a temporary cash shortage of his own.

It was then that a Syrian emissary showed up in the Egyptian camp, bringing a personal message from Shirkuh.[18] The timing, the contents, and the reverberations it produced in the Egyptian command suggest that Shirkuh must have been aware of Shawar's difficulties with his Christian allies. In a straightforward manner Shirkuh declared that neither he nor his associates held any hostile designs with regard to Egypt. Their concern—he pleaded—was the victory of Islam over the Crusaders. If only Shawar would join forces with Shirkuh, they could deal a fatal blow to the Franks. "I do not think that Islam will ever have another chance like this," Shirkuh concluded his arguments.[19]

Shawar was irked by that demarche. "What's wrong with the Franks; what about the Franks?" he remarked angrily.[20] Still, it was rather difficult for him to dismiss outright Shirkuh's emotional declaration. For by emphasizing his anti-Crusader stand, Shirkuh upgraded his Egyptian intrusion to a *jihad,* a holy war, the outcome of which Shirkuh now argued rested with Shawar.

Obviously, Shawar needed some advice, for he met with his son al-Kamil, his brother Najm al-Din, and al-Qadi al-Fadil. The presence of the Qadi—the source, incidentally, of our information—suggests he enjoyed the highest degree of Shawar's confidence. The conference revealed a great divergence of opinions. Al-Kamil advised an attack on the Crusaders. Najm al-Din proposed that Shawar withdraw with his supporters to Salim and farther beyond. Significantly enough, in his account al-Qadi al-Fadil omitted mention of his own attitude. At any rate, Shawar remained unconvinced by these suggestions. He made his own position clear when he exclaimed pathetically: "I shall continue fighting the intruders until I die." A momentary impasse was resolved by the sudden arrival of a delegation from the palace. The strong man of the palace, major domo Saniat al-Mulk, and the chief Ismaili missionary, Ibn Abd al-Qawi, entered the tent, bringing the funds Shawar so desperately needed.[21] That was all Shawar required. He answered Shirkuh by putting to death the Syrian emissary, then he informed the Franks about Shirkuh's appeal and his rejection of it.[22] As in 1164 timely palace intervention enabled Shawar to prosecute his policy against Shirkuh.

In spite of ample tangible evidence of Shawar's commitment to the Frankish-Egyptian alliance, Amalric insisted on a more formal treaty. Perhaps he knew the part played by the palace establishment. In any event, the Crusader king demanded that a treaty of alliance between Egypt and the Kingdom of Jerusalem be ratified by the caliph himself. Since Shawar by then had reached the point of no return in his pro-Frankish policy, he had no choice but to arrange for a special ceremony at the palace.[23]

Saladin at the battle of al-Babain and the defense of Alexandria

While the palace forces lined up with Shawar and Amalric, the Alexandrians came out in support of Shirkuh. They had received an appeal from him, concerning the Frankish peril, and responded by promising resources and weapons to fight the enemies of Islam. The leadership over what amounted to a rebellion against the caliphate and the vizirate was assumed by Najm al-Din, a son of a former Egyptian vizir who had been hiding from Shawar in Alexandria.[24] Even with such support, Shirkuh's situation was critical. Under mounting enemy pressure he was compelled to evacuate his position at Giza and retreated hastily as far south as Ashmunain. The long weeks of inactivity, followed by a strenuous march with the aggressive enemy on their trail, demoralized some of Shirkuh's commanders. A military success of some sort was so badly needed that Shirkuh decided to give his pursuers a battle.

What the Syrian leader lacked in numbers he hoped to make up with the quality of his troops and a daring battle plan. He split up his army into two contingents, one of which was to serve almost suicidally as a tactical bait. Positioned to protect the baggage, it was to bear the first onslaught of the charging enemy. When pressed, this contingent was to fall back and draw the enemy in pursuit, and then to counterattack in turn, as the fight might allow. The second contingent, composed of picked horsemen commanded by Shirkuh himself, was to cut up the enemy's rear, which consisted of the less martial Egyptians. It was obvious that the outcome of the battle—if not the very fate of Shirkuh's expedition—hinged upon the proper execution of the bait maneuver. Shirkuh's choice of commander for this first contingent fell on Saladin.

The opposing armies clashed on 18 April 1167 at al-Babain. The battle proceeded as Shirkuh had anticipated. Saladin drew the Franks away: the Egyptians were cut up and routed; and when the Crusaders, returning from the pursuit, found their allies routed, they also fled for their lives. Their king narrowly escaped captivity.

In spite of the victory, Shirkuh had no time to relax because the enemy, quickly recovering from the debacle, prepared to resume offensive operations. As in the first campaign, Shirkuh needed an operational base and, since Bilbais was in hostile hands, he marched northwards to friendly Alexandria. The leaders of the rebel city lived up to their pledge. Najm al-Din, in handing his command over to Shirkuh, placed at his disposal rich financial resources and supplies, prepared for this purpose by the head of the local ministry, al-Qadi Rashid al-Din Ibn al-Zubayr.[25] These assets permitted the Syrian commander to evolve a new strategy: Alexandria was to function as static bait to tie up the army of Amalric and Shawar, while Shirkuh would turn south, to Upper Egypt, in search of additional troops. Alexandria was well fortified, with troops of her own; her population was hostile to Shawar, and, above all, to the Crusaders. The local garrison was reinforced by a contingent of Syrian soldiers, in addition to all the incapacitated men from the expeditionary army. Once again there arose the crucial question of a suitable, experienced, and inspiring leader who could weld these diverse elements into a unified command. And once again the choice fell to the hero of al-Babain, Saladin.[26] Around the end of April or the beginning of May 1167, the bulk of the Syrian expeditionary force departed south, while Saladin remained on his own, bracing himself to carry out his dangerous assignment.

He did not wait for long. Hardly had Shirkuh left when the Franks and Egyptians of Shawar closed in on Alexandria and with their powerful forces and siege machines engaged the isolated and outnumbered garrison in heavy fighting. It soon became apparent that Shirkuh had chosen his commander-in-chief wisely. In spite of relentless attacks, the defensive perimeter of Alexandria remained unbroken. Both the defenders and the populace behind the front line, aroused by the valor, determination, and inspiring leadership of Saladin, dug in and resisted the murderous onslaughts. They suffered many casualties, their supplies were running short, but after nearly three months of fighting Saladin's men remained unconquered.[27] With the siege thus dragging on during the oppressive summer months, the attacking troops must have been tiring. In the meantime, in the last days of July Shirkuh with fresh supplies and locally recruited Bedouin and other volunteer forces, marched north to threaten Cairo.[28]

The prospects of opening yet another front, after seven months of inconclusive siege, appealed neither to Shawar nor to Amalric. Since they proved amenable to negotiations, Shirkuh proposed his price for cessation of hostilities. On 4 August 1167 an official treaty was concluded whose basic clause provided for the evacuation of the foreigners from Egypt. Shirkuh was also paid 50,000 dinars by Shawar, while the Franks pretended to be satisfied with a lesser amount of 30,000 dinars.[29] Special arrangements were made for Alexandria, the negotiations for which Saladin conducted.[30] The heroic commander's reputation must have, by then, been firmly established among Moslems and Crusaders as well, because Amalric invited Saladin to pass a few days in the Frankish camp, pending implementation of the armistice agreement. Accepting the invitation, Saladin met in person his Christian adversary and his knights.[31] It also gave him an opportunity to exercise direct influence on the king, to prevent Shawar from abusing the terms of the agreement. According to its terms Saladin's troops were to evacuate the battered city of Alexandria. The able-bodied soldiers were to depart by land, but the wounded or incapacitated ones were to be transported aboard Frankish ships to Acre, to spare them the desert trip. The rebel Alexandrians were to open their gates and allow the hated Shawar and Amalric to take possession of the city. That this was not simply a sellout for the safe-conduct granted to Saladin and his men became evident from a special article which guaranteed personal immunity to all who had joined the rebellion.[32] Although Shawar and Amalric must have relished their triumphant entry into the city, they soon found that the spirit of the men who had rallied around Saladin remained unbroken. When Shawar castigated the city elders for their armed revolt against the legitimate government, the scholarly jurist, Shams al-Islam Abu al-Qasim spoke up unequivocally: "We fight everybody who comes under the sign of the Crusaders' cross, no matter who he is!" [33]

Shawar did not delay retributions. Even before Saladin left the Crusader camp, he had received disturbing news about the vizir's large-scale retaliatory measures against all those implicated in the rebellion. Najm al-Din managed to escape to Syria; other Egyptians contemplated similar steps. It took Saladin's personal intervention with King Amalric to bring about suspension of Shawar's repressive measures. Indeed, Shawar adopted a more conciliatory attitude which made many people abandon their plans to leave Egypt. There were others, however, who did not trust their vizir, preferring to seek political asylum in Syria or even at the court of the Crusaders.[34]

Saladin upon his return from the expedition

On 6 September 1167 Shirkuh returned to Damascus, having failed once again to achieve the submission of Egyptian resources to Nur al-Din's control. Once again Shawar had foiled the Syrian attempt by enlisting King Almaric's support. However, Shirkuh's mission could not be regarded as a failure. By successfully applying superior strategy the Syrian leader forced through a peace treaty with Shawar which prevented Egypt from falling into the hands of the Crusaders. A major factor in achieving it was the performance of Saladin. Whether in the running battle of al-Babain, or in the static defense at Alexandria, Shirkuh's nephew revealed himself not only as a competent and courageous field commander, but as an inspiring leader of men, military and civilian alike.

Veteran of two Egyptian campaigns, Saladin returned to Syria as an experienced warrior. He had watched his soldiers gloating over their early victory, but he had also seen them hungry, crippled, and dead, in the siege of Alexandria. As one of the chief armistice negotiators, Saladin was introduced to the intricate art of diplomacy. He was quick to learn that these agreements were shortlived diplomatic expedients observed only as long as none of the signatories were strong enough to violate the solemnly pledged treaties.

Back in Syria his outstanding accomplishments did not remain unrecognized. Saladin's material reward was two military appanages, one in the district of Aleppo, another in that of Kafartab.[35] More satisfying to personal prestige was his rise to prominence in the entourage of Nur al-Din. Resuming his former function as an aide-de-camp, Saladin displayed great skill in various cultural and political activities at court.[36] As a constant companion of Nur al-Din, Saladin exerted himself in sharing his master's passion for polo. From that period also dates Saladin's friendship with the famous poet Imad al-Din al-Isfahani;[37] their tombs stand side by side. More significant for the historian was the urge Imad al-Din felt to immortalize the exploits of his great friend and hero, Saladin, which he did in several extremely interesting (if overly flamboyant) eyewitness accounts of the campaigns against the Crusaders.

A new crisis in Egypt

Saladin's leisure preoccupations at the court of Aleppo were not to last long. About the time Shirkuh arrived in Damascus, Muslim public opinion in Egypt and Syria was shocked by another perfidious act Shawar perpetrated. There existed, apart from the official tripartite treaty, a secret agreement with Amalric, which Shawar had made without the knowledge of the palace establishment,[38] or even of his son and principal advisor, al-Kamil. The deal, ostensibly intended to ward off Nur al-Din's attacks against Egypt, provided for annual payments of 100,000 dinars to the chest of the Crusaders in return for military assistance. Moreover, much to the indignation of Caliph al-Adid and to the horror of the inhabitants of the capital, Amalric was ceded an enclave within the fortified precinct of Cairo, to be manned by a Frankish military contingent under their own Christian command.[39]

Shawar's high-handed and cynical policy not only flouted Muslim public opinion but invited further Frankish efforts towards asserting direct control over Egypt. Conspiracy-prone Egyptian politicians wasted no time. Before the end of 1167 a new conspiracy had come into existence, with Shawar's own son, al-Kamil among its leading members. It was their turn to approach Nur al-Din for assistance, using as intermediary a prominent Kurdish commander and maternal uncle of Saladin, Shihab al-Din al-Harimi. Writing on behalf of the conspirators, al-Kamil appealed to the Syrian sultan asking him to restore law and order in Egypt as well as to unite the forces of Islam.[40] Such a stipulation showed the new conspiracy to be directed not only against the vizir but against the Ismaili caliphate as well. As an economic inducement, the conspirators promised to pay an annual tribute to Nur al-Din. To prove their serious intent, they sent a considerable amount of cash to Damascus as soon as they received an encouraging reply from Nur al-Din. In addition to that group of conspirators, other enemies of Shawar, like Yahya ibn al-Khayyat, Ibn al-Nuhhas, and Ibn Qarjalah (Farajallah?) were also active, but they preferred to base their hopes on Frankish rather than on Syrian support. These conspirators, after escaping from Egypt, betook themselves to the court of King Amalric.[41]

Obviously sensing the spread of hostile political ferment, Shawar instituted a regime of terror. In violation of his earlier pledge, the vizir ordered the arrest of all people suspected of favoring Shirkuh or Nur al-Din. It is said that many innocent persons were summarily executed in the garden of the vizirial palace, in the very presence of Shawar.[42] Among the most notable victims were two erudite poets, officials, and juridical experts, al-Muhadhdhab ibn al-Zubayr and his brother al-Rashid ibn al-Zubayr; the latter had been prominent in the Alexandrian revolt.[43]

Then employing the same Shihab al-Din who had previously interceded on behalf of the anti-Shawar conspirators, the vizir promised Nur al-Din rich economic rewards if he could succeed in diverting Shirkuh's attention from Egypt. Much to his satisfaction Nur al-Din let him know, around the middle of 1168, that he had made Shirkuh give up his Egyptian plans, in return for an increase in his feudal appanage consisting of Homs and its provinces.[44]

Despite these precautionary measures, Shawar still felt insecure in office. Trusting neither the efficacy of diplomatic arrangements nor the fighting ability of his troops, he decided to strengthen the belt of fortifications around the capital and ordered speedy construction of a wall and moat around the old city of Fustat.[45]

The third campaign

If the first two campaigns had witnessed Saladin's gradual rise to fame and authority, the third expedition was all Saladin; from the initial mobilization to the final triumph of Shirkuh, he served as his uncle's right hand in military, political, and administrative matters.

In contrast wth the earlier campaigns, this one was provoked by the Crusaders. Yielding to pressure from the barons, the Hospitalers, and the Pisans, King Amalric attempted to establish direct control over the country of the Nile. In the middle of October 1168 the land and naval formations of the Crusaders, having feigned preparations for an offensive in Syria, moved westward from Ascalon to Darum.[46] The news about the Frankish advance arrived in Cairo around 20 October. Immediately Shawar dispatched one of his commanders, Zahir al-Din Badran, as a special envoy to Amalric, demanding explanation. The envoy reached the Frankish headquarters at Darum only to be bribed by Amalric, who asked him to persuade the vizir that the Crusaders were marching to place their services at the disposal of the Egyptian government.[47] Shawar, however, was not deceived and delegated another envoy, this time the prominent politician Shams al-Khilafah himself; but the king continued with deceptive excuses: the Christian advance had been precipitated by the greed of the Crusaders from overseas; he had joined them to serve as a mediator; a tribute of two million dinars would satisfy the invaders. More startling was his statement that the Crusaders had been alarmed by the news that a Syrian jurist, Isa al-Hakkari, had gone to Egypt to arrange for a wedding between Shawar's daughter and Saladin.[48] Although categorically denied by Shams al-Khilafah, this allegation was not void of historical significance. As it will be seen later, Isa al-Hakkari did serve as a go-between in Syria's relations with Cairo.

Furthermore, the mentioning of Saladin in the context of diplomatic intrigues indicated that the Frankish leaders by then regarded him as a potential threat to their interests.

Shawar also received a diplomatic note from Darum, in which the Crusader king asserted that he was coming to Egypt to collect his annual tribute as stipulated in the treaty of 1167. The vizir merely replied that the circumstances calling for continuous implementation of the treaty articles no longer obtained.[49] Obviously, Shawar by then was perfectly aware that various diplomatic excuses offered by the Franks were nothing but a smoke screen for their move to capture the country. Under the circumstances, there was nothing left but to face the grim task of meeting the Crusader challenge. While the fortification work at Fustat feverishly continued, Egyptian troops were being mobilized. Hoping to prevent a Frankish thrust against the capital, Shawar decided to stand at Bilbais, dispatching troops and supplies to that fortress. Command over that exposed garrison was given to his son Tari.[50]

The Crusader invasion of Egypt

Shawar's plan did not work at all. On 4 November 1168, Frankish units closed in on Bilbais and the following day they took the fortress by storm. There followed plunder, conflagration, and massacre of civilian population—though not as widespread as the Latin version of the events tends to indicate.[51] Half the captured population and prisoners of war were distributed as slaves among the victorious troops. The other half, which included Shawar's sons Tari and Sulayman, were retained by the king.[52] To add insult to injury, Amalric sent a message to the vizir in which he boastfully announced his next objective: "Your son Tari wondered whether I thought that Bilbais was a piece of cheese to be eaten by me. Yes, indeed: Bilbais is my cheese and Cairo my butter." [53]

The bloody defeat at Bilbais epitomized the utter failure of Shawar's foreign policy. Through various payoffs, concessions, and promises he had bought the cooperation of the Crusaders in an effort to keep Egypt independent of Syrian domination. Now the Christian forces themselves were threatening the independence of Egypt. Obviously, the total fiasco of his pro-Frankish orientation called for new diplomatic arrangements; for the moment, however, it was the rapidly deteriorating military situation that required immediate attention. After a stay of five days in Bilbais, the invaders resumed their offensive toward Cairo. Since the fortifications around Fustat were not yet complete, its inhabitants were ordered to evacuate it without delay. Familiar with the grim fate of Bilbais, the panic-stricken people of Fustat sought shelter in the congested city of Cairo.[54] To prevent the town from serving as an enemy base, Shawar issued a dramatic order to set Fustat on fire. On 13 November much of the first Muslim capital of Egypt was engulfed by fire, as if the entire old city were irrevocably doomed to perish in the fiery immolation.[55]

The siege of Cairo

A day later, the Crusader army came within sight of Cairo. Once again the vizir delegated Shams al-Khilafah to dissuade them from further aggression. He found Amalric encamped at Birkat al-Habash. The emissary pointed to the awesome spectacle of billowing smoke over Fustat and added that Egyptian willingness to burn their opulent and historical city was the best indication of their determination to defend Cairo against the Crusaders. The exhortation failed to deter Amalric. Bypassing the burning area the Crusaders approached the walls of the capital near the Barqiyah gate and quickly launched their attack.[56]

Despite their hostile feelings toward Shawar, the citizens of Cairo were determined not to share the fate of Bilbais. So instead of a quick victory the Crusader army found itself stalled outside the walls of Cairo. Several weeks of fighting failed to achieve a breakthrough; the intended blitzkrieg had degenerated into a war of attrition.[57] What was frustration to the Franks offered hope to the Fatimid state. The precious time gained by Cairo's tenacious resistance permitted the Egyptians to look for an ally.

The appeal to Nur al-Din

Initiative for a new diplomatic move came from Shams al-Khilafah. Assessing the situation on the basis of his experience as negotiator between Shawar and Amalric, the astute politician doubted the vizir's will to resist continued Crusader pressure. Only a relief expedition from Syria could, in his opinion, avert the impending disaster; however, Shawar could hardly be expected to favor such an idea. There remained the palace establishment, except that it, too, had twice decisively supported the anti-Shirkuh forces. In view of Shawar's ruthless suppression of political dissent Shams al-Khilafah had an extremely difficult task to perform. He chose Shawar's son al-Kamil as his emissary to the court, knowing—or at least, suspecting—him of sympathy toward a Syrian diplomatic solution.[58] Al-Kamil found the caliph receptive to the idea, so both of them sent urgent messages to Nur al-Din. To stir sympathy for the plight of his people al-Adid enclosed some of his wives' hair with his letter. Since the secret message was bound to leak out, the caliph informed Shawar that he was requesting Syrian help which couldn't be less desirable than the Christian assistance Shawar had brought down on Egypt.[59] Shawar in his reply pointed out al-Adid's delusion, for the caliph himself was most likely to suffer from Syrian intervention.[60]

But the palace was no longer disposed to heed Shawar. The gravity of the immediate situation made long-range considerations irrelevant. The catastrophic results of Shawar's policy were all too apparent: the treaty had been cynically violated, Bilbais captured and devastated, Fustat destroyed, Cairo besieged, and Egypt on the verge of Christian occupation. "As long as Egypt remains Muslim, I am ready to become the price of the Muslims!"[61] was al-Adid's reported reply to Shawar. Nor was the caliph alone in his appeal to Syria; several high dignitaries sent similar messages. Obviously the palace had reversed its stand.

Reaction of Nur al-Din, Shirkuh, and Saladin

News of the critical situation in Egypt caused energetic reaction in Aleppo. At a special meeting of top military commanders it was decided to send a relief expedition to Egypt, once again under Shirkuh's leadership. Saladin was instructed to hasten to Homs, to inform his uncle about these developments.[62] Hardly had Saladin left Aleppo when he ran into his uncle, who had also received some Egyptian appeals and was hurrying to be of service to Nur al-Din. "Get ready to march to Egypt," Shirkuh was crisply informed.[63]

In spite of his notorious interest in Egypt, Saladin's uncle hesitated. Perhaps he thought an expedition too risky, in view of the advanced Frankish penetration; perhaps the strain of earlier campaigns was taking its toll; at any rate, Shirkuh quibbled about fearing another trap of Shawar and about lack of funds with which to pay his troops. In reply, Nur al-Din stressed the magnitude of the issue: "If you keep delaying a march into Egypt, I'll lead personally the relief expedition. If we neglect this matter, the Franks are bound to capture Egypt and that, in turn, will lead to our loss of Syria and other territories." [64] Moreover, to soothe Shirkuh, he furnished clothes, weapons, animals, and 200,000 dinars in cash to finance an effective fighting force. But Shirkuh needed additional assurance: he demanded Saladin should be on his staff. Saladin is said to have protested, too horrified by his Alexandrian experience to go.[65] But Shirkuh was adamant,[66] and Nur al-Din supported his request. The sultan even met Saladin's last demur by supplying him, too, with the necessary funds.

Once having accepted the command, Shirkuh proceeded vigorously. In addition to his own feudal contingent, consisting of 500 *mamluk* (slave) and Kurdish soldiers, he selected 2,000 troopers from Nur al-Din's regular army and hired 6,000 Turkmen cavalry.[67] With this army he marched, in early December, from Aleppo to Damascus, where his staff was joined by a number of outstanding high-ranking officers designated by Nur al-Din, including Shihab al-Din al-Harimi, Izz al-Din Jurdik, Gharas al-Din Qilij, Sharaf al-Din Buzughsh,

Nasih al-Din Khumartigin, Ayn al-Dawlah al-Yaruqi, and Qutb al-Din Inal ibn Hassan al-Manbiji.[68] In a convincing gesture to show the importance of their task, Nur al-Din gave each soldier twenty dinars in addition to their regular allowance.[69] Finally, on 14 December 1168 Shirkuh—with Saladin at his side—set out on the fateful mission to Egypt. By now his earlier trepidation must have given way to high hopes and high confidence, for Saladin reputedly promised to pay a prominent poet, al-Arqalah, 1,000 dinars upon the conquest of Egypt.[70]

About this same time—around the fifth week of the siege of Cairo—Shawar received a letter from the sultan of Syria, announcing his decision to send a relief expedition to Egypt. The bearer of the letter was Isa al-Hakkari, the very same jurist Amalric had referred to during his first conversation with Shams al-Khilafah.[71] What Shawar ignored was the fact that al-Hakkari had secretly delivered another letter from Nur al-Din to al-Adid, raising a number of issues not to be revealed to the vizir.[72]

Shawar focused his attention on how to manipulate the arrival of the relief army. He was convinced that by diplomatic blackmail he could use the Syrian intervention to preserve Egyptian independence and perpetuate his own authority. Consequently, he immediately sent Shams al-Khilafah—whose part in the initial exchanges between the caliph and Aleppo remained undetected—to the Crusader camp to communicate Egyptian armistice proposals. The Egyptian envoy informed the king that as both sides had mounting casualties from the futile Crusader attacks, Egypt favored a peaceful solution. In return for Frankish evacuation, Shawar offered to pay 400,000 dinars. And in an obvious attempt to restore positive relations with Amalric, Shawar insisted that only fear of al-Adid and his Muslim supporters had kept him from greater cooperation in the latest conflict. Experienced diplomat as he was, the vizir also tried to intimidate the king by hinting at Nur al-Din's possible intervention.[73]

As if aware of the tension between palace and vizir, Amalric insisted he would negotiate only with the caliph or his representatives. And so the supreme judge and Ismaili official, Ibn Abd al-Qawi, and the major domo, Saniat al-Mulk Jawhar—the very men who in 1167 had represented the palace in support of Shawar—appeared in the

Christian camp to serve notice of disillusionment with the vizir's policy. They found the terms the Crusaders proposed extremely hard: 400,000 dinars, 25 percent to be delivered forthwith, the balance in yearly installments involving a 10 percent surcharge, plus 10,000 *irdabb* (about 2.5 bushels) of grain to be furnished without delay. The palace intended to procrastinate, anticipating an early arrival of the relief force; Shawar, on the other hand, pressed for an immediate settlement. Fortunately for him, one court official revealed to him the existence of a palace cache containing 200,000 dinars; in addition, the inhabitants of Cairo and the refugees from Fustat managed to scrape up 5,000 dinars. With this cash in hand, Shawar pressed the palace to meet the Frankish terms. Avoiding a premature showdown with the vizir, the palace gave in and delivered 100,000 dinars to Amalric.[74] Although the Crusaders grumbled about being short-changed, they agreed to suspend hostilities. After some eight weeks the Franks lifted the siege and established their camp at Birkat al-Habash,[75] where they awaited more money before they would totally evacuate the country.

Arrival of the relief army and retreat of the Crusaders

On 1 January 1169 Shirkuh's army entered Egypt, raising the curtain on three dramatic weeks in the history of the Fatimid caliphate. Not only was the Frankish invasion ended, but an important realignment was made in the political structure of the Cairo government.

News of the approaching relief expedition spurred Shawar on 2 January to proceed with his diplomatic maneuver. He decided to ask Amalric to modify the terms of the armistice agreement. The vizir must have regarded his bargaining position as strong, because he did not use the palace intermediaries but sent his own envoy, Shams al-Khilafah. Shawar now asked Amalric to return the cash earlier delivered by the Egyptians as a price buying Frankish withdrawal. The vizir also asked the king's formal permission to use some money otherwise marked for the Crusaders as funds to obtain Shirkuh's withdrawal from Egypt. Finally, the Egyptians expected the king to release military prisoners of war, including Shawar's sons and to respect the remaining civilian property in Bilbais. In return the vizir promised to observe the truce, which implied that the Egyptians would not harass the Crusaders during their evacuation.

After two months of campaigning, Amalric was in no mood to meet a new challenge—this time from the fresh and always dangerous army of Shirkuh—or to pass up an opportunity to regain Shawar's confidence. Consequently, he complied with the demands and on 4 January 1169 the Frankish army began its retreat, moving first to Bilbais, then to Fakus, finally fading away in the direction of Palestine, but not without dragging along some 12,000 captive civilians, men, women, and children.[76]

Political intrigues in Cairo and liquidation of Shawar by Saladin

Hardly had Shawar declared his nonbelligerency toward the Franks, when he joined Shirkuh to propose immediate military action against the Christian invaders. Having retrieved the money and obtained the release of his sons and the other captive soldiers, Shawar was now eager to pursue the Crusaders, so he could later claim credit for the liberation of Egypt. But he was in for an ominous disappointment. Shirkuh shrugged off the idea of a joint military operation and continued his advance toward the capital, without showing any concern about the withdrawing Crusaders. The Syrian allies got to al-Luq, outside Cairo, where Shirkuh decided to set up his headquarters.[77] The departure of the Crusaders and the arrival of the relief expedition meant for Cairo a much-welcomed turn toward peaceful recovery. Also, the lawlessness which for fifty-four days had prevailed in the deserted city of Fustat would finally be brought to an end.

On 8 January 1169 Asad al-Din Shirkuh entered Cairo amid the acclaims of the jubilant populace to receive a hero's reception from the caliph at a special audience in the palace. Both capital and country were delivered from the Frankish invaders by the Syrian intervention, but Shirkuh's mission was not finished. The caliph assigned some of his own commanders to the staff of the Syrian leader to deliberate regarding the future of the vizirate.[78]

The friendly relationship between Shirkuh and the caliph could not have escaped Shawar's attention. Having earlier alienated many segments of the Egyptian population, he was now falling into the court's disfavor. Hitherto he had managed the tightrope of Egyptian politics by using the support of the court establishment and by exploiting diplomatically the rivalry between Amalric and Shirkuh for control of Egypt. Now, however, the Franks were gone, the Syrian army stood in front of Cairo, and the palace turned against him. In spite of the handwriting on the wall and a warning transmitted to him by Isa al-Hakkari,[79] Shawar refused to step down—or, rather, to run for his life. Instead, he began to contrive yet another scheme to extricate himself from the desperate situation. He intended to arrest Shirkuh and his lieutenants at a banquet ostensibly given in their honor. Once Shirkuh and his entire staff were rendered harmless, Shawar would be able to take command of the entire expeditionary army and thus regain control over Egypt. The vizir confided this plan to his son al-Kamil, who emphatically rejected the idea and even threatened to denounce his father to Shirkuh.[80] With his own son turned against him, all Shawar's hopes were gone. Indeed, on 18 January 1169—only ten days after Shirkuh's triumphant entry into Cairo—Shawar's life abruptly ended.

The vizir, trusting the protection of his bodyguards, rode out of Cairo to visit Shirkuh, but was met instead by Saladin and Izz al-Din Jurdiq, accompanied by a group of their own followers. The two Syrian commanders managed to isolate their Egyptian guest from his soldiers, and, while the Syrians suddenly attacked and dispersed the latter, Saladin arrested the hapless vizir and led him away to Shirkuh's camp. As soon as the caliph learned about Shawar's seizure, he dispatched an aide to the Syrian leader, ordering him to finish the job. On the same day the head of the executed vizir was delivered to the palace.

The following day the caliph invited Shirkuh to the palace. On his way, he met a tumultuous mob riotously celebrating the downfall of the hated vizir. The crowds were getting so completely out of control that Shirkuh, fearing for his own safety, told them to take possession of the masterless vizirial palace.[81] While the mobs ravaged those premises, Asad al-Din Shirkuh received his reward at the court of the caliph. In al-Adid's presence and acting as his spokesman, the major domo Saniat al-Mulk Jawhar expressed regrets for earlier opposition to the guest of honor and satisfaction at his victory over the foes of the Fatimid house. After Shirkuh had proclaimed his readiness to serve the caliphate loyally, he was officially installed as the new vizir and commander-in-chief of the Fatimid armed forces. His appointment was confirmed by an elaborate document of investiture, composed and written by al-Qadi al-Fadil,[82] countersigned by the caliph, and read out to the new vizir by the supreme Ismaili judicial and theological dignitary, Ibn Abd al-Qawi.[83] Finally, on 28 January, a special missive, written by al-Qadi al-Fadil on behalf of the caliph, was sent to Nur al-Din, in full recognition of the latter's contribution to the new political development in Egypt.[84]

Thus, Shirkuh's third expedition to Egypt attained complete success: the Crusaders lost the most dramatic round in the battle of Egypt, and Shirkuh himself emerged holding the highest executive office in the Fatimid state organization. As it turned out, this was the climactic finale to a long and ambitious public career.

Saladin's role in Shirkuh's rise to the vizirate

Medieval Arab chroniclers are not unanimous on the details of Shirkuh's coup d'etat.[85] Notwithstanding discrepancies on some points, available evidence reveals a number of interesting aspects of his accession, which have so far remained unnoticed, misunderstood, or unappreciated.

Although ten days separated Shawar's execution from Shirkuh's triumphant entry, that period was enough to confirm Saladin's reputation as a man of trust, of intrepid action, who accepted bloody extermination as a political tool. Shirkuh's recognition of Saladin's outstanding abilities, as well as his insistence that his nephew participate in the Egyptian expeditions, was amply vindicated. Without Saladin the first two Egyptian campaigns might have ended in disaster for Shirkuh; without Saladin's participation in the third expedition Shirkuh might not have achieved his triumph so easily. For, in spite of minor variations, all sources agree that Saladin played an essential and prominent part in the actual planning and implementation of Shawar's capture and killing. Shirkuh demonstrated his full trust in Saladin further by the authority he gave Saladin to handle various matters falling within his jurisdiction as vizir and commander-in-chief.

On the other hand, contrary to a popular version presented by Lane-Poole,[86] it is quite apparent that Shawar's overthrow was precipitated, not by a clash of interests following Shirkuh's arrival, but by a prior and premeditated decision of the Fatimid palace establishment which had become utterly disappointed with the appalling performance of its vizir. Al-Adid's appeal to Nur al-Din may even have included a request for Shawar's elimination.

The role palace establishment assumed during this critical period is most important. After playing second fiddle to a series of autocratic and arrogant vizirs, the Fatimid court politicians made a move to regain effective political authority by taking advantage of the critical situation. Despite initial reservations respecting Shirkuh, they found him amenable to political cooperation. He decisively helped the caliphate get rid of its nefarious vizir; in return, the caliphate rewarded him with an appointment which formally recognized his prominent status in the ruling regime of Egypt.

In this light, the fate of Shawar's son al-Kamil acquires specific significance. Hearing of his father's execution, he and a few other members of Shawar's immediate family sought asylum at the Fatimid court. The move was not illogical, since al-Kamil had on a number of occasions demonstrated his loyalty to Egypt, to the Fatimid caliphate, and to Islam, even conniving with the palace establishment, or with Nur al-Din, against his own father. So al-Kamil had good reason to hope that the caliphate would reciprocate by protecting him from the Syrians. It is further possible that he counted on the help of his friend al-Qadi al-Fadil. Yet he was fatally wrong. The palace establishment resolved to base its plans for political regeneration on cooperation with Shirkuh and considered any male survivor of Shawar's family a political liability. On the other hand, Shirkuh seemed to be anxious to see al-Kamil spared, perhaps in grateful recognition of his pro-Syrian and anti-Crusader sentiments. As it was, the poor refugee chose the wrong haven. When, on 3 February, Shirkuh inquired at court concerning the fate of Shawar's son, he received in reply a silver container with the head of al-Kamil inside.[87]

Contrasting with al-Kamil's tragic end was the career of his close friend and Shawar's confidant, al-Qadi al-Fadil. Sometime after the second Egyptian campaign, he was delegated by al-Kamil to deputize as the head of the Fatimid chancellery for the ailing Ibn al-Khallal. During the siege of Cairo, al-Qadi al-Fadil took part in court consultations concerning the negotiations with Amalric.[88] After Shawar's overthrow, he was assigned the prestigious task of composing and writing Shirkuh's diploma, as well as handling the correspondence of the caliphate with the sultan of Syria. His influence, however, was not sufficient to save al-Kamil; besides, by that time, the resilient dignitary may have already begun service as the chief secretary of the new vizir.[89] At any rate, it is obvious that—his professional competence apart—al-Qadi al-Fadil's success lay in his ability to guess accurately the power shifts in Egyptian political life. With such an asset he could confidently anticipate long indefatigable service in Egypt's cause.

Nur al-Din's dissatisfaction with the new Egyptian situation

Cooperation between the Ismaili caliph and the Sunni commander worked out to their mutual advantage. Shirkuh's new capacity allowed him to enjoy the rewards and shirk the responsibilities of the high governmental position. He liked to converse with the caliph and appreciated the company of Ibn Abd al-Qawi.[90] Administrative affairs he delegated to Saladin[91] and al-Qadi al-Fadil. Except for personally initiating and encouraging the rehabilitation of fire-scarred Fustat,[92] the new vizir showed complete political passivity, complacently accepting the *status quo*—much to the satisfaction of the Fatimid establishment.

In relation to Nur al-Din, the entrusting of the vizirate to the leader of the expeditionary army takes on an interesting color. To secure dispatch of the relief force, al-Adid promised the sultan of Syria huge economic rewards which some reports placed at one-third the entire produce of Egypt. Shirkuh's appointment provided a way out of this heavy financial obligation, for when Nur al-Din was officially informed of Shirkuh's new position,[93] the caliph served notice that henceforth the sultan's own commander, not the caliphate, was responsible for Egypt's wartime financial commitments.

This would explain Nur al-Din's reported irritation at the news from Cairo.[94] The sultan had been interested in what Egypt could contribute to the struggle against the Crusaders. Furthermore, as a zealous Sunni Muslim, he entertained ideas about suppressing the Ismaili domination in that country. The campaigns his troops waged in Egypt were intended to implement this policy, and the military success of the third intervention made entirely feasible the prosecution of political schemes going beyond the economic payment pledged by Cairo. Several weeks had passed by and Nur al-Din's hopes and plans remained unfulfilled. Neither money nor other supplies arrived from Egypt and Shirkuh, that trusty right hand of the sultan, had managed to accommodate to the Ismaili caliphate of the Fatimids. In vain did Nur al-Din prevail on al-Adid to effect Shirkuh's return to Syria.[95] As a disciplinary measure, Nur al-Din ordered the confiscation of Shirkuh's feudal holdings in Syria,[96] but that failed to influence the position of the man in Cairo.

The conflict did not last long. Familiar with the pattern of political developments of that decade, some people in Cairo were convinced that Shirkuh's death was imminent.[97] On 23 March 1169 Asad al-Din did die, victim not of bloody purge, however, but simply of obesity. The prosaic end of this outstanding member of the ambitious Kurdish family opened another chapter in the story of Saladin.

4 Saladin's accession to the Fatimid vizirate

". . . it was this opinion of Saladin's docility that had procured him an office where a tractable tool was wanted."—Lane-Poole

Saladin's rise misrepresented

Like so many other aspects of Saladin's career, the story of his promotion to the vizirate has been either played down as devoid of historical relevance or oversimplified as the following quotations from Lane-Poole plainly illustrate:

Saladin had been dragged to Egypt against his will, foreseeing nothing but misery; and now the very step he had tried to avoid was to lead him to the pinnacle of fame. . . . The Fatimid Caliph chose him from among all the Syrian captains. . . . His comrades in arms, many of whom were older and more experienced than himself, were not easily reconciled to the promotion of the young man of thirty over their heads. They thought him a well behaved and intelligent subaltern, too quiet and unambitious for high command;—it was indeed this opinion of Saladin's docility that had procured him an office where a tractable tool was wanted:—but to raise him above the warworn captains of Nur-ed-din's campaigns was more than they could stomach. It needed all Saladin's tact and diplomacy, supported by the specious arguments of el-Hakkary the lawyer, and a liberal opening of treasury coffers, to induce the jealous warriors to submit; and several of them returned to Syria rather than serve under their junior.[1]

Such a treatment of Saladin's promotion is absolutely inadequate and quite misleading. Although Saladin succeeded to the vizirate only three days after Shirkuh's death, his promotion was not immediately assured. First came a series of political maneuvers among a number of pressure groups, each of which tried to impose its own resolution. These crucial if bloodless events deserve a thorough investigation, because they form an essential part of Saladin's rise to power, because they tellingly reveal the intricate nature of the political scene in Cairo, and because they initiated a number of dangerous developments which later were to test the political wisdom and stamina of the new vizir. Above all, the elevation of Saladin to the vizirate once again revealed his reputation of being an experienced, trustworthy, and ambitious leader of men.

Election of Saladin as the commander-in-chief of the Syrian expeditionary forces

Although shortly before his death Shirkuh nominated Saladin as his successor,[2] this designation was not formally recognized by any political or legal hierarchy, so the Syrian expeditionary army found itself without a leader in a foreign country and the Fatimid state had no vizir. Since Nur al-Din himself had appointed Shirkuh, the ultimate selection of his successor would normally have belonged to the Syrian sultan. And yet the emergency arising from Shirkuh's death was much too serious, and Aleppo too far away, to allow the Syrian forces to wait for word from their overlord. Consequently, a new commander-in-chief had to be selected on the spot by consensus among the leading Syrian commanders, who need not consult the Egyptian caliph.

The appointment of a new vizir, on the other hand, presented a more complex problem, since any candidate the Syrian contingent proposed, or imposed, had to be officially invested by the caliphate; and the caliph was hardly in a position to choose a vizir unacceptable to the powerful Syrian pressure group.

Unfortunately the Syrian camp and the palace establishment were far from unanimous on a suitable candidate. The Syrians were split in two basic blocs: the Nuriyah, or the people belonging to Nur al-Din's own feudal contingent, and the Asadiyah, or the people of the contingent of Asad al-Din Shirkuh. In the Nuriyah bloc were several eager contenders, among whom one should mention Shihab al-Din Mahmud al-Harimi, Qutb al-Din Khusraw ibn al-Talil, Sayf al-Din Ali ibn Ahmad al-Mashtub, and above all, Ayn al-Dawlah al-Yaruqi. On the other hand, all 500 men of the Asadiyah contingent favored Saladin, on the strength of Shirkuh's recommendation.

Of the two blocs, the Asadiyah was politically stronger because it supported a single contender, because it claimed to be executing the will of the deceased leader, and finally, because one of its leading members happened to be Isa al-Hakkari. Acting on behalf of Saladin, al-Hakkari came to an understanding with Baha al-Din Qaragush, the commander of the 3,000 man Syrian cavalry force, thus securing military backing for the otherwise outnumbered Asadiyah bloc.[3] Hoping to achieve Saladin's election without bloodshed, the diplomatic jurist then engaged in a number of secret negotiations, during which he shrewdly exploited the rivalry among the Nuriyah contenders, appealed to feelings of solidarity between the Kurds, and capitalized on the family connections of his candidate. He first went to Sayf al-Din Ali al-Mashtub and swung him over to Saladin, by arguing that "this command will never be yours in the presence of Ibn al-Talil, al-Harimi and al-Yaruqi."[4] The negotiator then got in touch with Shihab al-Din Mahmud al-Harimi, appealing to his family ties with Saladin. Al-Hakkari insisted: "He is the son of your sister, and his cause is your cause. The command has been reserved for him. Don't be the first of those who want to deprive him of that, especially since you yourself will not attain it anyway."[5] Al-Harimi was quite aware that in hoping to succeed Shirkuh, he faced opposition from Ayn al-Dawlah al-Yaruqi and others, who might use violence to frustrate his ambitions. Consequently, he yielded to al-Hakkari, satisfied that if Saladin were successful, military and political leadership would, after all, remain in the family.

In negotiating with the third contender, the Kurd Qutb al-Din Khusraw ibn al-Talil, al-Hakkari used an anti-Turkish line: "Verily, everybody is for Saladin, except you and al-Yaruqi. What is needed now, above all, is an understanding between you and Saladin, especially because of his Kurdish origin, so that the command does not go away from him to the Turks."[6] And, after promising additional fiefs to Qutb al-Din, the negotiator secured his cooperation as well.

But al-Hakkari tried in vain to obtain the approval of al-Yaruqi.[7] The ambitious Turkish commander refused to accept Saladin's election, though his opposition could not prevent it. Saladin's supporters were now strengthened by many of his former rivals; the leading officers in the Nuriyah camp voiced their support for him.[8] After acclaiming him their new commander-in-chief the Syrians naturally assumed that the palace establishment would install him as the new vizir of the Fatimid caliphate.

A conflict at the Fatimid court and the nomination of Saladin as the new vizir of Egypt

The appointment of a new vizir caused a clash of opinions at the court of al-Adid. While all were determined to preserve political advantages regained after Shawar's overthrow, they disagreed about who would best suit the political interests of the palace establishment. One party, headed by the leading member of the court, Saniat al-Mulk Jawhar, advocated a radical plan aimed at further increasing the authority of the caliphate. According to that plan, the caliph would assume direct control over the 3,000 Ghuzz cavalry, commanded by Baha al-Din Qaragush. These units were to be given feudal allotments in the province of Sharqiyah and would thus be transformed into locally settled border troops, protecting Egypt's eastern frontiers against Crusader attacks. The vizirate would go to a local Fatimid military man who would serve the interests of the caliph, acting as a liaison between the sovereign and the Egyptian people, without infringing on the authority of the ruler or interfering with his affairs.[9]

This policy echoed an idea earlier entertained by Shawar,[10] when it stressed the necessity of utilizing Syrian troops for the exclusive benefit of Egypt's own security. The ineligibility of non-Egyptians for the vizirate, as well as the proposed limitations on that office, revealed the aspiration of the palace establishment to increase the prestige and effective sovereignty of the supreme Ismaili institution.

However, Saniat al-Mulk's plan ran into opposition from another palace group, which acted as if it had been hired to serve Saladin's interests. This group insisted the caliph should appoint the man who had done the actual administering for Shirkuh. They maintained further that if Saladin were confirmed as vizir, then Qaragush and other prominent Syrian commanders would stay on in Egypt to serve him.[11] With the palace politicians so divided, an opportunity arose for young al-Adid to assert his own authority. In obvious rejection of the radical solution, he sent for Shihab al-Din al-Harimi to consult about the choice made by the Syrian camp, and when the latter advised the caliph to appoint the new commander-in-chief to the vizirate, the matter was definitively settled.[12] Only then, on 26 March 1169 did Saladin, son of Ayyub, officially become the vizir of the Fatimid caliphate in Egypt.

Saladin's qualifications and ambitions

Saladin's elevation consisted of two decisive stages. The first was his election as Syrian commander-in-chief; the second, his official promotion to the vizirate. But why had Saladin's candidacy for commander-in-chief come up in the first place? Why did al-Adid or his coterie regard Saladin as an acceptable candidate for the crucial job of vizir? These questions arise because of popular misconceptions concerning Saladin's qualifications and personal ambitions. Lane-Poole, quoted above, refers to Saladin as "the young man of thirty," "a well-behaved and intelligent subaltern, too quiet and unambitious for high command"; Saladin's success is attributed to "docility that had procured an office where a tractable tool was wanted."

To what extent can these allegations withstand serious criticism? Could Saladin's age per se, for instance, constitute a handicap? At the time of his election, Saladin was, indeed, only slightly over thirty, but he already had some sixteen years' experience of regular service in the military state organization of Nur al-Din; some of those years were spent in an administrative capacity, others in a highly responsible position as the sultan's aide-de-camp. At the age of twenty-eight, he held independent command during the Frankish-Egyptian siege over the entire garrison and city of Alexandria; before Shirkuh's death, he had acted as de facto vizir, in place of his relaxing uncle. After all, Nur al-Din became sultan of Aleppo when he was twenty-nine, and Amalric was crowned king at thirty-one.

It is difficult to establish the meaning of "well-behaved" or "too quiet," but one is bound to observe that as the *shihnah* of Damascus in 1164, and later, when he resisted joining the third Egyptian campaign, Saladin did not appear exceptionally "well behaved." His indulgence in wine and other questionable pleasures which, according to Arab sources, he gave up following his vizirial nomination, do not show him too quiet either.

Was he "unambitious for high command?" It is true that Baha al-Din, the consistent idolizer of Saladin, claimed that his hero resisted nomination to the vizirate, and that it took much persuasion to change his mind.[13] However, this assertion of the Arab biographer is absolutely incompatible with the consistent nature of Saladin's striking rise to prominence. Had he not been ambitious, he could hardly have gotten increasingly more responsible and demanding command positions in Shirkuh's army. Had he really been unambitious, lukewarm, or indifferent to high command responsibility, no one would have made him commander-in-chief of the Syrian expeditionary army. Above all, had Saladin not desired the career to which his earlier exploits and successes seemed to predestine him, Shirkuh's death gave him a good opportunity to prove it. Certainly, he was not bound to assume his uncle's political and military legacy in Egypt; indeed, there are many indications that the sultan of Syria would have been far more delighted to see Saladin return forthwith to Aleppo.

This is the very crux of the issue. As long as Shirkuh lived, the army under his command enjoyed an official status as a military unit serving the Fatimid vizir. His death, however, placed the expeditionary forces in the odd situation of being stationed in a foreign country, without regular status, either military, political, or economic. Also, with the death of Shirkuh, the Kurdish ethnic faction lost the leader who had protected its interests against those of the Turks. Finally, the relatives and affiliates of the house of Shirkuh and Ayyub were concerned about losing the influence which they had enjoyed. For these reasons, the election of a mediocre man to Shirkuh's position was out of the question. Shirkuh's family clique, the Kurdish contingent, the rank and file of the expeditionary army, all needed a trustworthy and outstanding leader —and they had every reason to believe that Saladin was their man. Besides the prestige he enjoyed as Nur al-Din's favorite liaison officer and aide-de-camp and also as Shirkuh's confidant, Saladin more than once demonstrated his leadership during the three Egyptian campaigns. He led his men successfully in all kinds of military assignments; he inspired them to heroic efforts in the face of deadly enemy pressure; he cared for the well-being of his men, the healthy and the wounded alike; he proved a capable negotiator; and he showed no mercy to those who dared obstruct any cause he supported.

Although there were several contenders for the position of commander-in-chief, Saladin appeared to be Shirkuh's natural successor. Whether the initiative to elect him originated with Shirkuh, or with someone else in the Kurdish or the family group, Saladin was absolutely prepared to accept the responsible function. His prestigious maternal uncle, Shihab al-Din al-Harimi, stepped down, mostly because he feared the intrigues of some Turkish rivals,[14] but Saladin had no such qualms. Indeed, such was his authority and prestige that those who envied his elevation saw no possibility of dislodging him or dominating him. Their only alternative was to pack up and leave Egypt for Syria.

But what motivated the palace establishment to appoint Saladin as the new vizir? The simple answer to this may be that al-Adid, or the politicians behind the throne, had no means of challenging the choice of Saladin. The expeditionary army constituted the most effective military contingent in Egypt, and Shirkuh's earlier appointment to the vizirate had established a precedent which the palace was in no position to change, nor the Syrians in a mood to stop. There are certain indications, however, that in spite of Saladin's dynamic personality, al-Adid hoped to bring him under the influence of the palace establishment. According to Arab chroniclers,[15] the palace establishment rightly anticipated that Saladin's elevation would split the Syrian camp, producing a subsequent exodus of some commanders and their own units, protesting the choice of the vizir. The defection of these units was expected to weaken the expeditionary army to such a degree that Saladin would have to cooperate with the Fatimid establishment.

Saladin's official investiture took place at a solemn ceremony in the vizirial palace. Attended by much of the Fatimid and local Syrian elite, the son of Ayyub, addressed by the new honorific name of al-Malik al-Nasir,[16] received sumptuous vizirial garments, his sword of office, and several precious gifts from the caliph. Finally, a pompous investiture diploma, again composed and written by al-Qadi al-Fadil, was read [17] proclaiming Saladin's nomination and outlining various governmental responsibilities he was to perform, including the obligation to wage holy war against enemies of the Ismaili sovereign.[18] The ceremony concluded with the new vizir bestowing various honors and gifts on the members of the audience.[19]

This solemn event in Saladin's career was marred by the recalcitrant attitude of Ayn al-Dawlah al-Yaruqi. Embittered by his failure to succeed Shirkuh, Ayn al-Dawlah decided to lead his contingent back to Syria rather than serve the son of Ayyub.[20] One can well imagine what kind of report the envious commander passed on to Nur al-Din. Indeed, according to one source, the sultan of Syria was greatly upset at the news of the high honors conferred upon his former favorite.[21]

Ayn al-Dawlah's departure, which was followed by a few other defections,[22] might have been interpreted as demoralization in the Syrian expeditionary army. If real, this debilitation would have served the palace in controlling the political ambitions of the new vizir. As it later turned out, those who suffered from such delusions had grossly underestimated the dynamic personality of Saladin.

5 Saladin as Fatimid vizir

" . . . Saladin's personal position and qualities, the spirit in which he approached his task, and the methods he employed were utterly different from those possessed and displayed by the founders of great military empires."—H. A. R. Gibb

Contrary to popular romantic notions, exemplified by the above epigraph, Saladin's political behavior did not differ in spirit and methods from that of other medieval military leaders. Conditions in Egypt hardly allowed for experimentation. His accession to the vizirate meant the fifth change in that office within six years. In February 1163 Shawar had become vizir only to be ousted and succeeded that August by Dirgham. In May 1165 Shawar again became vizir, after Shirkuh defeated Dirgham, and 19 January 1169 Shirkuh became vizir after Shawar's execution. Finally on 26 March 1169 Saladin succeeded Shirkuh. The last event marked the beginning not only of a new phase in Saladin's career, but of a significant chapter in the history of Egyptian vizirate. For, unlike his predecessors, Saladin managed to maintain himself in the hitherto vulnerable position and ultimately succeeded in converting his vizirial prerogatives into absolute powers. Also, having secured political and military stability in Egypt, he created conditions which made it possible for Egyptian society to begin social and economic recovery.

The most crucial phase in Saladin's consolidation of his position was unquestionably the first two and a half years. Saladin's masterly policy during that period, when he overcame complex difficulties in many sectors of the degenerate Fatimid state organization, was at the foundation of his later international military and political career.

Saladin's military and political position at his accession to the vizirate

At his accession, Saladin's position left much to be desired. Militarily, he could depend only on the expeditionary army which at the time of its departure from Syria had counted 8,500 men, but was now reduced by the defection of Ayn al-Dawlah al-Yaruqi. Most of Saladin's commanders, particularly those belonging to the Asadiyah contingent, or to the Kurdish faction supporting the house of Shirkuh, were trustworthy, but the loyalty of certain top Turkish officers of the Nuriyah regiment, envious of the new commander's successes, had as yet to be tested.

Apart from its numerical limitation, the expeditionary army was weakened by its uncertain economic position in Egypt. Original cash resources were running short, and Nur al-Din's attitude being what it was, no cash subsidies could be expected from Syria. It is true that, even before Shirkuh's death Saladin had begun to distribute feudal assignments to the Syrian commanders and their troops, but that program did not go beyond its initial phase.[1]

On the other hand, the regular Egyptian army numbered several regiments of cavalry, some Armenian infantry units, and from 30,000 to 50,000 Sudanese guards serving the palace establishment. As the decade had demonstrated, the Fatimid army was less effective in defending Egypt against foreign invasions than in adding to the confusion caused by factional struggles, but unlike the expeditionary army, the Egyptian forces had a regular economic base consisting of special cash allocations, coming either from the treasury of the vizir or from the palace establishment. Furthermore, in an emergency, it was possible to recruit fighting units of Bedouin warriors, although such troops were notoriously fickle. Finally, the ease with which the Christian fleets attacked Egyptian coastal towns indicated that the Egyptian navy, which had once dominated the Eastern Mediterranean, was virtually nonexistent.

Saladin's political status was also complex. Although he professed the strict Shafiite brand of Sunni (orthodox) Islam, he assumed the obligation of serving an Ismaili caliphate. This was no novelty in Egypt, however Saladin's appointment was special, since it had been achieved mainly through the support his Sunni expeditionary army had given him. And Saladin in his capacity as commander-in-chief of the expeditionary force remained officially subordinate to Nur al-Din, well known for his dedication to Sunni Islam. Because of his own religious convictions, because he depended on his Sunni military supporters in Egypt, and, finally, because of his status in respect to the Syrian sultan, Saladin belonged ideologically and formally to a Muslim bloc determined to obliterate the Ismaili caliphate of the Fatimids. With this kind of liability, how could Saladin be expected to last as vizir?

Saladin had to contend not only with young al-Adid but with all the local Egyptian elements making up the palace establishment. Although the Ismaili caliphate was degenerating, it still benefitted various people and factions who would wish to preserve it. The palace establishment controlled a considerable proportion of Egyptian resources, possessed relatively strong military forces, and dominated the judiciary as well as the chancery (*diwan al insha*). Different religious (Ismaili and Sunni Muslims, the Copts) and ethnic groups (Arabs, Armenians, Sudanese) participated in this palace life. Although political rivalry often generated bloody internal conflicts, which sometimes involved direct outside intervention, the palace establishment wisely observed one fundamental principle: the preservation of the Fatimid caliphate. Men are institutional animals; and the Fatimid caliphate of Egypt provided the useful cohesiveness of legality. In spite of their political and personal shortcomings, the last Fatimids continued to confirm major governmental appointments and ratify important diplomatic agreements. The splendor of the court, backed by its accumulated treasures, both commanded respect and acted as a psychological shield protecting the status of the dynasty. Physical protection was offered by the strong walls of the palace grounds and the special military units. The Fatimids maintained popular prestige through their participation in public ceremonies (e.g., the New Year procession in the streets of the capital) and the ritual invocation of their names and titles (the *khutbah*) every Friday in all the mosques of Egypt.

Saladin's initial relations with the Fatimid caliph and with Nur al-Din

As if to allay establishment misgivings, Saladin made a real effort to impress the people at court and in the streets of the capital with his respect for the Fatimid sovereign. He gained al-Adid's confidence, occasionally even staying as the guest of the palace for several days at a time.[2] The caliph appeared satisfied with Saladin's positive attitude and yielded without protest to various requests he made. To demonstrate publicly this official harmony, the caliph and vizir jointly participated in the solemn processions staged at the opening and closing of Ramadan, A.H. 564 (28 May–27 June A.D. 1169).[3] Also, on each Friday of that Moslem month of fasting, Saladin accompanied the caliph on religious visits to different mosques, including al-Azhar, the focal center of the Ismaili theological and missionary activities.[4]

But in his relations with Nur al-Din the new vizir ran into difficulties. To Saladin's reiterations of loyal respect the sultan reacted with obstructionist measures or gestures calculated to undermine Saladin's prestige and even his effective authority in Egypt. Within one month of Saladin's appointment, Nur al-Din ordered total confiscation of all Shirkuh's and Saladin's feudal appanages in Syria, including Homs and Rahba [5]—a drastic economic uprooting of the Asadiyah in retaliation for their opposition to the Nuriyah. When Saladin asked that his brothers be transferred to Egypt, his request was denied.[6] Instead, the sultan ordered the Nuriyah commanders to leave Saladin and return forthwith to Syria.[7] This caused defection of a few more commanders, such as Qutb al-Din Inal, Nasih al-Din Khumartigin, Ibn Yaruq, and Izz al-Din Jurdiq, who were said to have been irked by Saladin's cooperation with al-Adid.[8] Furthermore, although Saladin had added the name of the Syrian sultan in the official *khutbah* invocations in Egypt, Nur al-Din refused to recognize Saladin as vizir. Whereas many people in Egypt, impressed by the achievements and new status of Ayyub's son, referred to him in regal terms, the sultan's letters did not even mention the title of vizir and were addressed deprecatingly "to the

Amir Salah al-Din, commander-in-chief, and to other amirs"; [9] obviously, Nur al-Din intended his former aide to function solely as his agent in Egypt, entrusted with channelling her economic resources to Syria.

Saladin's new army and its economic base

Saladin was far from accepting such an interpretation of his mission. As the top executive official in Egypt, he had no intention of relinquishing any of his prerogatives. But to maintain himself he needed strong land and naval forces of his own. The possibility of using the local Egyptian units had to be ruled out, partly because they were of inferior quality and partly because they were specifically committed to defending the palace grounds. On the other hand, the expeditionary force, even reduced in size by the Nuriyah departures, was available for the backbone of a new army. Saladin failed to get his brothers into Egypt, but he still had several trustworthy commanders, eager to participate in the program of large-scale military expansion.

How to finance the recruitment and upkeep of this expanded military establishment created a real problem. Some cash, found in Shirkuh's treasury, helped Saladin to buy time necessary to launch his ambitious program.[10] Any cash forthcoming from tax collection could also purchase military slave-recruits (*mamluks*), equipment, and other military stocks. Sporadic financial assistance from the caliph might come in times of foreign invasion, but could not be counted upon, especially as the palace establishment supported between 30,000 to 50,000 Armenian and Sudanese guard troops.

Exact figures of the military build-up Saladin envisaged in 1169 are lacking, but it is possible to make plausible estimates by comparison with the size and/or cost of Egyptian land forces some years later. In 1181 the reorganized regular land forces in Egypt counted 8,640 men and the annual budgetary allocation for its maintenance amounted to 3,670,500 dinars.[11] These figures show an average per capita cost of about 425 dinars a year. This level of allocation seemed to remain constant over the subsequent decade, judging by the figure of 3,462,424 dinars assigned to the regular troops in 1189.[12] In spite of the Nuriyah exodus, Saladin still had the entire Asadiyah regiment of 500 men, as well as 3,000 Ghuzz cavalry, commanded by Baha al-Din Qaragush. Disregarding those Nuriyah officers and troops who may have stayed on in Egypt, one may surmise that the nucleus of Saladin's new regular forces amounted to at least 3,500 men, calling for annual expenditures of approximately 1,487,500 dinars. These land forces were quickly expanded. Before even the summer of 1169 was out, Saladin had already formed a personal guard regiment, called the Salahiyah, and commanded by the amir Abu al-Hayja.[13] Although its size is unknown, it is fair to assume it was not smaller than the Asadiyah regiment. Two years later, in September 1171, the total regular cavalry troops numbered approximately 14,000,[14] calling for annual expenditure of about 5,850,000 dinars. Even allowing a substantial overestimate of 20 percent, the resulting figure, over 4.5 million dinars, required for the maintenance of the regular army represented an onerous demand on the Egyptian economy. In 1145, before the steady economic recession of the second half of the twelfth century, land taxes—by far the most productive fiscal item of Egyptian revenue—amounted to 1,200,000 dinars.[15] Moreover, the estimates of 1171, of 1181, and 1189 took account of important additional military allocations necessary to cover administrative and logistic personnel, the auxiliary forces (e.g., the Judham Arabs in the service of Saladin, whose number in 1171 reached 7,000 men),[16] the fleet, and a variety of static defense establishments, all of which must have substantially augmented the tremendous burden on Egypt's economy.

Though the budgetary data are expressed in monetary units, the military forces in Egypt were not financed by cash. Because of the shortage of hard currency, medieval Near Eastern administrations since the end of the ninth century had depended on a feudalistic system of *iqta* grants, or various sources of revenue assigned in lieu of cash salaries, to the civilian and military personnel. Even the opulent Fatimid regime was forced, in its later period, to reward some of its land and naval forces with the *iqta* assignments instead of cash.

His long experience with the feudalistic army organization of Nur al-Din had acquainted Saladin well with the *iqta*. Indeed, he himself had been an *iqta* holder. Consequently, he would have had no qualms about applying the *iqta* system, if such a measure was necessary to finance his military expansion. In fact, even before Shirkuh's death he had begun to assign some Egyptian lands as *iqtas* to members of the expeditionary army, avoiding, however, any infringement on the existing *iqta* privileges of the Fatimid army officers.[17]

Total mobilization of economic resources was the price Egyptian society had to pay for external security and internal stability. But even with such a total subordination of the Egyptian economy to this maximum military effort, the maintenance of substandard or redundant units and establishments could no longer be tolerated. In other words, the Egyptian economy could not sustain two parallel armies: the obsolete Fatimid contingents and Saladin's projected army. Consequently, after gaining the caliph's confidence, Saladin abandoned his earlier restraint and began to phase out the old Egyptian army, by withdrawing from the Fatimid commanders their *iqtas* and the military units attached to them.[18] The released feudal holdings were then integrated with the new military organization. With this new measure, Saladin disturbed the delicate balance of power between the palace establishment and the vizirate, which had prevailed during the shortlived regime of Shirkuh. The upholders of the Fatimid cause became alarmed. In an effort to protect themselves, jeopardized as they were by the army reorganization, Fatimid military commanders rallied around Saniat al-Mulk, the same palace major domo who had strongly objected to Saladin's nomination. Many an arrogant vizir had learned a hard lesson from the palace establishment, and Saladin—in their view—was definitely asking for one.

New Crusader threat and cooperation between Saladin and Nur al-Din

Immediate reinvigoration of Egyptian military strength became particularly necessary when news began to circulate that the Crusaders planned to launch another attack against the Fatimid state. To King Amalric and his advisers, the accession of Shirkuh and Saladin to the Fatimid vizirate could only appear as an extension of Nur al-Din's authority over the country of the Nile. To all intents and purposes, Muslim Egypt and Syria were united, and the Crusaders had to move quickly to prevent Nur al-Din from consolidating his newest strategic advantage. Because Egypt had been so militarily vulnerable of late, it was the objective of a new Christian offensive. This time the Franks enjoyed the cooperation of the Byzantine emperor who placed an impressive army and navy at the Crusader king's disposal.

Naturally Nur al-Din, for his part, was determined not to lose the strategic advantage achieved by this last successful intervention in Egypt. Putting aside his reservations concerning Saladin's ambitions, the sultan proceeded with appropriate measures to strengthen Egyptian defensive capability. In an obvious attempt to bolster Saladin's position, Nur al-Din now allowed the other sons of Ayyub to join their distinguished brother in Egypt. Accompanied by their families, they arrived in Cairo on 29 July 1169 under the leadership of the oldest brother, Fakhr al-Din Shams al-Dawlah Turan Shah, and bringing badly needed military reinforcements.[19]

Fatimid conspiracy and open rebellion in Cairo

Saladin had hardly greeted his relatives, when he suddenly discovered a conspiracy directed against him. Saladin's soldiers had apprehended a suspicious-looking man, who had concealed letters addressed to the Crusaders in a brand new pair of shoes. Interrogation of the prisoner and examination of the letters revealed not only treacherous relations with the Franks, but the identity of the scribe who had actually written the messages.[20] With such a lead, Saladin and his staff could now get exact information about the conspiracy.

As could be predicted, Saniat al-Mulk had masterminded the conspiracy. Although he could count on the support of the numerically superior Fatimid contingents, he must have doubted Saladin's troops, for the conspirators preferred an alliance with the Crusaders. According to their plan, they would wait for an attack of the Frankish army which would inevitably draw Saladin and his army to the eastern frontier. Then the conspirators were supposed to strike, attacking

Saladin's forces from the rear. Trapped between them, Saladin could not escape destruction.

Not only its premature disclosure but also Saladin's reaction to it turned this first attempt to overthrow his young regime into a bloody failure. Tipped off that Saladin knew of the plot, Saniat al-Mulk went into hiding behind the well-protected walls of the Fatimid palace. Contrary to his fears, Saladin made no effort to extradite him. Indeed, Saladin pretended to ignore the whereabouts of the frightened major domo. This feigned indifference deceived the refugee who made the fatal mistake of leaving his asylum on 20 August 1169 to visit his summer residence near Qaliub. Seizing the opportunity, Saladin sent a special detachment after him. On that same day, the head of Saniat al-Mulk was brought back to the vizir. The elimination of the treacherous major domo was followed up by the appointment of the trustworthy Baha al-Din Qaragush to his post.[21]

The crisis was not yet over. Next day, the Sudanese slave soldiers, enraged by the summary execution of the popular Saniat al-Mulk, rose in arms against the vizir and his people. They were joined by Fatimid commanders and their units stationed inside Cairo. Totalling over 50,000 people, they began to advance toward the vizirate palace. Before they reached their objective, Saladin's recently arrived brother Shams al-Dawlah and his soldiers furiously assaulted them. In the meantime, Saladin rushed in reinforcements, consisting mainly of his Salahiyah regiment under the command of Abu al-Hayja. By then, the rebels had been joined by the Armenians, as well as local groups from different quarters of Cairo. The main confrontation took place in the wide quadrangle called Bain al-Qasrain. After some heavy fighting, the Sudanese, spearheading the rebel forces, appeared to be gaining the upper hand over the outnumbered troops of Saladin.[22]

Caliph al-Adid watched the battle from a pavilion overlooking the Bain al-Qasrain. At one moment, when the Sudanese slaves were gaining advantage, Saladin's hard-pressed forces came under a barrage of arrows and stone missiles from the palace walls. Obviously believing the battle was going to the rebel army, the caliph's entourage decided to join actively on the winning side. Although the sudden attack added to the predicament of Saladin's exposed warriors, they refused to be written off. With a quick decision the impetuous Shams al-Dawlah called on the *naffatin* (people manning special catapults for projecting fireballs) and, displaying no respect for the caliph's person, ordered them to zero in on his pavilion. However, before the first fiery missile reached its destination, an official of the palace appeared bringing a message for Shams al-Dawlah. "The Commander of the Faithful," he said, "sends his greetings to Shams al-Dawlah, and tells him to go on fighting against the wretched slaves, until they are driven out of the country." [23]

This was a shock to the Sudanese soldiers. Shortly before this incident they had lost one of their leaders,[24] and now they saw the very symbol of the whole Fatimid establishment, for which they were laying down their lives, contemptuously turning his back on them.

Saladin's bloody suppression of the rebellion

While the battle was raging in the Bain al-Qasrain area, Saladin proceeded with a gruesome measure against the mutinous Sudanese. With only women and children left in the Sudanese barracks outside the Zuwayla Gate, Saladin's soldiers suddenly appeared and set fire to the entire area. The news of this terrible act against their defenseless families caused understandable consternation among the Sudanese soldiers.[25] The original momentum of their attack was lost. They began to yield ground, retreating in the direction of the Zuwayla Gate, offering only sporadic resistance. To destroy nests of resistance, the pursuing troops had to burn house after house sheltering the fleeing Sudanese. At one stage, Armenian archers, shooting from their quarters near the Bain al-Qasrain, tried to contain the advance of the pursuers, but their place was immediately ignited so that all perished in flames.

When finally the slave soldiers reached the Zuwayla Gate, they found their only escape route cut off. After two days of fierce fighting, the Sudanese agreed to lay down arms if Saladin would offer them a safe-conduct. Their request was granted on condition that they promise to leave Cairo. The defeated and disarmed Sudanese marched out and set up their camp in Giza, where—in a cynical violation of the safe-conduct pledge—they were massacred in cold blood by Shams al-Dawlah, Saladin's brother. Only a small fraction of the original slave guard regiments survived the blood bath, and escaping to Upper Egypt, they were hunted down by Shihab al-Din al-Harimi who was assigned that mission by Saladin himself.[26]

These successful countermeasures not only liquidated the conspiracy of Saniat al-Mulk, but also eliminated the main body of Fatimid regular infantry forces. Saladin's victory was everywhere evident. The burnt-out houses between Bain al-Qasrain and the Zuwayla Gate testified to his troops' savage efficiency. Outside the Zuwayla Gate, the smoldering ruins of the Sudanese barracks poignantly illustrated the kind of retaliation Saladin would mete out to those who dared to challenge his authority. Indeed, to erase all vestiges of the long predominance of the Sudanese guards in Cairo, the barrack area of al-Mansura was ploughed over and later turned into a garden.[27]

Saladin's men seized such property, formerly that of Sudanese, Armenian, and other Fatimid forces implicated in the revolt, as remained intact.[28] There was similar confiscation all over the country.[29] Not only was Saladin's authority decisively affirmed, but the task of financing his new army was made easier by this quick if bloody elimination of some 50,000 Fatimid soldiers.

Deprived of his security forces, Caliph al-Adid found himself dependent on the mercy of the vizir.[30] However, though some people maintained that the caliph himself ordered the sudden arrow attack from the palace walls, Saladin took no overt retaliatory measures beyond ordering Baha al-Din Qaragush to maintain strict control over the entire palace precincts. It is possible that Saladin's restraint was motivated by his reluctance to break openly with the palace establishment before he had further extended his influence and authority in the Egyptian state organization. It is more likely, however, that the victorious vizir intended to restore some cooperation between the Fatimid establishment and his own camp in anticipation of another Crusader attack against Egypt.

Crusader attack defeated

Reports coming from Syria were not the only source of information about the preparations of the Crusaders. In the spring of 1169 Saladin dispatched a naval squadron to patrol possible routes they might take. His precautions were soon rewarded. In July a powerful Byzantine task force sailed from Constantinople to Palestine. On its way, the task force met six ships of the Egyptian fleet off Cyprus. In the ensuing clash the Byzantines captured two ships, but the remaining four escaped to Egypt bringing news of the formidable Byzantine armada.[31]

Fortunately for Saladin, the departure of this invasion force was delayed because the Crusaders and their Byzantine allies had to settle certain diplomatic and logistic questions. That delay allowed Saladin to proceed with precautionary measures, involving military personnel, equipment, and—unavoidably—expenditure. Two of his close relatives, his nephew Taqi al-Din Umar and the renowned Shihab al-Din Mahmud al-Harimi, were given command of the garrison of Damietta which was to defend the route of expected Crusader penetration. They were provided with money, weapons, and supplies. To strengthen their loyalty to the vizir, extra money was distributed to the army. Such measures kept Saladin in full control of the situation when, in the last days of October 1169, the Crusaders appeared off Damietta. The invaders found access to the port barred by a chain, which prevented a direct, frontal attack from the sea. It also prevented the Christian ships from sailing up that branch of the Nile to blockade Damietta. Although the exposed fortress was cut off by land and sea, Saladin maintained communications with it by means of the Nile. At the same time, he put pressure on both al-Adid and Nur al-Din, asking the caliph for more financial support and the sultan for active military cooperation. Both requests were successful; the caliph provided over one million dinars in cash together with quantities of clothing and Nur al-Din launched a diversionary operation against the Crusaders in Syria.

Saladin's sound strategy, in which logistic planning played such a prominent role, resulted in total success. The Crusaders and their allies withdrew from Damietta in mid-December 1169, after thirty-five days of futile siege operations.[32] Once again, Saladin's superior leadership foiled Crusader plans to conquer an Egyptian coastal fortress. The repulse of this invasion brought at last a spell of peace to Egypt's Mediterranean border, which, from the fall of Ascalon in 1153, had been suffering recurrent attacks by various Christian enemies.

Saladin's political restraint toward the palace establishment after crushing the Saniat al-Mulk conspiracy paid off during the crisis of Damietta. He encountered no difficulties with the remaining contingents of the Fatimid army and the caliph was persuaded to help finance the war costs—a contribution the grateful Saladin emphatically acknowledged.[33]

Once the external crisis was over, Saladin could turn back to internal reorganization. Although he had engineered the victory at Damietta, it was Caliph al-Adid who received a congratulatory message from Nur al-Din. Obviously, when wishing to register his satisfaction at the repulse of the Crusaders, the Sultan would send his congratulations to the nominal head of the Egyptian state. But this recognition accorded the caliph must have given rise to ill-conceived hopes in the palace concerning possible exploitation of Nur al-Din's authority to promote their own cause. This was evident in a letter where the caliph asked Nur al-Din to recall the "Turks" from Egypt and to curtail Saladin's powers. It was also evident in the persistent efforts—if only diplomatic—to undermine the vizir's authority and in the caliph's personal involvement in anti-vizirial plotting. But the maneuver failed completely. In answering al-Adid, Nur al-Din stated in no uncertain terms that the presence of the "Turks" in Egypt was absolutely essential to the safety of the country.[34] The point about Saladin was left unanswered, as if to indicate that questions pertaining to the sultan's authority over his representative in Egypt lay outside the caliph's concern.

Continued military reforms and the first offensive against the Crusaders

Following the Damietta battle, efforts at military reorganization resumed. Phasing out of redundant Fatimid units continued, not without provoking armed resistance. According to some reports, in the winter of 1169-70, some Fatimid forces perished by drowning in the province of Buhaira and Ashmunain.[35] In the district of Qus in Upper Egypt, a Fatimid commander, Abbas ibn Shadhi, started an abortive rebellion. Other areas in Upper Egypt suffered unrest caused by the Bedouins and the Sudanese fugitives.[36] However, these difficulties did not slow the new regime's take-over. Confiscated lands kept being redistributed as *iqta* assignments to the personnel of the new army and fleet.

Anxious to strengthen further his family group in Egypt, Saladin asked the Syrian court to transfer his father from Damascus to Egypt. Nur al-Din's reaction this time was favorable; very likely he expected Ayyub to influence Saladin positively on his behalf. Ayyub left early in April 1170, arriving 16 April in Cairo, where he received a royal welcome, as befitted the father of Egypt's virtual ruler. The streets of the capital were festively decorated. Even al-Adid himself rode out to meet the father of the vizir, an honor never accorded anyone by the Fatimid suzerains. In addition to many magnificent gifts, Ayyub received from the caliph a new honorific name, al-Malik al-Afdal, the Most Virtuous King. In an ostentatious display of reverent respect, Saladin proposed to surrender the vizirate to him, but Ayyub refused, reportedly saying: "My son, God had not chosen you for this great position had you not been fitted for it; it is not well to play with one's luck." [37]

Although declining the vizirate, Ayyub did accept appointment as head of all treasury departments. Saladin could now feel certain that no efforts would be spared in providing adequate resources for his armed forces. Predictably, the Ayyubid family, whose eager cooperation was so essential to the new military regime, received extensive feudal assignments. While Saladin presumably inherited the fiefs and revenues of the Egyptian vizirs, his father received as *iqta* Alexandria, Damietta, and al-Buhaira, and his oldest brother, Shams al-Dawlah, was assigned the southern provinces in Upper Egypt (Qus, Aswan, and Aidhab), to which were later added an entire quarter in Cairo, as well as Bush, Giza, and Sammanud.[38] The total value of *iqta* grants assigned Ayyub and Shams al-Dawlah alone exceeded 1,000,000 dinars, sufficient to finance over 2,000 armed men. Significantly, the Upper Egyptian provinces assigned to Shams al-Dawlah had belonged to Shams al-Khilafah,[39] the influential Fatimid politician who at the time of Amalric's attack against Cairo had performed several difficult diplomatic missions.

The military reorganization appears to have been completed toward the end of 1170, when Saladin led his new army on an offensive against the Crusaders.[40] Although limited in scope, this first independent offensive operation confirmed Saladin's outstanding grasp of military strategy, tactics, and logistics. The main strategic objective was Ailah, situated at the head of the Gulf of Aqabah, which was the southernmost Crusader outpost in the fortress chain they had built from the southern tip of the Dead Sea to the Red Sea to interfere with Muslim trade and military movement between Egypt and Syria. The task force assigned this operation consisted mainly of mobile troops which included some Fatimid units, a contingent of sailors and marines, and considerable ordnance with a number of shipwrights. The ordnance men were to transport supplies, mangonels, and prefabricated ship sections, specially built in Cairo for this expedition. The tactical plan was ingenious and imaginative. It called for a combined naval and land assault against Ailah, to be preceded by diversionary terrorist raids against the southernmost Crusader fortresses on the Mediterranean coast.

The army left Cairo on 26 November 1170 and marched to the western shore of the Gulf of Suez. There the building materials and ship sections, transported on camels, were assembled into a flotilla. The crews assigned to the naval contingent received orders to sail toward Ailah. The main force, under Saladin's personal command, marched toward Palestine. At a point halfway between the Mediterranean and the Gulf of Aqabah, Saladin set up his headquarters, from which he dispatched a tactical force, equipped with mangonels, to carry out the diversionary mission. It fell out exactly as Saladin had expected. On 10 December his raiders attacked Darum. Despite the surprise attack and punishing bombardment, the fortress garrison held out. The time bought by the defenders of Darum allowed King Amalric to organize a strong relief force which set out from Gaza to counterattack the besieging Muslims on 12 December. This was the very effect Saladin had planned. On the night of 13 December Saladin's raiders disengaged from the enemy and under cover of darkness executed a swift thrust against Gaza. Although the citadel resisted, the raiders captured the town of Gaza, killed or captured many of its inhabitants, and set Muslim prisoners free. After plundering the town, the raiders returned with their spoils to Saladin's headquarters by the evening of 21 December.

With Crusader attention focused on this area of sudden hit-and-run Egyptian attack, Saladin could safely proceed against his principal target. On 31 December 1170 he launched a simultaneous sea and land attack against Ailah; the assault ended in complete success. Before the end of 1170 Saladin had wiped out the Christian garrison, thus attaining the principal objective of his campaign. He remained in the field a few more weeks to take care of the military needs of the reconquered fortress and to offer protective escort to the large caravan which was bringing the rest of his family from Syria.[41] After its arrival Saladin set out on the return trip, arriving at Cairo with his victorious army on 4 February 1171.

This first offensive campaign was certainly a significant accomplishment. Apart from attaining its specific objective, his success indicated that in less than two years Saladin had transformed the armed forces of Egypt into a homogeneous operational entity, capable of carrying effective war to the Crusaders.

To complete his military build-up, Saladin took care of the static defenses of Egypt. After an inspection tour of Alexandria on 1 May 1171, he ordered construction of walls, towers, and curtain-walls.[42] Needless to add, he was enthusiastically greeted by the people of Alexandria, who remembered well the heroic leader of their defense against Shawar and Amalric in 1167. Also in 1171 Saladin instructed Baha al-Din Qaragush to put the walls of Cairo into shape, repairing both war damage and neglect.[43]

Saladin and the termination of the Fatimid caliphate

Having established a solid military foundation, Saladin could now improve his political status, for, whatever his effective power, he was still ostensibly under the formal authority of the Ismaili caliph. Considered in terms of religious ideology it was a paradoxical situation. As a Shafiite Muslim, Saladin recognized the supremacy of the Sunni caliphate of the Abbasids in Baghdad; and yet, by virtue of his vizirial appointment in Egypt, he was officially serving the cause of their archenemy. Naturally, Saladin was flexible enough to compromise religious convictions for the sake of political expediency, as was shown by his positive attitude toward al-Adid immediately after he assumed the vizirate. But once relations with the Fatimid figurehead deteriorated, once the master of the palace was no longer politically useful, Saladin wasted no time in promoting the interests of Sunni Islam at the expense of the Shiite caliphate, especially since such a policy would improve his own position in Egypt. In addition, he may have believed in the rich treasure that popular gossip ascribed to the Fatimid caliph, which a complete take-over of the palace grounds would naturally deliver to him.

In considering action against al-Adid, Saladin had a powerful if distant ally in Nur al-Din. As a fervent Sunni, Nur al-Din was interested in seeing Egypt return to the fold of the Abbasid caliphate and had been urging Saladin for some time to do away with the Fatimid structure. However, while Saladin and Nur al-Din held similar religious views with regard to the heterodox Ismaili caliphate, they did not share ideas concerning the subsequent political arrangements to be derived from promotion of the Sunni cause. To Nur al-Din, abolishing the Fatimid caliphate meant the integration of Egypt into the Sunni bloc and total subordination of Egyptian resources to his command for the struggle against the Crusaders. As long as he had these objectives, he was not overly concerned about the subsequent internal organization of Egypt. To Saladin, however, removing the Fatimid caliphate meant that prestigious institution would no longer shield him from the pressure of his Syrian overlord. Thus, Saladin was careful not to bring about a situation in which his own position might be undermined to the obvious benefit of Nur al-Din. Handling al-Adid did not present much of a problem. Following the execution of Saniat al-Mulk and the extermination of the Sudanese and Armenian guards, al-Adid—restricted to the palace grounds under the omnipresent surveillance of Saladin's men—was not expected to offer any effective resistance. Getting rid of him might easily jeopardize Saladin's strong and semi-independent relation to Nur al-Din and perhaps even provoke the diehards of the decaying Ismaili regime into a desperate rebellion. In spite of his military build-up, Upper Egypt remained restive, and even as late as February 1171 Shams al-Dawlah had to undertake punitive raids against Bedouin warriors.[44] The mood of Cairo was not predictable either, particularly considering the riots which had erupted after Shawar's fall. Furthermore, one could not disregard possible negative public reaction to a change in the official political and ideological character of the Egyptian state. After all, Egypt had lived for over two centuries under the Fatimid dynasty, during which she had experienced a political hegemony and economic prosperity unheard of under earlier administrations. If the twelfth century caliphs did little governing, the cause of the caliphate itself was upheld by pro-Fatimid politicians and various groups with entrenched interests in the reigning establishment. Nur al-Din might have underestimated the importance of these factors, but Saladin was too good a politician to attempt uprooting a well-entrenched system prior to controlling most departments of the Fatimid state organization. When he finally pulled the curtain down on 202 years of Egyptian history, he did it only after meticulous planning and preparation. Despite its momentous significance, the details of Saladin's coup d'etat have neither been reconstructed nor thoroughly analyzed. It is true that modern historians have discussed various preliminary measures Saladin took, but in treating the dramatic coup itself, they have repeated uncritically the old clichés, which portray Saladin's action as a slight formality. The remark of Ibn al-Athir that "there was not so much as the butting of two goats"[45] when the name of the Fatimid caliph was dropped from the khutbah seems effectively to have influenced modern historians. That they have regarded the execution of the coup as an easy affair can be seen from the following representative quotations: "Then, one fine day, the name of the Abbasid caliph of Baghdad was proclaimed in Cairo in an atmosphere of complete indifference."[46] "The order was obeyed, with no immediate outward disturbances."[47] "This ecclesiastical revolution took place without a sign of opposition."[48] ". . . The advent of the new regime was received among the masses with the same passivity which they had shown to its predecessors."[49]

Contrary to these statements, the final assault against the Fatimid regime was a more complicated affair. Available source materials reveal that the smooth liquidation of the Fatimid caliphate was achieved not because of al-Adid's "timely" demise, but because Saladin and his supporters planned and prosecuted the anti-Fatimid action so well. Examination of this drama sheds light on al-Adid's downfall and, above all, on the personality of Saladin himself.

Anti-Fatimid measures

Saladin began a systematic anti-Fatimid policy soon after his father's arrival in April 1170. In sending Ayyub to Cairo Nur al-Din hoped Saladin's father would press the Syrian sultan's political demands,[50] including radical action against al-Adid. The sultan's assumption was borne out by a number of anti-Ismaili measures Saladin initiated following his father's appearance. For instance, the Shiite invocation *Hayy ala khayr al-amal* ("Come to the best of work") was ordered eliminated from the calls of the muezzins.[51] Beginning 25 August 1170 the first three orthodox caliphs were put back in the *khutbah* invocations and mentioned ahead of Ali's name.[52] On the other hand, the reference to al-Adid was to include the statement *Yahtamilu altalbis ala al-shiah* ("He brings confusion upon the Shiites").[53] To enhance Sunni influence further, in the fall of 1170 Saladin founded a Shafiite and a Malikite college (*madrasah*) in Cairo.[54] Yet another well-endowed Shafiite *madrasah* was set up in April 1171 by his nephew Taqi al-Din Umar.[55]

Other anti-Fatimid measures pertained to the Egyptian judiciary. In August 1170 a close associate of Saladin, Isa al-Hakkari, was appointed judge in Cairo.[56] At the same time, Saladin reinstated Diya al-Din Ibn Kamil to the post of judge in Fustat, from which he had been dismissed by Shawar in 1164.[57] The vindication of that pro-Fatimid official did not last for long. On 2 March 1171 Saladin dismissed al-Awris, the supreme judge of Egypt, and conferred that dignity upon Sadr al-Din ibn al-Darbas al-Hadhabani, a Shafiite jurist and a Kurd like the vizir himself.[58] The new *qadi al-qudah* wasted no time in substituting other Shafiite officials for the Ismaili ones.[59] The judicial purge was followed by the abolishment of the Ismaili theological and missionary sessions from al-Azhar and other mosques of the area.[60]

A further significant step extending Saladin's influence in the civil administration took place in early March 1171. On 4 March Ibn al-Khallal, a prominent judge and chief of the Fatimid chancellery, died in Cairo. He was immediately succeeded by al-Qadi al-Fadil,[61] whose high reputation was already firmly established. In spite of being a Sunni Muslim, he proved quite successful as civil servant in different departments of the Fatimid bureaucratic system. In addition to his outstanding professional competence, al-Qadi al-Fadil also proved politically flexible, for despite his close association with Shawar and al-Kamil he survived their extermination and emerged as Shirkuh's chief secretary. Although nothing explicit is known about his attitude towards Saladin prior to 1171, it is fair to assume they were well acquainted. As Shirkuh's secretary, al-Fadil must have cooperated with Saladin, and since al-Fadil continued to serve in the chancery during Saladin's vizirate, he must have comprehended prevailing political trends and developments. He could neither fail to see through Saladin's policy, nor remain unaware of the various palace opposition groups. Having witnessed the careers of several vizirs, yet conscious of Egypt's desperate need for security and stability, he could properly estimate Saladin's chances of ultimate success. Had he held any doubts, he could have declined the new promotion. For his part, Saladin was quite consistent in placing "his" men in key positions. Over two years of acquaintance with al-Qadi al-Fadil had apparently been enough to test his political trustworthiness and reliability. Had Saladin doubted al-Fadil's loyalty, he would not have made him chief of chancellery. As it happened, this marked an official beginning of a close personal and professional association between the two men, the harmonious character of which remained undisturbed as long as Saladin's policy favored Egypt's interests.

By August 1171 Saladin completed a number of crucial strategic measures necessary in phasing out the Fatimid establishment. Its leading members were by then kept under surveillance, their messages intercepted. There was now plenty of Egyptian speculation that Saladin contemplated eliminating the Fatimid dynasty, deposing and assassinating al-Adid, and reinstating the Abbasid suzerainty in Egypt.[62] Their misgivings must have grown when some Egyptian commanders were arrested as they were leaving their homes, the members of their households promptly evicted, and their properties confiscated for the benefit of Saladin's men. When al-Adid complained about those arrests, Saladin explained that the imprisoned commanders constituted a rebellious element, harmful to the interests of the caliphate.[63] By now Saladin hardly needed to account for his actions to al-Adid whose political, economic, and even personal freedom he had greatly curtailed. The royal domains and feudal estates of the caliph were confiscated, Fatimid emblems removed, and the palace grounds in Cairo subjected to Qaragush's authority.[64] With the forces of the establishment softened up and the royal quarry cornered, Saladin could move in for the kill.

The suppression of the name of the Fatimid caliph from the khutbah

Shortly before the end of August 1171 Saladin, under constant pressure from Nur al-Din, informed his staff that the final hour of the Ismaili regime was at hand.[65] Significant news coming from the entourage of the Fatimid caliph seemed to demand immediate action. In the last days of August or in the first days of September 1171 al-Adid began to show symptoms of an acute illness which rapidly sapped his physical strength.[66] Because the caliph's death would normally result in a power struggle over the succession and to prevent further perpetuation of the Fatimid dynasty, Saladin had to move quickly. However, while some of the commanders concurred with Saladin's opinion, others were still apprehensive.[67] Possibly they were concerned that a number of prominent establishment members remained in the capital. Intimidated, or even terrorized, as they were, they might react desperately." [68]

The difference of opinions notwithstanding, all the commanders agreed they could not ignore the order of Nur al-Din.[69] To ease his supporters' consciences about suppressing the prestigious Fatimid caliphate, Saladin sought to obtain moral support from the legal authorities; but it goes without saying that he limited this consultation to Sunni jurists. Among them was one al-Khabushani, a controversial Shafiite scholar, who for some time had been trying to promote himself. At odds with Hanbalite jurists, as well as with some of his Shafiite colleagues, he was eager to seize any opportunity to further his personal career.[70] At last came a time he could exploit. Of all the jurists Saladin consulted, al-Khabushani issued the strongest legal opinion (*fatwa*) justifying termination of the Fatimid caliphate.[71] That Saladin felt obligated to al-Khabushani for his enthusiastic response was indicated by the subsequent career of the ambitious jurist. Apart from asserting his authority among the Ayyubid supporters and being showered with gifts by the vizir, al-Khabushani was later appointed to the chair of yet another Shafiite *madrasah*, founded and endowed by Saladin in 1176.[72]

Backed by his military staff and legal authorities, Saladin could proceed with the coup d'etat. Amid rumors that al-Adid's condition had deteriorated, troops were concentrated in or near the capital. The traditional festivities of the Muslim New Year, the solemn Shiite celebrations of the Tenth of *Muharram*, or preparations for the anticipated expedition against the Crusaders could serve as a plausible pretext for the troop movement.[73] Although no traditional procession took place, on Tuesday, 7 September (4 *Muharram*), the caliph held an official audience in the palace. His appearance confirmed the rumors. Afflicted by fever, he was losing strength and control over his limbs.[74] As the first Friday of the new Muslim year was approaching, the *khutbah* required immediate attention. Authorities reporting on that historic week agree it was then Saladin decided to eliminate the invocation honoring al-Adid, and to replace it with one to the Abbasid caliph, al-Mustadi, but they do not agree about the details of that momentous change.

One of the better known accounts, that of Ibn al-Athir, is accepted as the standard version by medieval and modern historians. According to Ibn al-Athir, while Saladin and his men were discussing their move, a non-Egyptian theologian offered to initiate the new *khutbah*. *"Ana abtadi bi-al-khutbah la-hu!"* ("I'll begin saying the *khutbah* in his name!") he stated to that effect.[75] Then on Friday, 10 September

1171, he managed to precede the regular preacher in ascending the *minbar* and made an invocation in the name of al-Mustadi. No one objected.[76] Ibn al-Athir, who was not always innocent of "news management," [77] substantiated his story by stating that he had personally seen this handy intruder, known as al-Amir al-Alim, on many occasions in Mosul.[78]

This detail is contradicted by other authorities who maintain that the first to invoke the *khutbah* in the name of the Abbasids was a certain Muhammad ibn al-Muhsin ibn al-Husayn ibn Abi al-Mada al-Baalbakki.[79] Abu Shamah also refused to be satisfied with Ibn al-Athir's account. He introduced his narrative by stating succinctly: "Saladin opened the new year by establishing a pro-Abbasid *khutbah* in Fustat, on the first Friday, and in Cairo, on the second Friday of the year." [80] Then, after producing the story offered by Ibn al-Athir, Abu Shamah presented a different version of the same incident, based on the authority of Ibn Abi Tayyi.[81] In this version Saladin is said to have ordered his father, Najm al-Din, to proceed to the cathedral mosque (*al-jami*) accompanied by the supporters and military commanders of Saladin's regime. This happened on the first Friday of the new year. Najm al-Din was to ask for the preacher (*khatib*) to communicate a task assigned to him. Fearing that the plan might fail and the enemy retaliate, Saladin entrusted this matter to his father, so that he himself would appear innocent.

When Najm al-Din reached the mosque, he had the preacher brought into his presence, and said to him:

"If you invoke the resident of the palace, I will cut off your head!"

"Whom shall I exhort?" the preacher asked.

"Al-Mustadi al-Abbasi."

The preacher ascended the *minbar* and proceeded with the *khutbah*. However, when he got to the crucial point, he invoked no one, referring instead to the divinely guided imams and Sultan al-Malik al-Nasir. Upon stepping down, he was questioned about it, and explained: "I was not familiar with the full name of al-Mustadi, or with the details of al-Adid's obituary. This matter has not been cleared with me before this Friday. Next Friday—*in sha Allah*—I shall do what is necessary as regards the formulation of the personal and honorific names according to the procedural custom applicable in such circumstance." [82]

In spite of considerable discrepancy between the two versions, it is nonetheless possible to reconstruct certain fundamental facts about the event, as implied by Ibn al-Athir and Abu Shamah. No official deposition of the Fatimid caliphate was proclaimed on Friday, 10 September 1171. Only one isolated attempt was made to replace the name of al-Adid with that of al-Mustadi on that date, in the mosque of Amr ibn al-As.[83] The fact that Saladin preferred to stay ostensibly uninvolved seems to indicate the probing, tentative character of even this action. However, the fact that this did not provoke any remonstrances from the congregation must have spurred Saladin and his party on to the further prosecution of the coup d'etat.

Whether the people in the capital were favorably disposed toward the change, whether they were indifferent or intimidated, one thing is certain: Saladin was prepared to deal with any emergency. Indeed, having his army contingents concentrated in the capital district, Saladin proceeded with an impressive show of force one day after the action in the mosque. "Saladin held a review of all his troops, old and new, in the presence of Greek and Frankish envoys. The total number of *tulbs* (cavalry detachments) reviewed was 174. . . . The total number of these horsemen was approximately 14,000. . . . At the same time, the Judham Arabs in the service of the Sultan were reviewed, these numbered 7,000 horsemen. . . ."[84] While the Greek and Frankish envoys might have been assessing the significance of that show for the international balance of power, local observers were obviously discovering the true master of Egypt.

Death of al-Adid

Two days later, on the night of the Shiite holiday of the Tenth of *Muharram* (on Sunday night, 12 September, or in the early hours of Monday, 13 September) al-Adib passed away.[85] According to Ibn al-Athir, the family and friends of the ailing caliph preferred not to inform him about the *khutbah* episode. "If he recovers," they said, "he will learn about it. If he dies, it is not proper to torment him during the waning days of his life."[86]

The consensus of medieval historians is that the date of al-Adid's death appears certain, but not its cause or circumstances. This is not surprising considering that even in the present century historians do not always agree on the circumstances surrounding a prominent political figure's sudden death. More disappointing than surprising is the realization that modern historians have as a rule accepted the popular account of Ibn al-Athir, without examining its veracity in the light of other testimonies.

Actually, medieval historians recorded a number of variants relating to al-Adid's death. First his death has been attributed to the serious illness with symptoms of paralysis which is said to have afflicted the caliph in the last days of August 1171.[87] This version agrees with the account of Ibn al-Athir.[88] Another version claims that al-Adid's death was brought about by mental depression caused by his learning of the *khutbah* incident [89] (which contradicts the version of Ibn al-Athir), or by his realization of the hopeless situation of his affairs.[90] Yet another variant attributes the death to a freak accident; having learned about the *khutbah* incident, Al-Adid is said to have stumbled and fallen down while entering the palace. A fatal illness ensued, causing his demise five days later.[91] (This version contradicts the story of al-Adid's paralytic condition prior to the *khutbah* incident. It also implies 15 September and not the generally accepted 12 September as the earliest date of his death.) There exists also the suicide version, according to which al-Adid poisoned himself,[92] and its counterpart, which has the caliph assassinated by poison.[93]

In spite of such divergent reports, it is possible to offer the following reconstruction. Whatever its primary cause, al-Adid's illness was in an advanced stage before 10 September. The fever spread all over his body especially affecting his limbs. It was then that Ibn Sadid, a famous doctor and member of a pro-Fatimid family of physicians, withdrew his services and suspended medication. "He abandoned al-Adid to his own fate, conforming thus with the trends of the day." [94] Ibn Sadid, despite his pro-Fatimid affiliations, continued to prosper until his death in 1193.[95]

The news about the dropping of his name from the *khutbah* did reach the ailing caliph. "Whose name was invoked?" al-Adid is said to have asked. "No one was named at all," was the answer. To this he remarked: "Next Friday they will come up with naming a new man in the *khutbah*." [96] He then requested the presence of Saladin, but the latter refused to come, suspecting a trap.[97] Before the week was over the young caliph had died. As Ibn Taghri Bardi stated: "The day of his death constituted a supreme moment for Egypt, and the greatest blow to the Misriyin [the Fatimids and their supporters]." [98]

Upon learning the news, Saladin displayed unusual grief and allegedly stated: "Had I known that he was going to die in the course of this week, I would not have crushed him with the removal of his name from the *khutbah*." To which al-Qadi al-Fadil retorted: "Had he known that you would not have removed his name from the *khutbah*, he would not have died." "By that he meant that al-Adid had killed himself," commented Ibn Abi Tayyi.[99] The body of the deceased was washed by his son Dawud and wrapped in a shroud.[100] Saladin went to view the deceased and had proper authorities (*shuhud*) and notables examine the body. Not unpredictably the examination did not reveal any trace of assassination.[101] The funeral of al-Adid, which Saladin arranged and attended, was the last official state privilege granted the Ismaili dynasty in Egypt.[102]

The mystery of al-Adid's death may never be solved with certainty. One thing, however, appears obvious: al-Adid would always have served as a rallying point for the diehard supporters of the Fatimid regime. Considering Saladin's thorough planning, doubtless al-Adid was doomed the moment Saladin decided to overthrow the Fatimid caliphate. He had to eliminate the caliph without giving him a chance to nominate a successor. As the planning of Saladin's action was excellent, so was its execution. Operation al-Adid was a complete success—because the patient died. The day which the chroniclers report as the date of the mysterious demise of the last caliph of the Shiite dynasty, a dynasty whose ideological beginnings were connected with Husayn ibn Ali ibn Abi Talib, seems to convey a significant message: it was the tenth of *Muharram*, or the anniversary day of the martyr death of that Shiite imam.

The aftermath

Upon the death of al-Adid, Dawud inquired of Saladin concerning his succession. The little boy—since the caliph died at the age of twenty-one, his oldest son could have hardly reached the age of ten— obviously did not make political demands on his own. Part of the palace establishment still hoped to salvage the Fatimid dynasty. The answer came addressed to Dawud. "I am the deputy of your father in the matters of the caliphate," categorically stated Saladin. "And he did not order me to make you his successor." [103]

On the evening of 14 September Saladin made a public appearance at a palace gathering, which included members of religious congregations as well as divines. After being served food, they expected Saladin to announce a new caliph from the family of al-Adid. They waited in vain.[104]

The anti-Fatimid action reached its climax on Friday, 17 September 1171. By then the preachers in Fustat and Cairo had received orders from Saladin to invoke al-Mustadi in the *khutbah*. The orders were carried out, provoking no public protests. Saladin dispatched similar instructions all over the Egyptian provinces.[105] The historical distinction of being the first to invoke an Abbasid caliph in the mosque of Amr, after a lapse of two centuries, fell upon Muhammad ibn al-Muhsin ibn al-Husayn ibn Ali Abi al-Mada.[106]

While mosques of the capital proclaimed the restoration of Sunni supremacy, Saladin's forces were taking over the palace grounds. They rounded up the deceased caliph's family and their retinue and committed them to protective custody in a special area of the palace precinct. The members of the new regime then divided their houses, slaves, and treasures.[107] The purge was not limited to the living. On that same Friday, the corpses of a brother of Shawar, of al-Kamil, and of his brother, were exhumed and taken away from the palace burial place.[108]

In the meantime, a real anti-Fatimid persecution was in progress in the Cairo streets. The Sunnis were out to settle accounts with the people of the establishment. The Ismailis were so hounded and abused they did not dare to leave their abodes. Whenever they were apprehended by Turkish soldiers, they were stripped of their clothes. So great was their misfortune that most sought refuge in the countryside, much to the rejoicing of the Sunni population in the capital.[109]

News of the successful coup arrived in Damascus and Baghdad, where it caused great jubilation.[110] On 8 December 1171 Egyptian coinage appeared, struck in the name of the Abbasid sovereign.[111] The final ceremonies marking the reinstallation of Abbasid sovereignty were held in March 1172. On 10 March Saladin made a public appearance in the decorated streets of the capital. He was dressed in a ceremonial robe and appropriate insignia, received from Baghdad in triumphant recognition of his contribution to the Abbasid cause.[112] On the following day, there were special services in the mosques of Fustat and Cairo. The black Abbasid banners decorated the *minbars* and the preachers dressed in black robes just received from Baghdad. The regime publicly cautioned the faithful not to be late or miss the Friday service. Those who transgressed these instructions would face stiff penalties. Under the circumstances, the ceremony honoring the triumph of the Abbasids was attended even by those "who did not wish it at all." [113]

6 The new master of Egypt and Nur al-Din

"Guileless himself, he never expected and seldom understood guile in others."—H. A. R. Gibb

As a result of his suppressing the Shiite caliphate, Saladin became known as an idealistic leader dedicated to the cause of Islamic unity—a reputation which has influenced some of his modern admirers. In reality, Saladin was a pragmatist pursuing power-oriented self-serving ambitions. This motivation guided his policy towards Nur al-Din, which pushed the Muslim forces of Egypt and Syria to the brink of bloody confrontation.

Egypt in the strategy of Nur al-Din

Nur al-Din's military intervention in Egypt had aimed at two major strategic goals: to prevent it from falling to Amalric and to secure total subordination of its resources to the Syrian war effort against the Crusaders. Success of this strategy could mean a decisive step in the realization of historic Zangid aspirations. The military and economic resources of his Syrian and Mesopotamian feudal dominions had helped Nur al-Din to cripple the Christian Kingdom of Jerusalem. And by exploiting Egypt's potential, he would be able to attempt total liberation of Muslim territories from Crusader domination, a triumph which would tremendously enhance the political power and prestige of the Zangid dynasty.

Nur al-Din had both economic and military plans for Egypt. Of immediate economic concern was the question of direct cash payments to his treasury. Nur al-Din's claims here were well justified in view of the solemn pledges made both by Shawar in 1164 and by

Caliph al-Adid in 1168. And in the light of the high cost of financing Shirkuh's third expedition, his demands for monetary compensation were also warranted.

Prior to the overthrow of the Fatimid caliphate, Nur al-Din received absolutely no cash shipments from Egypt, except for 50,000 dinars which Shirkuh had obtained from Shawar by the 1167 armistice agreement.[1] While Shawar and al-Adid simply violated their financial agreement with Nur al-Din, Saladin's failure to meet Egypt's obligations could be explained by his unusually high political and military expenses. His expensive military reorganization, the costs of defending Damietta, and, finally, the considerable proportion of Egyptian revenue necessary to support the Fatimid court made it impossible for Saladin to transfer any funds to Syria. However, by the end of 1171 all these impediments no longer existed. Following the Crusaders' abortive expedition against Damietta, they suspended their destructive attacks against Egyptian territory; the military build-up was essentially complete—in fact, early in 1172 Saladin was able to demobilize some Bedouin units;[2] and, finally, the onerous Fatimid establishment no longer weighed down Egypt's fiscal structure. In the light of these propitious developments Nur al-Din was justified in expecting Saladin to begin discharging the long overdue monetary obligations towards Syria.

Nur al-Din's dissatisfaction with Saladin

Much to Nur al-Din's annoyance, Saladin never reached the level of economic cooperation desired by the court of Syria. In April 1172 Saladin dispatched 100,000 dinars to Aleppo, to which were added a ceremonial turban and robe of one of the early Fatimid caliphs, a few other valuable objects confiscated from the treasury of al-Adid, and a quantity of incense. Although the envoys from Egypt brought also a statement outlining the schedule of Saladin's subsequent payments to Syria, Nur al-Din could not conceal his disappointment with the delivery. "By God! We have no need for all this," said he, with obvious reference to the valuable gifts. "This dispatch hardly amounts to one percent of the money we spent on fitting out the troops sent to conquer Egypt. And, after all, we undertook the conquest of Egypt with the sole purpose of recovering the Syrian coast and of evicting the infidels." [3]

On 30 May 1173 Saladin sent off another caravan to Nur al-Din, delivering 60,000 dinars, gold and silver vessels and utensils, crystal objects, precious stones of extreme rarity both in size and quality, luxurious clothes, incense, perfumes, and finally, an elephant. Once again, Nur al-Din objected, reiterating his need for gold. [4]

After waiting in vain for a few more months Nur al-Din began to run out of patience. In the spring of 1174 he decided to send his trusted vizir, Ibn al-Qaysarani, to Cairo. He was to audit the Egyptian fiscal records to determine the exact amount of money Saladin should transfer to Syria. [5] When Ibn al-Qaysarani explained his task to Saladin, the latter appeared shaken. "Have we stooped so low?" [6] he exclaimed and proceeded to argue his case, detailing the state of Egyptian economy and the cost of maintaining effective control over the country. But having failed to convince Ibn al-Qaysarani, Saladin ordered a special fiscal report prepared and—in an apparent rebuff to the Syrian envoy—chose his trustworthy and diplomatically experienced supporter, Isa al-Hakkari, to deliver it personally to Nur al-Din. [7] It is certain Saladin tried to placate his Syrian overlord, for he sent with the two envoys another rich caravan to Damascus. However, this caravan did not reach its destination before Nur al-Din's death.

In addition to direct cash payments, Nur al-Din had also hoped to receive from Saladin indirect economic contributions to the holy war. These involved supporting land and naval forces stationed in Egypt, ready for deployment against the Crusaders. In a certain sense Saladin fulfilled this obligation, because the costs of his military build-up and its maintenance were borne by the Egyptian economy alone. Also, Saladin's transformation of Egypt from a defenseless, moribund state into a potent entity was accomplished at no cost to the Syrians.

In active military contribution Saladin again disappointed Nur al-Din. Having saved Egypt from Frankish occupation, Nur al-Din's strategy called for maximum utilization of Egyptian war potential in coordinated military actions against the Crusader kingdom. That Nur al-Din was in earnest became evident during the 1169 Damietta crisis, when he carried out diversionary attacks in Syria,[8] as well as in the fall of 1171 when he launched a violent raiding campaign into the county of Tripoli, in retaliation for Crusader seizure of two Egyptian merchant ships at Ladhiqiya.[9] Caught between the new administration in Egypt and the army of Syria, the Crusaders faced the grim and imminent prospect of simultaneous attack on more than one front. Indeed, to counterbalance this menace, King Amalric made an effort to obtain the help from Byzantium. In the spring of 1171 he came to Constantinople to elicit from Emperor Manuel solemn pledges of Franco-Byzantine cooperation.

One basic requisite of joint military effort by Syria and Egypt was the improvement of communication lines between the two countries, which the belt of strategic Crusader fortresses between the Dead Sea and the Gulf of Aqabah blocked. It became imperative to conquer or at least contain these Crusader garrisons. Saladin's capture of Ailah in 1170 obliterated one such base at the southernmost tip of the blockade belt. As a logical follow-up Nur al-Din intended to eliminate the fortresses of Kerak and Shaubak, situated in the northern sector. But Nur al-Din never saw the capture of these fortresses, which was partially Saladin's fault. The first attempt against the Christian targets was undertaken in the fall of 1171. According to a plan Nur al-Din conceived in consultation with Saladin, the armies of Syria and Egypt were to converge on Kerak to launch a joint assault against the fortress. Apparently in accordance with that plan, on 25 September, almost immediately after the overthrow of the Fatimid caliphate, the new master of Egypt set out with his army against Kerak. Hearing the Egyptians were on the move, Nur al-Din led his own troops to a camp off Kerak where they awaited the army of Egypt. However, instead of joining his overlord, Saladin suddenly interrupted his advance and on 16 November 1171 returned to Cairo, thus causing the failure of the project.[10]

On 30 May 1173 Saladin again invaded the territory of Kerak and Shaubak, but though staying in the field for over two months he returned home without having attacked the two fortresses.[11]

According to Ibn al-Athir, Saladin's failure to fulfill his share in the joint operation provoked Nur al-Din's bitter resentment, which ultimately led to a state of explosive tension.[12] Viewed from a historical perspective, however, the vigorous policies of the new master of Egypt were bound to cause the deterioration in relations between the two leaders.

Saladin and the Egyptian economy

In interpreting Saladin's conduct toward Nur al-Din one must be aware of the economic factors influencing him. Doubtless replacing the degenerate, onerous Fatimid establishment by a vigorous, dynamic regime was conducive to an economic revival of Egypt. The success of these people who had demonstrated their political and military stamina during the rebellion of the Sudanese or the dangerous Crusader attack against Damietta must have inspired confidence in the prospects of internal stability and external security, so essential for the normal economic activities. The constructive interest of the new administration in economic matters was indicated in an important decree, solemnly proclaimed on 6 October 1171,[13] which not only invalidated most noncanonical nuisance taxes (mukus) but declared null and void all indebtedness to the state treasury, incurred through the nonpayment of the taxes in question.[14] Apart from its propaganda value, abolishing these taxes injected about 100,000 dinars annually into the economy for the benefit of investors and consumers.

It appears that Egyptian economy did indeed react favorably to the new political situation. The agricultural sector was unaffected by the substitution of militaristic iqta holders for the Fatimid class of large landowners or administrators of the feudal allotments. However, the new regime accomplished a great deal in pacifying the countryside. After overcoming scattered Fatimid resistance, Saladin's forces handled sporadic flare-ups in Upper Egypt efficiently if brutally. That agricultural production seems to have functioned normally is suggested by the remarkable stability of grain prices.[15]

It is manufacturing activities which must have been stimulated by the consolidation of Saladin's position in Egypt. His crash military program necessarily stimulated those productive forces catering to army and navy needs. Whatever supplies Saladin might have had inherited from the previous regime, the rapid expansion of his land and naval forces must have created an immediate and heavy demand for uniforms, weapons, and equestrian and naval equipment. Saladin's naval needs spurred the ship-building industry. As early as 1170 Egyptian shipyards were called upon to supply Saladin with pre-fabricated ship sections for use in the Ailah operation. Further expansion of naval production followed, so that by the spring of 1179, only eight years after Saladin's final take-over, the Egyptian Mediterranean fleet, which had been virtually wiped out during the punishing attacks of the Crusaders and their Norman and Byzantine allies, counted as many as eighty operational units, including sixty galleys and twenty transports.[16]

Under the new administration the building industry also entered a period of boom. To a considerable extent that industry responded to civilian demands, such as the rehabilitation of Fustat, the replacement of houses the Crusaders destroyed in Bilbais, or the reconstruction of Cairo where it was damaged in the destructive street fighting during the Sudanese rebellion. On the other hand, various defense projects such as the fortification works in the capital and in Alexandria must have absorbed a large proportion of skilled and unskilled labor.

Finally, Egyptian trade, transit, export, and import, reacted favorably to the prospects of stability and security, as well as to the staggering defense requirements generated by Saladin's regime. Especially beneficial to Egyptian commerce was the fiscal decree of 1171, in which one clause was designed as an incentive to traders in the heavily populated metropolitan area. That clause exempted the people of Cairo and Fustat, as well as all exporters and importers in those two centers, or those passing through the Nile ports of al-Maqs and al-Minya, from all customs dues and from vexatious formalities.[17]

A usual level of commodity prices on the home market suggests normal internal trade.[18] Documents from that period also reveal a flow of mercantile traffic between the Mediterranean and the Red Sea.[19] Furthermore, thanks to the protection of military convoys Saladin furnished, merchant caravans reappeared on the Transjordanian trails running across the hostile territory between Egypt and Syria. On the maritime front, the seizure in 1171 of two Egyptian cargo ships at Ladhiqiya attested to the revival of the Egyptian coastal trade.[20] Saladin was also determined to protect traditional merchant interests in Egypt from European, especially Italian, competition. Thus he would not allow the Italians officially and directly into the interior markets of Egypt, including those of her capital.[21] On the other hand, obviously motivated by certain economic and logistic considerations, Saladin did favor regulated commercial intercourse with the Italians, if it was confined to the Mediterranean coastal area. A treaty in 1173 permitted the Pisans to set up a colonial factory in Alexandria, which included the establishment not only of commercial, housing, and bath-house premises, but of a church as well.[22] Similar privileges were subsequently extended to other Italian mercantile republics. In a letter written as early as 1174–75, Saladin could boast that the port of Alexandria was full of Italian ships supplying him with war material.[23]

Despite these promising trends, the Egyptian economy was still inadequate to meet Saladin's current needs. And it certainly was not capable of satisfying the monetary demands of Nur al-Din, on top of Saladin's own military expenditure. One of the most acute economic problems confronting the new master of Egypt was a severe lack of gold reserves. In this respect his situation differed greatly from that enjoyed by earlier administrations.[24] In the first half of the eleventh century, the Fatimid administration still had plentiful gold stocks. These had accumulated because the Fatimids enjoyed a favorable balance of foreign commerce, intensive transit trade, the inflow of gold tribute from regions recognizing Cairo's suzerainty, access to the mining areas of Nubia and Western Sudan, cash revenue derived from customs and from taxes imposed by Fatimid mints on bullion they converted into the official Egyptian currency, and, finally, a solvent fiscal policy of the ruling regime.

By the time Saladin took over, however, the gold reserves had vanished. The operations of foreign and transit trade, disrupted by the Crusader victories, could hardly offset the gold loss military expenditure necessitated. Ever since the loss of Sicily to the Normans in the second half of the eleventh century, Egypt had to depend on European merchants for iron. Instead of receiving tribute, Egypt was recurrently compelled to make gold payments to the Crusaders.

The mines of Nubia were exhausted, and Egypt was cut off from West Sudanese gold ore by the powerful Almohad state in North Africa. The Crusaders tried monetary subversion by disseminating pseudo-Fatimid debased dinars all over the Mediterranean markets,[25] which undermined public trust in the official Egyptian gold currency. This circumstance, as well as the omnipresent insecurity, produced widespread hoarding. The production of Egyptian mints dropped to a very low level and were suspended altogether with the overthrow of the Fatimid regime. By then the Egyptian gold shortage was so acute that one medieval Arab author wrote "to say the name of a pure gold *dinar* was like mentioning the name of a wife to her jealous husband, while to get such a coin in one's hand was like crossing the doors of paradise."[26] Contrary to Saladin's hopes, the confiscated palace treasury turned out to be a disappointment. Though yielding impressive quantities of jewels and other valuable objects, it did not include ready cash.[27] Apparently Shawar's payments to the Crusaders, funded by the Fatimid establishment, and the lavish monetary contribution of al-Adid to the battle of Damietta, completely depleted the last cash reserves of the caliphate.

The critical gold shortage detrimentally affected the status of the new regime's official coinage. Traditionally, the accession of new dynasties or regimes in Islamic Egypt was accompanied by modifications in coinage, and for propaganda reasons Saladin should have flooded the markets with coinage whose quality excelled that of the overthrown Fatimid dynasty. However, on 28 November 1171 when the mints of Egypt resumed production, their output was extremely limited.[28] Despite an effort to scrape up adequate quantities of silver— the mosques of the capital, for instance, were stripped of all pro-Fatimid silver inscriptions [29]—Saladin's new dirhams resembled the low quality Fatimid silver of irregular, reduced weight.[30] Indeed there are indications that Saladin's administration had to depend on glass-paste jetons, used as fiduciary currency, to expedite internal market operations.[31]

And yet in spite of monetary stringency Saladin managed to carry out sweeping military reforms which in turn stimulated Egyptian economic productivity. To a certain extent he accomplished this by economy measures such as dismissal of redundant military units, reductions in administrative personnel,[32] and, above all, in getting rid of the fabulous Fatimid court. However, the main reason for this success lay in the large-scale use of military *iqtas*[33] and the improvement in collection of canonical taxes.[34] Although illegal taxes were immediately abolished in principle, the treasury department (at one stage headed by Saladin's father) was not above questionable practices such as selling operating licenses to brothels in Alexandria, collecting fees from producers of wine,[35] and imposing taxes on transfers of property.[36]

This background of economic stringency explains some aspects of Saladin's relations with his nominal overlord. And while it is true that Saladin disappointed Nur al-Din regarding the cash tribute, he nevertheless exploited all available resources to restore the defensive and offensive effectiveness of Egyptian military forces, fulfilling thus one important strategic objective of the Syrian sultan. Paradoxically enough, instead of the regenerated army of Egypt combining in a joint strategy against the Crusaders, it brought Islam to the brink of another suicidal struggle.

Did Saladin evade his obligations at Kerak and Shaubak?

As stated earlier, the first test of Nur al-Din's strategic use of Egyptian units for joint offensive operations against the Crusaders, undertaken in the autumn of 1171, ended in a fiasco because Saladin suddenly returned to Egypt. According to Ibn al-Athir, Saladin claimed troubles at home required his withdrawal, but Nur al-Din did not accept that excuse.[37] The same chronicler claimed this failure was at the root of tension between the two leaders.[38] Whatever the true measure of Nur al-Din's disappointment, Ibn al-Athir's analysis of Saladin's sudden decision is not borne out by other sources. The entirely sufficient reason for Saladin's withdrawal was that even before reaching the rendezvous point, his forces had suffered a major defeat at the hands of hostile Bedouin warriors collaborating with the Crusaders. Having lost substantial equipment, horses, and camels, Saladin had no alternative but to withdraw.[39]

It was to avenge this humiliation that Saladin, in the last days of

May 1173, launched an offensive operation in the area of Kerak and Shaubak. Contrary to the story found in Lane-Poole,[40] there was no question of a joint operation on that occasion, because Nur al-Din had headed north to intervene in a struggle between the Muslim princes of Anatolia. As Saladin duly reported to Nur al-Din, the main objective of his expedition was not a direct attack on the Crusaders but to destroy their partnership with the Bedouin.[41]

On the other hand, it is true that this 1173 expedition to Transjordan ended prematurely because Saladin's father suffered a fatal accident. On 31 July 1173 Najm al-Din Ayyub fell off his horse and died nine days later, even before Saladin's speedy return from the expedition. The interrupted campaign was but a minor consequence of Ayyub's death. More important was the fact that Saladin was now senior member of the ambitious Kurdish family, not so much on the ground of his age, as on the basis of his actual political power.

Saladin's actual performance appears to indicate he made an effort not to antagonize Nur al-Din. Although he failed to furnish satisfactory amounts of gold, he did send rich gifts to Syria; although Kerak and Shaubak remained unconquered, Saladin actively pressed these strategic targets. Moreover, Saladin carefully observed all the protocol expressing his subordinate status toward his Syrian overlord. The Syrian sultan was included in the *khutbah* invocations, as well as in the inscriptions on the new Egyptian coinage.[42] Finally, Saladin scrupulously reported to Nur al-Din about his activities in Egypt. And yet, in spite of such expressions of loyalty, the relations between the two leaders grew steadily worse—reaching an explosive point in the spring of 1174.

The roots of the conflict

Not only did Ibn al-Athir maintain that Saladin's alleged evasion of military obligations [43] had caused this conflict, but he also insinuated that Saladin deliberately obstructed Muslim offensive plans because he had preferred Kerak and Shaubak in Crusader hands where it would serve as a buffer against Nur al-Din himself.[44]

A much more persuasive and sophisticated interpretation of the tension between the two has been offered by H. A. R. Gibb:

> At bottom, the causes of the strain lay more probably in a divergence of political views. Nur al-Din regarded Syria as the main battlefield against the Crusaders, and looked to Egypt firstly as a source of revenue to meet the expense of the jihad, and secondly as a source of additional manpower. Saladin, on the other hand, judging from the former competition for Egypt and the attempt on Damietta in 1169, and probably informed of the tenor of Amalric's negotiations with the Byzantine emperor in 1171, seems to have been convinced that for the time being, at least, the main point of danger lay in Egypt. He was more conscious also than Nur al-Din could be of the dangers arising from the hostility of the former Fatimid troops and their readiness to join with the Franks. In his view, therefore, it was his first duty to build up a new army strong enough to hold Egypt in all contingencies, and to spend what resources he could command on this object.[45]

Persuasive as it is, Gibb's thesis calls for further elaboration. The crux of the matter is that Nur al-Din realized not all Egyptian economic and military potential was being applied to the holy war. On the other hand, Saladin, while openly professing his attachment to Nur al-Din, refused to make Egypt the object of quasi-colonialist Syrian exploitation so long as it benefited not his own but Zangid ambitions.

Saladin got where he was not so much through Nur al-Din as through the decisive support of several pressure groups convinced that he would safeguard the interests they had vested in Egypt. To surrender totally to Nur al-Din's demands would jeopardize the interests of Saladin himself, of his immediate family, of his relatives, of his Kurdish, Turkish, and Arab supporters, and of all the local people who saw in the new regime a chance for Egypt's recovery. To fulfill that trust, Saladin had to act as a true ruler of Egypt, following a policy dictated by the interests of Egypt, not by those of a foreign power.

It is with such an interpretation of Saladin's policy that one can

best understand why Egypt and Syria once again found themselves
on a collision course.

The project of westward invasion

Though a principal factor underlying Egypt's new security was the
strength of the army, and though the army did stimulate the country's
productivity, the maintenance of Saladin's large land and naval forces
weighed heavily on the fiscal potential of Egypt. Some economy was
achieved in the winter of 1171–72, by an almost 20 percent reduction
of Bedouin tribal units,[46] though here Saladin may have been motivated by bitterness over the defeat inflicted by the Transjordanian
Bedouins. In February 1172, however, it proved necessary to raise by
20 percent the fiscal allocations for the fleet.[47] Thus, soon after Saladin's
coup, it became apparent that despite extensive reliance on the *iqta*
system, the new regime had to find additional expedients to preserve
a healthy balance between Egypt's military needs and economic means.

Indeed, on 18 April 1172 Saladin went to Alexandria to consult on
the grave problem of military expenditure. On that occasion the idea
of a military expedition against Barqa in Libya appears to have been
conceived. Barqa, Saladin was told, enjoyed the reputation of being a
rich region, sparsely populated with defenseless Bedouins.[48] Such a
deployment of idle army units outside his own domain, which would
bring political and economic advantages to Egypt, would certainly
have appealed to Saladin. Consequently, a special war council of
Saladin, his father, Ayyub, his uncle al-Harimi, and his nephew Taqi
al-Din Umar decided to launch a westward invasion. The council entrusted Taqi al-Din with the task of organizing and leading an expeditionary corps consisting of 500 troopers in addition to his own
feudal contingent.[49] Instead of concentrating on the anti-Crusader
front, Saladin chose to commit a sizeable part of his tactical troops
to an invasion of Muslim territories in the West. The actual launching of the expedition, however, was delayed, because disturbing news
arrived about an aggressive push of Nubian warriors against the
southern frontier of Egypt.

Victory over the Nubians

This delay was a wise decision. During the summer of 1172 Nubian troops crossed the frontier and laid siege to Aswan. Its governor, Kanz al-Dawlah, sent for help to Saladin who immediately dispatched a relief force under the command of al-Shuja al-Baalbakki. At the approach of the relief expedition the Nubians retreated, spreading havoc and destruction in the countryside, but they were finally overtaken by the pursuing Egyptian troops, who after a bloody battle drove the invaders out of Egypt.

Informed of the Nubians' destruction, Saladin resolved to teach them a lesson. In the last days of December 1172, his impetuous brother, Shams al-Dawlah, set out from Cairo with a task force of cavalry units backed by support troops transported up the Nile on especially provided cargo ships. This retaliatory operation ended in a success. After entering Nubia the Egyptian army attacked and captured Ibrim, liberated some Muslim prisoners, laid waste surrounding territories, left a Kurdish garrison in occupation of Ibrim, then turned back to Egypt, laden with booty. Upon reaching Qus, Shams al-Dawlah received an embassy from the king of Nubia suing for peace. The Nubian conflict ended with Saladin's consolidating Egypt's domination in the regions of the Upper Nile.[50]

Invasion of North African regions

The counteroffensive against Nubia seemed to prove the viability of reducing military expenditure by sending Egyptian troops on predatory expeditions, even if such a policy entailed reduction of efforts against the Crusaders. The victory of Shams al-Dawlah, besides resulting in rich booty, reopened the southern land and river routes connecting Egypt with the gold, ivory, and slave trade of the African hinterland. However, Nubia itself was too poor and too rugged a country to appeal to Saladin or his men. (Even the Kurdish garrison stationed in Ibrim, unable to stand the local conditions, returned to Egypt after two years of occupation).[51] The westward expedition, finally launched in 1173 under the leadership of Sharaf al-Din Qaragush, a commander on the staff of Taqi al-Din, turned out to be an outstanding success. The advancing army of Qaragush swept over Barqa and adjacent communities to reach Jabal Nafusa in Tripolitania. There it was joined by Bedouin warriors rising against Almohad authority in North Africa. With their support the Egyptian troops captured Tripoli and pushed on into the territory of Tunis.[52]

Some two decades later, when trying to obtain naval assistance from the powerful Almohad state, Saladin cynically disclaimed responsibility for the attack on North Africa,[53] but in 1173 he boasted of his army's exploits in a letter to Nur al-Din who, in turn, relayed the news to the caliph in Baghdad.[54] Assessed from Saladin's vantage point, this westward invasion of Moslem territories certainly paid off. It kept part of his mobile troops occupied while providing for their upkeep with no cost to Egypt; it supplied Saladin with large booty; and finally, it reestablished Egyptian political and military influence over the coastal and sea routes along which the lucrative commercial and pilgrim traffic between North Africa and Egypt moved. If stabilized and consolidated, this extension of Saladin's authority might restore many advantages enjoyed by Egypt during the better days of the Fatimid caliphate. Such a prospect had strategic value for Saladin's navy, as it would bring Egypt within direct reach of the North African forests, facilitating acquisition of lumber required for ship-building. And the success of Saladin's troops would aid recruitment of experienced North African sailors for the Egyptian fleet.[55]

Invasion of the Red Sea eastern littoral

The new master of Egypt also wanted to extend his political power over the eastern approaches to his country. One should remember that since the reconquest of Ailah in 1170, Egypt controlled the navigation in the Gulf of Aqabah. Subsequently, in 1173 Saladin, striving to improve security for caravans going between Syria and Egypt, led his troops against the Transjordanian Bedouins. In 1174 another powerful army embarked on a difficult and costly expedition aimed at reasserting Egypt's influence over the eastern coast of the Red Sea. Once again Saladin downgraded the Crusaders on his list of political and military priorities.

The very idea of this new expedition had an unusual conception, involving Saladin's ambitious brother, Shams al-Dawlah, and a brilliant poet, Umarah al-Yamani. Although Shams al-Dawlah had played an essential part in the elimination of the Fatimid caliphate, he did not mind associating with some prominent members of the overthrown establishment, who somehow had escaped the repressive measures of the new regime. One of them was al-Sharif al-Jalis, the foremost councillor and official of the last Fatimid caliph; [56] another was Umarah, the court poet of the abolished caliphate. Indeed, it was through Sham al-Dawlah's protection that Umarah escaped punishment for composing poems eulogizing the bygone Fatimid era.[57] The same protege of Shams al-Dawlah now began to advocate the conquest of Yemen.[58]

Although treated preferentially as far as his *iqta* allocations were concerned, Saladin's driving brother reacted enthusiastically to the projected predatory campaign in the Arabia Felix, which sounded more promising than his earlier invasion of the poor Nubian regions. Saladin approved the proposed expedition, since a successful extension of Ayyubid influence over Yemen would further enhance Egypt's strategic position. After securing Nur al-Din's permission,[59] Saladin ordered his brother to go ahead with preparations. In addition to his own feudal contingent, Shams al-Dawlah received a regiment of 1,000 horsemen, as well as a fleet of transport ships to carry heavy weapons and supplies. To finance the initial expedition costs Shams al-Dawlah was allowed to utilize the proceeds from that year's entire crops sale in the province of Qus.[60]

Toward the end of February 1174 Shams al-Dawlah, accompanied by a number of outstanding commanders, led his army on a new Ayyubid conquest. The combined land and sea units moved from Egypt to the Hejaz. After a brief stop in Mecca, Shams al-Dawlah continued his advance southward to reach Zabid on 13 May 1174. Overpowering resistance by the local ruler, the invaders pushed further south and succeeded in establishing Ayyubid mastery over Sana, Aden, and other places in Yemen.[61] As in the expansive period of the Fatimid regime, Egypt once again dominated the Red Sea and its important commercial and pilgrim traffic.

A new pro-Fatimid conspiracy

While his oldest brother was extending Ayyubid domination in Arabia, Saladin faced a new large-scale conspiracy aimed at restoring the Fatimid caliphate. The plot was hatched among different groups hostile to Saladin's regime. Leading members of the conspiracy included Ibn Abd al-Qawi, formerly chief Ismaili missionary and a pillar of the Fatimid establishment; two prominent Fatimid judges, Ibn al-Kamil and al-Awris, dismissed during Saladin's judicial reform of 1171; the poet Umarah and the aristocratic al-Jalis, both noted for personal relations with Shams al-Dawlah; Shubruma, a high official in the Fatimid chancery; Abd al-Samad, a Fatimid military commander; and, finally, Qadid al-Qaffas, the head of a clandestine Fatimid faction in Alexandria. This subversive movement was also joined by some descendants of two former Fatimid viziers, Ruzzayk and Shawar, as well as by other local Egyptian malcontents.[62]

More disturbing, however, was the fact that the conspiracy included leaders in the new regime—a number of Saladin's own commanders and warriors,[63] as well as the Sunni theologian Zayn al-Din, and a prominent Egyptian politician, Ibn Massal.[64] It is difficult to determine why Saladin's military people should join this rebellious movement. As for Zayn al-Din, a divine belonging to the Hanbalite rite of the Sunni Islam, it is possible the conspirators approached him through his antagonism toward al-Khabushani,[65] that controversial Shafiite jurist Saladin favored in reward for his *fatwa* endorsing the Fatimid deposition. Apparently the conspirators were unaware that Zayn al-Din had participated in the secret negotiations of 1164 between Shirkuh and Egyptian Sunni theologians proposing the overthrow of the Fatimid regime, and they may have trusted Ibn Massal, although he had been most instrumental in advancing Shirkuh's cause in Alexandria during the campaign of 1167, on account of his pro-Fatimid family background.

As is often the case with revolutionary movements representing diverse religious, family, and ethnic groups, the new conspiracy suffered from internal squabbles and rivalries, but it was nonetheless dynamic enough to evolve an ingenious plan of action. Bearing in mind how the rebellion of 1169 was crushed, the plotters realized that a military revolt stood no chance as long as the army of the new regime remained concentrated in Egypt. It was for this reason that Umarah persuaded Shams al-Dawlah to embark on the Yemen expedition.[66] Considering that over 500 troops were in North Africa, the effective strength of Saladin's army was reduced by over 1,500 men and the services of one of its most brilliant field commanders. To further minimize easy countermeasures, the conspirators decided to start their uprising during the harvest season when most military personnel would be dispersed to supervise the collecting and marketing of crops on their feudal estates.[67] To ensure the success of their coup, the conspirators continued on Crusader naval and land attacks, which would divert Saladin's attention and troops from the capital. To this end the plotters entered into secret negotiations with King Amalric, using the influence of that same Ibn Qarjalah who had once fled from Shawar's persecutions and helped the Crusaders plan their 1168 invasion of Egypt.[68] In their clandestine communications with Amalric the rebels relied on a Christian, by the name of George, who was already—officially—the diplomatic courier between the court of the Crusaders and Saladin. Interestingly enough, there existed rumors that the conspirators had asked an uncle of Ibn Qarjalah to approach the Assassin sect in Syria to obtain their cooperation in the proposed pro-Ismaili revolt.[69]

In spite of its widespread ramifications and elaborate preparations, the conspiracy failed because Saladin learned of it even before the plotters completed their plans. One informer was Ibn Massal,[70] but the main credit went to Zayn al-Din. Once approached by the conspirators, the Hanbalite theologian wasted no time in exploiting that circumstance to his own material advantage. He reached Saladin through al-Qadi al-Fadil, informed him of the conspiracy, and agreed to serve as a double agent.[71] In reward for his services Zayn al-Din requested all the house property possessed by Ibn al-Kamil, one of the conspiracy masterminds.[72] With intelligence of this kind, Saladin was able to crush the internal subversion.

The conspiracy throws additional light on the dispatch of Shams al-Dawlah to Yemen. While Umarah had urged the brilliant commander to go in order to weaken Saladin's military position in Egypt, it is likely, considering Saladin's knowledge of the plot, that Saladin used the invasion of Yemen to remove his brother from Egypt, lest he interfere with the ruthless punishment Saladin planned for his brother's Fatimid proteges.

Saladin planned and executed his moves with typical skill. On 12 March 1174 the Fatimid royal internees, who until then had been kept in a section of the palace, were placed under strict house arrest to prevent them from serving the interests on the conspirators.[73] Mass arrests followed in the first days of April. One after another, the chief conspirators were sought out and brought before Saladin to confess meekly their subversive involvement. They pleaded that their hostility to the new regime had been caused by severe economic deprivation. A special tribunal of Sunni jurists was then set up, which sentenced the principal offenders to death by crucifixion and their followers to banishment.[74]

For several days beginning 6 April, Cairo residents witnessed a gruesome spectacle, where much of Egypt's former elite were crucified one after another.[75] The first to go was the brilliant poet, Umarah. With his patron away in Arabia, he stood no chance of escaping Saladin's vindictiveness. When led past the residence of al-Qadi al-Fadil, the condemned man made a desperate plea for intercession of the influential secretary, but to no avail. Umarah's crucified body was displayed in the central square of Cairo, the famous Bain al-Qasrain, along the western facade of the Fatimid palace.[76] The body of al-Awris hung at the entrance to the Street of the Chain.[77] Another conspirator, Ibn Abd al-Qawi, was believed to have known the whereabouts of hidden Fatimid treasures, but he did not reveal the secret and shared the others' fate.[78] Also executed in Cairo were Abd al-Samad, Shubruma and his accomplices, a number of Saladin's commanders and regular soldiers, and some slaves and followers of the conspirators.[79] Between 15 and 25 April the royal Fatimid prisoners were taken out from the palace grounds and committed to protective custody in the Barjuwan district.[80] On 29 April, Qadid al-Qaffas was arrested in Alexandria where he was also executed.[81] The last to perish, on 23 May, was Ibn al-Kamil.[82] Those sentenced to banishment were branded and sent to the most distant regions of Upper Egypt.[83]

By this well-planned, bloody operation, Saladin destroyed the last remaining nerve center of Fatimid opposition and averted the outbreak of new fighting and internal disorder in Egypt and her capital.

The threat of hostilities between Nur al-Din and Saladin

While Saladin was endeavoring to crush this conspiracy, Ibn al-Qaysarani arrived in Cairo as special envoy from Nur al-Din.[84] His request to audit the fiscal records of Saladin's administration in order to assess the proportion of revenue which should go to Syria could only be regarded as an arrogant, provocative demarche, intended to remind the master of Egypt of his inferior status in respect to the Syrian sultan.

By then Nur al-Din must have been fully aware that Saladin had been placing the interests of his administration in Egypt above the immediate needs of his overlord. The successes of Egyptian troops on different fronts contributed to Saladin's glory without adding directly to Nur al-Din's effective power. In fact, these successes had absorbed a lot of Egyptian manpower and economic resources which might otherwise have been used against the Crusaders. Obviously, Saladin did not consider the war against the Crusaders as the dominant or exclusive factor in his policy. Why, then, did Nur al-Din allow Saladin to send a major and costly expedition to Yemen? The answer may be that, like the conspirators in Cairo, Nur al-Din had an interest in seeing Saladin's forces reduced by the departure of Shams al-Dawlah and his army. Nur al-Din's plans may well have coincided with those of the rebels, for he had been preparing an armed intervention in Egypt aimed at removing Saladin. In the spring of 1174 the Syrian headquarters issued special orders to that effect.[85]

Nur al-Din's aggressive plans were not unknown to Saladin.[86] Although he continued to reiterate his loyal submission to his overlord, his forces were determined to defend Egypt's independence from Syria. These tactics were easily recognized by Ibn al-Qaysarani who reported to Damascus that Saladin's apparent respectful composure was but a diplomatic mask covering a "guileful and dissentful" disposition toward Nur al-Din.[87] Thus, ironically enough, Saladin's successful salvaging of Egypt from complete chaos and possible Crusader occupation led to a situation where once again the forces of Syria were pitted against those of Egypt. Because of Saladin's policy in Egypt the Muslim front encircling the Crusader kingdom now faced another disruption. As it happened, however, this possibility disappeared with the opportune death of Nur al-Din on 15 May 1174.

7 Saladin's first campaign in Syria

"Nothing makes me so sad except the thought of what will befall my family on the part of Yusuf, the son of Ayyub."
—Nur al-Din on his death bed

The death of Nur al-Din produced a political situation similar to that prevailing on the eve of Shirkuh's Egyptian expeditions, except the roles of Syria and Egypt were now reversed. While Saladin's Egypt was dynamic and unified, Syria became the scene of intense factional struggle, revolving around al-Salih, Nur al-Din's eleven-year-old son, now acclaimed as the new ruler in Damascus. But there the analogy ended. Unlike Nur al-Din in Syria, Saladin did not need substantial outside resources to shore up his military position. Nor did Saladin face the threat of an imminent Crusader offensive. In the 1160s, Nur al-Din had to consider the possibility that Egypt might fall into the hands of the Christian enemy, but in the summer of 1174 this danger no longer existed. With the death of King Amalric on 11 July 1174, the Crusader kingdom lost its last leader capable of effective expansionist pressure against Muslim territories. Nor could the Crusaders now count on the support of their traditional allies. The crushing defeat inflicted on Emperor Manuel by the Saljuqids of Iconium, in the battle of Myriokephalon (17 September 1176) eliminated the Byzantines as an active ally in future Crusader campaigns in Syria or Egypt. Furthermore, Venice, Pisa, and Genoa, having established colonial outposts in the Syrian littoral and having reopened commercial connections with Egypt, were not interested in supporting an expansion inland of the Crusader kingdom. Thus, barring the large-scale intervention of fresh Crusader forces from Europe, neither Damascus, Aleppo, nor Cairo had much to fear from the Christian Kingdom of Jerusalem.

Saladin's position looked more promising than ever. He had successfully overcome all challenge to his government. And with none of its resources being siphoned off, Egyptian society—benefitting from the internal stability Saladin established—was expected to strengthen his base economically. But to perpetuate this state of affairs Saladin had to watch the new developments in Syria.

Medieval Egyptian rulers had always displayed keen interest in Syria; they had missed no opportunity to exploit her fiscally and to use her territory as a staging area for north and eastbound military expeditions. Furthermore, they had consistently tried to maintain direct control over southern Syria, especially Palestine, to serve as a buffer zone guarding Egypt's eastern approaches. On the other hand, they neither had attempted transferring the political center of their power to Syria, nor had they indulged in a Syrian policy which would endanger the economic stability of their Egyptian base. In the twelfth century this pattern of relations between Egypt and Syria had undergone a dramatic reversal. Syria's economy suffered badly from the prolonged struggle between the Muslims and the Crusaders. Her leaders, Muslim and Christian alike, regarded Egypt as a source of supplementary revenue. Egypt's territory had become the target of many invasions coming from Syria, which were facilitated by the early disappearance of an Egyptian presence in Palestine. Now, in 1174, a crisis in Syria presented the ambitious ruler in Cairo with a chance to resume the traditional policy for the benefit of his Egyptian power base.

This chance was not wasted on him. Before the end of 1174, he rode into Syria and laid claim to those regions which had seen the rise of Shirkuh and Ayyub. A decade earlier the Syrian intervention had revealed Saladin as an outstanding military leader, a meticulous planner, and a stern ruler. His present involvement was destined to unveil his true ambitions and to add larger dimensions to his leadership. It also showed him definitely more active against Muslim rivals than against the Crusaders.

Saladin's initial reaction to the new regime in Damascus

On the very day of Nur al-Din's death, political and military circles in Damascus, led by the commanders Ibn al-Muqaddam, Ibn Isa al-Jarrahi, and Jamal al-Dawlah Rayhani, by the prestigious court officials

Ibn al-Ajami and Ismail the treasurer, and by the prominent judge Ibn al-Shahrazuri, formally acclaimed al-Salih the new ruler of Syria. Because of his minority, Nur al-Din's son was placed under the tutelage of Ibn al-Muqaddam who got himself appointed commander in chief of the Damascus armed forces.[1] The post of vizir was taken over by Ibn al-Ajami, in obvious displacement of vizir Ibn al-Qaysarani, who at that time had not yet returned from his diplomatic mission to Cairo.[2]

In spite of this smooth transition of authority in Damascus, the new regime felt far from secure. It alienated the population by quickly reintroducing various noncanonical taxes which Nur al-Din abolished.[3] Such measures must have displeased the revered judge Ibn al-Shahrazuri. Nor could the returning Ibn al-Qaysarani have shown any enthusiasm for those who had ousted him from the vizirial post.[4] The regime also faced opposition in northern Syria, particularly in Aleppo. There, the Banu al-Dayah or sons of Ibn al-Dayah, who had served for twenty-three years as governor of Aleppo, insisted that they should have the wardship of young al-Salih.[5] The Shiite population of Aleppo, headed by Ibn al-Khashshab, whose religious freedom Nur al-Din had sharply curtailed, could be expected to exploit the tenuous hold of the new regime in Damascus.[6] Also of concern to the new regime must have been the attitude of the fanatically militant Assassin sect of Syria, headed by the "Old Man of the Mountain," the notorious Sinan of Masyaf.[7]

In addition to these internal difficulties, three external forces jeopardized the new government's security: the regime of Saladin in Egypt; the court of Mosul under the rule of Sayf al-Din Ghazi, nephew and vassal of Nur al-Din; and of course the Crusader kingdom. Saladin most worried the leaders in Damascus. After all, they knew well his accomplishments and the prowess of his military forces as well as the tense, almost explosive, relations between Damascus and Cairo when Nur al-Din died. Consequently, on the advice of Ibn al-Shahrazuri—once noted for bitter criticism of Saladin but now respecting his military might—the ruling clique wasted no time in seeking Saladin's diplomatic recognition. On the very day of Nur al-Din's death, a letter Imad al-Din al-Isfahani composed and the youthful al-Salih himself signed was dispatched to Cairo informing

Saladin of the new regime and asking him to respect the suzerainty of his deceased overlord's son.[8] Some of the more bellicose Damascus commanders—one suspects these must have included the Nuriyah officers opposed to Saladin's elevation in Egypt—condemned such a soft policy towards Cairo. There are even indications that pro-Saladin commanders in Damascus were imprisoned during the critical change-over.[9] Cairo's official reply, however, allayed the apprehensions of the new regime. Saladin's letter, composed by al-Qadi al-Fadil and dated 6 June 1174, assured the court of Damascus that as of that date Cairo had recognized the suzerainty of al-Salih and that his name would be solemnly invoked in all the mosques of territories belonging to the Egyptian ruler.[10] As an additional expression of the recognition, Saladin sent new Egyptian dinars showing the name of al-Salih included in their inscriptions.[11] Shortly after this official letter arrived, there came another note from Cairo, in which Saladin once again emphasized his willingness to support the new ruler in Damascus.[12]

Reaction of Mosul and of the Crusaders

The relations with Sayf al-Din Ghazi of Mosul posed a more complicated problem. Shortly before his death, Nur al-Din ordered his nephew to come to Syria with his Mesopotamian contingent, in preparation for an invasion of Egypt. While leading this army west, Sayf al-Din received the news of Nur al-Din's death. Considering himself released from vassalage, Sayf al-Din promptly annexed various places between the Tigris and the Euphrates, which had been subject to the sultan of Syria. One after another, the governors of such important towns as Nisibin, al-Khabur, Harran, Edessa, Raqqa, and Saruj were compelled to submit to Sayf al-Din. Though he did not extend his drive west of the Euphrates, Sayf al-Din's annexations significantly diminished the heritage of Nur al-Din.[13]

Nor was this opportunity lost on Amalric. Within two weeks of the death of Nur al-Din, the Crusaders in a quick thrust besieged Banyas, situated within striking distance of Damascus. Unable to handle the Frankish threat militarily, Ibn al-Muqaddam resorted to diplomacy. He sent an envoy to King Amalric, threatening him with Saladin's intervention on behalf of Damascus. In a way, this move paralleled those employed during the battle of Egypt, except the roles were reversed. At any rate, the policy of Ibn al-Muqaddam achieved its effect. The Crusaders agreed to terminate hostilities and even signed an armistice in return for a sizeable ransom and the release of a number of Christian prisoners.[14]

The Frankish menace to Damascus subsided when on 11 July 1174 King Amalric died, to be succeeded by his son Baldwin, a boy of thirteen afflicted with leprosy. Saladin emerged as the ruler most capable of filling the power vacuum which the deaths of Nur al-Din and Amalric created.

Conflict between Damascus and Aleppo

Hardly had these external pressures subsided when a power struggle developed between Damascus and Aleppo, which ultimately precipitated Saladin's intervention in Syria. The new conflict originated in Aleppo where the Banu al-Dayah led by Shams al-Din and many Nuriyah associates overcame the Shiite resistance, forced their leader, Ibn al-Khashshab, into hiding, and established themselves in control of the town and the citadel.[15] They then pressed Damascus to transfer al-Salih's residence to the capital of northern Syria. In presenting their demands, the clique of Shams al-Din maintained that such a move had been ordered by the late sovereign himself.[16] Furthermore, Shams al-Din insisted the presence of al-Salih in Aleppo was imperative to thwart the aggressive designs of Sayf al-Din of Mosul.[17] Valid though such arguments might have sounded, the Banu al-Dayah's real motivation was naturally a determination to use the young sovereign to legalize and extend their own authority over all Syria.

Direct negotiations in Damascus were entrusted to one of the younger Banu al-Dayah, Sabiq al-Din. But the most dynamic negotiator was a certain Gümüshtigin, a former commandant of the citadel of Mosul, who entertained notions of political self-aggrandizement. It was due to Gümüshtigin's persuasiveness that the negotiating parties reached an agreement which should have pleased Aleppo: the ruling clique in Damascus consented to move al-Salih's residence to the northern metropolis. Moreover, Ibn al-Muqaddam agreed to relinquish wardship of the young ruler in favor of Shams al-Din Ibn al-Dayah.[18]

In a prompt implementation of the settlement, al-Salih left Damascus on 25 July 1174, accompanied by Sabiq al-Din, Gümüshtigin, and representatives of the Damascus clique.[19] Among these were Ibn al-Ajami, Ismail the treasurer, and Izz al-Din Jurdiq,[20] who had played such a prominent part in helping Saladin eliminate Shawar.[21] In spite of this auspicious beginning, Shams al-Din's hopes of asserting control over al-Salih failed to materialize. Instead of delivering the royal ward, the arriving party managed to capture and imprison the Banu al-Dayah and their backers. It is true that the young successor to Nur al-Din settled in the castle of Aleppo, but it was Gümüshtigin who emerged as the real master of the northern capital. To forestall potential opposition from Shiite troublemakers in Aleppo, the new master commissioned Jurdiq to eliminate the sectarian leader, Ibn al-Khashshab. As in 1169 Jurdiq demonstrated his reliability in such matters. Having lured Ibn al-Khashshab out of his concealment, Jurdiq invited him up to the castle. Shortly afterwards, the head of the Shiite leader was seen hoisted out from a tower of the citadel. The new establishment in Aleppo appeared to be secure.[22]

Saladin's concern about events in Syria

It is possible that al-Salih's removal to Aleppo had been motivated by a fear of Saladin. "Nothing makes me sad except the thought of what will befall my family on the part of Yusuf, the son of Ayyub," Nur al-Din allegedly stated in the final days of his life.[23] At stake, of course, were the interests not only of the late sovereign's family, but of all the people attached to the Zangid dynasty, particularly those hostile to the Ayyubid master of Egypt. Indications that Saladin, despite his declarations of loyalty to al-Salih, was displaying an active, mounting concern for the current developments in Syria may well have aroused these people's apprehensions. Once Saladin learned of Sayf al-Din Ghazi's acquisitions beyond the Euphrates, he sent an angry note to Damascus, criticizing the leaders for not informing him of the advance, so that he might prevent this loss of territory.[24] Also, to counteract the military and political ascendancy of Sayf al-Din, Saladin entered into correspondence with his brother, Imad al-Din Zangi, the master of Sinjar. By exploiting jealousy between the two brothers, Saladin succeeded in securing diplomatic cooperation from Imad al-Din against the lord of Mosul.[25]

Before long, Saladin began to lay the diplomatic groundwork for direct intervention in Syria. This is evident from a communication addressed to Judge Ibn al-Shahrazuri and the military commanders in Syria, in which the master of Egypt went so far as to claim moral responsibility for Nur al-Din's legacy. Ignoring his explosive relations with Damascus just before Nur al-Din's death and disregarding the troops Nur al-Din had mobilized to attack Egypt, Saladin blatantly asserted that "if Nur al-Din had thought any one of you capable of taking my place or of being trusted as he trusted me, he would have appointed him to the government of Egypt, the most important of all his possessions. If death had not prevented him, he would have bequeathed to none but me the guardianship and bringing up of his son." Added to this preposterous assertion was a declaration of his intentions: "I perceive that to my hurt you have arrogated to yourselves the care of my Master, the son of my Master. Assuredly I will come to do him homage and repay the benefits of his father by service which shall be remembered forever; and I shall deal with each of you according to his work. . . ."[26]

Apparently hearing that such tactics were not altogether effective, Saladin engaged in an intensive correspondence stressing his commitment to the struggle against the Crusaders. The truce agreement Ibn al-Muqaddam concluded with Amalric furnished convenient material for the new propaganda line. In a number of letters to military commanders and notables of Syria, Saladin denounced the negotiations and claimed that he had already sent military assistance to help Damascus against the Crusader attack.[27]

Furthermore, in a message sent to Shams al-Din in Aleppo, Saladin hinted at the need for a common front to frustrate the aggressive designs of the Christian foe.[28] Following al-Salih's transfer to Aleppo, Saladin's diplomatic declarations—while reiterating his loyalty towards the house of Nur al-Din and condemning the usurpation of authority by Gümüshtigin—played up his obligations to the unity of Islam. This was particularly evident in a letter to Ibn al-Muqaddam, where Saladin remonstrated that the agreement with Aleppo set back the cause of Islamic unity and he reserved to himself the right to intervene. Ibn al-Muqaddam responded by cautioning Saladin against such intentions and urging loyalty to the house that had established him in Egypt.[29] The reply from Cairo, composed by al-Qadi al-Fadil, contained an unequivocal formulation of Saladin's political program:

> In the interests of Islam and its people we put first and foremost whatever will combine their forces and unite them in one purpose; in the interests of the house of the atabeg [i.e., Zangi] we put first and foremost whatever will safeguard its root and its branch. Loyalty can only be the consequence of loyalty. We are in one valley and those who think ill of us are in another.[30]

Norman attack against Alexandria and an uprising in Upper Egypt

Although Saladin had enough military forces in Egypt to convert his diplomatic dissatisfaction with Syria into forceful intervention, he remained passive throughout the summer of 1174. Even his assertion that the Egyptian army had been on the move during Amalric's attack against Banyas appears to have been nothing but diplomatic bluff. For, although Saladin kept his army mobilized and concentrated around Fakus,[31] this military preparedness was defensive, in anticipation of yet another Christian attack. The Crusaders, as part of their pledge to support the pro-Fatimid conspirators, had succeeded in securing the cooperation of the Normans in Sicily. While the liquidation of the pro-Fatimid plot in Cairo and the death of Amalric eliminated two important elements from the anti-Saladin alliance, the Normans, unaware of these developments, carried forward their offensive commitment against Egypt. On 28 July 1174 a powerful Sicilian armada approached the Egyptian coast and launched an assault against Alexandria. However, despite the size of the Sicilian task force—even the most conservative sources assert that it consisted of 200 galleys carrying 30,000 men, and more than 80 freighters for 1,500 horses, equipment, supplies, and war machines—the attack was doomed to failure.

The invaders found the harbor entrance blocked by a great number of sunken ships, which the garrison had sacrificed for that purpose. When they did manage to disembark troops and siege machines, the fortifications of Alexandria—strengthened by Saladin's order of 1171—proved too strong for the Normans to overcome by a direct frontal attack. Nor did a heavy bombardment bring the Normans closer to success. After three days of bloody fighting came news that Saladin's tactical forces were approaching. This was more than enough to dishearten the invaders and embolden the Alexandrians to launch counterattacks and night sorties. The commanders of the Christian armada, to avoid imminent disaster, sailed home on 1 August with the sad remnants of what, only three days earlier, had been the proud expeditionary army of the Norman king of Sicily. Only a small force of 300 knights, entrenched on a hill near the city, continued to fight, until the very last of them was either killed or captured.[32]

The Norman invasion was not the only threat absorbing Saladin's attention in Egypt. Whether by coincidence or by plan, a major pro-Fatimid revolt broke out in Upper Egypt in the first days of August 1174. Its leader was Kanz al-Dawlah who had been retained by Saladin despite his Fatimid affiliations and had even proved his apparent loyalty to the new regime at the time of the Nubian invasion of 1172. Now with the support of Ismaili partisans and various anti-Ayyubid elements, Kanz al-Dawlah launched terroristic activities throughout the regions surrounding Aswan and Qus. Since the local government troops were unable to cope with the rebels, Saladin was compelled to dispatch a sizeable well-equipped force to the area, under the command of his younger brother al-Adil. In carrying out this assignment al-Adil proved as dependable as Saladin's oldest brother. After overrunning various insurgent groups, he inflicted a crushing defeat on Kanz al-Dawlah in a major encounter fought 7 September 1174. With the rebel leader and most of his army annihilated, al-Adil was able to report the successful termination of what turned out to be the last armed uprising in the name of the overthrown Ismaili caliphate.[33] After the long crisis summer of 1174, all Egypt was assured of a period of internal and external security. At last Saladin felt free to engage actively in the affairs of Syria.

Saladin's successful expedition to Damascus

By the end of the summer, political conditions in Muslim Syria deteriorated critically. Gümüshtigin's ambitions and his rule in Aleppo so disturbed Ibn al-Muqaddam and most of the military commanders in Damascus that they decided to seek outside assistance. They first appealed to Sayf al-Din Ghazi, promising to deliver Damascus in return for military protection. However, the ruler of Mosul refused to intervene, fearing that his expedition to southern Syria might end in a trap set up by Damascus and Aleppo.[34] Under the circumstances, Saladin's intervention appeared the only safeguard for the Damascus clique against the pressure of Aleppo. Consequently, Ibn al-Muqaddam approached Saladin,[35] whom he found, not surprisingly, receptive to the idea of helping Damascus.

Most of September and early October were spent on preparations for this important operation. Saladin himself took care of personnel assignments and nominated his brother al-Adil, so effective in dealing with the rebellion of Kanz al-Dawlah, as his deputy in Cairo.[36] Meanwhile, in Damascus, Ibn al-Muqaddam and his associates were mobilizing public opinion to welcome the powerful ally from Egypt.

At the end of October 1174, Saladin finally set out with a detachment of 700 cavalry, accompanied by his brother Tughtigin and his chancellor, al-Qadi al-Fadil.[37] Judging by the relatively small size of his contingent, it is obvious that Saladin did not anticipate serious opposition. As he progressed towards Damascus he was joined by various local commanders, notably Sadiq ibn Jawala, the master of Busra. When Sadiq saw the number of soldiers accompanying Saladin, he expressed some doubts whether this expedition stood any chance of taking Damascus unless its leader had plenty of money to buy his way in. Trying to reassure Sadiq, al-Qadi al-Fadil remarked that they had brought 50,000 dinars, but Sadiq remained pessimistic. "You are through, and you will drag us down with you." [38] Saladin actually had only 10,000 dinars, but was confident that popular support would do the trick. Indeed, soon after passing Busra, he was met by his cousin, Nasir al-Din, the son of Shirkuh. Then, Saad al-Din, the son of Anar, whom Nur al-Din had ousted as master of Damascus in 1154, joined the newcomers. Every day Saladin's expedition saw the arrival of various important Syrian leaders with their military contingents. And when Saladin reached the vicinity of Damascus, the whole affair acquired the character of a popular mass movement hailing the hero of Egypt. The same was true of the capital city itself, whose gates were flung wide to receive the new master.

Saladin had every reason to be elated. Except for some token opposition by a small group of dissenters and the recalcitrance of Jamal al-Din Rayhani who shut himself up in the citadel, Saladin's entry into Damascus on 28 October 1174 took place amid enthusiastic popular acclamation.[39] Six years had elapsed since Saladin, at Nur al-Din's request, had left Damascus to assist Shirkuh in saving Egypt from Crusader domination. Now he had returned, the glorious conqueror of the Crusaders, with a dramatic contribution to the cause of the Sunni caliphate to his credit and backed by powerful Egyptian military and economic resources. As if to emphasize his longstanding affiliation with the Syrian metropolis, the jubilant hero set up headquarters in the house belonging to Ayyub, his deceased father and former military governor of Damascus.[40]

Saladin wasted no time in bringing political stability to Damascus. He established friendly relations with the city elders and administrators;[41] he abolished all illegal taxes and questionable fiscal practices reintroduced since the death of Nur al-Din;[42] he showed magnanimous respect for Judge Ibn al-Shahrazuri in spite of the animosity which had characterized their relationship during Saladin's tenure as *shihnah* of Damascus;[43] and he persuaded Jamal al-Din Rayhani to surrender the citadel without bloodshed, in return for a remunerative appointment.[44] To dissipate any fears as to his political intentions, the new master of Damascus declared that he had only come to guard the interests of al-Salih and his kingdom. He solemnly reiterated his recognition of al-Salih's sovereignty, claiming that he was but a regent and protector of the reigning dynasty. In accordance with this official announcement, Saladin ordered continuation of the young sultan's names and titles in the *khutbah* invocations as well as in the coin inscriptions.[45]

A conflict with Aleppo

Saladin's successful intervention in Damascus produced a dramatic deterioration in the military position of the Crusaders. Far from being able to continue its aggressive strategy, the Kingdom of Jerusalem, hemmed in between Cairo and Damascus, was now vulnerable to a joint Egyptian and Syrian attack. Fortunately for the Crusaders, the Ayyubid leader could not mount a large-scale assault against them; his full attention was demanded by Aleppo.

It is obvious that Saladin, despite his loyal submission, was hardly overcome with respect for the twelve-year-old al-Salih. But he was concerned about those who enjoyed the advantage of legitimate authority which effective charge of the Zangid prince conferred. Besides the ambitious Gümüshtigin, the ruling Nuriyah clique in Aleppo included Ibn al-Ajami who had earlier been vizir in Damascus, Inal ibn Hasan who had left Egypt in protest against Saladin's elevation,[46] and Ibn al-Qaysarani—the same Ibn al-Qaysarani who had accused the Ayyubid commander of having a "guileful and dissentful" disposition toward Nur al-Din.[47] That they viewed with hostility the latest turn of events in Damascus can be inferred from yet another message Saladin sent to al-Salih:

> I have come from Egypt in service to you, to fulfill an obligation out of respect for my deceased overlord. I plead with you not to heed the people around you, for they undermine your status and corrupt your authority. As to my aim, I strive only for the unity of Islam against the Franks.[48]

Predictably enough, the clique in Aleppo reacted with indignation. Al-Salih was told to reply condemning Saladin's aspirations and actions in no uncertain terms.[49] To drive home their attitude, the leaders in

Aleppo selected Ibn Hasan, well known for his dislike of Saladin, to carry this reply to Damascus.

He did not disappoint them. After delivering the message, Inal ibn Hasan made a strong statement expressing the sentiments of the Nuriyah warriors towards the self-proclaimed guardian of Nur al-Din's legacy.[50] Pointing to his hip, he declared to Saladin:

The swords which once conquered Egypt for you are still in our hands, and the spears with which you seized the castles of the Fatimids are ready on our shoulders, and the men who once seceded from you will now make you depart from Syria; whatever you try they will oppose you. You are arrogant and you have exceeded your limits. You are but one of Nur al-Din's *ghilman* (boys); whoever needs people like you to protect his son? [51]

This derisive and abusive defiance made Saladin explode in anger:

"By God," exclaimed he, "had you not come as ambassador I would have cut off your head!" [52]

Then, regaining his poise, he repeated to Inal what he had declared on several earlier occasions:

Be persuaded that I had come to Syria to close ranks in Islam, to bring order to its affairs, to protect the people, to defend its frontiers, to watch over the son of Nur al-Din, and to do away with injustice from its enemies.[53]

But Inal remained adamant:

You have come but to seize the kingdom for yourself; that is your only purpose, but we will not let you accomplish it. You had better go where you came from and desist from your covetous schemings. . . .[54]

Saladin maintained his composure. Preventing his men from assaulting the arrogant envoy, he reiterated calmly: [55]

God is my witness that I have not come to Syria coveting or seeking material gains for myself. In those, Egypt more than abounds. I am here to emancipate the boy from the control of you and of your associates, for you are the cause of the collapse of his kingdom.[56]

Aleppo's diplomatic attempt to impose its authority over Saladin had signally failed. Now preservation of harmonious cooperation between Muslim forces in Syria, and with it the prospects of major offensive campaigns against the Crusaders, depended on Saladin. Of course he refused to withdraw from Damascus, or even to tolerate the existence of a separate Muslim regime in Aleppo. As on earlier occasions, Saladin was less concerned about the Christian peril to Islam than the Zangid threat to his political ambitions. He ordered his troops in Syria to prepare for an expedition to Aleppo. For the first time since 1154—the year of Nur al-Din's annexation of Damascus—Syria once again was split into two hostile Muslim blocks. An open contest for supremacy between the Zangids and Ayyubids had begun.

Saladin's thrust against Aleppo

In the last days of November 1174, Saladin set out for northern Syria, leaving his brother Tughtigin in charge of Damascus.[57] The Ayyubid leader, evidently confident of the expedition's easy outcome, had not deemed it necessary to call up additional troops from Egypt. But he was in for bitter disappointment; once the new operation had begun, he soon learned that there were people in Syria disapproving of his bid for supremacy.

In contrast with his smooth and quick takeover in the south, the new expedition proceeded at a slow pace. Bypassing Baalbek, Saladin reached Homs on 10 December. It took him three days to subdue the town, but the citadel still resisted. After posting a sizeable contingent to lay siege to the citadel, Saladin moved northward.[58] About that time came the first major defection, reducing the effective strength of his army in Syria. Fakhr al-Din Ibn al-Zafarani, one of the Nuriyah commanders, had originally joined Saladin's cause in Damascus because he wanted an appointment as commander in chief. Since Saladin had not bestowed any special favors on him, he left the Damascus army and withdrew to his feudal possessions.[59]

In contrast, Ibn al-Zafarani's feudal subordinate in Hamah, Izz al-Din Jurdiq, proved amenable to cooperation. In spite of his own Nuriyah affiliations and his part in installing Gümüshtigin's regime in Aleppo,[60] Jurdiq had left Hamah in the care of his younger brother and ridden out to al-Rastan, half way between Homs and Hamah, to enquire about Saladin's real intentions. Following a lengthy meeting, the two men reached agreement. Saladin solemnly swore that he had come to protect the country for Nur al-Din's son, and Jurdiq promised to deliver Hamah to him. Exploiting Jurdiq's cooperative disposition, Saladin sent him to Aleppo to try persuading its leaders into submission. But once again the diplomatic maneuver misfired. Accepting Saladin's bid was so repugnant to Gümüshtigin and his clique that, far from answering this latest appeal, they arrested Jurdiq and put him in jail with Shams al-Din ibn al-Dayah and his brothers.[61] Saladin managed, however, to capitalize even on this. He hastened to Hamah and reported Jurdiq's imprisonment to his brother. The latter was so indignant about Aleppo's violation of diplomatic immunity that on 28 December 1174 he opened the gates of both the town and citadel of Hamah to Saladin.[62]

Following a quick march, during which Saladin was joined by Nasih al-Din Khumartigin[63] (yet another Nuriyah officer who had defected from Egypt in 1169), the army of Damascus reached Aleppo. On 30 December 1174 Saladin established his camp on the hill of Jawshan, his unfurled banners clearly visible to the inhabitants of Aleppo. But if he had entertained any hopes that this show of force would induce the town to open its gates, such illusions were quickly dispelled. The ruling clique, afraid Saladin might repeat his success in Damascus, managed to arouse the inhabitants in support of al-Salih. The boy-king himself made a public appearance at the city's main square and exhorted the people to protect him from Saladin. The dramatic appeal proved effective, because the citizens of Aleppo rallied to his cause, producing resources and men to help make a determined stand against Saladin's army. And because of the external danger, all suppressive anti-Shiite measures, which Nur al-Din had imposed in Aleppo, were now revoked to promote internal unity.[64]

Thus Saladin was forced to proceed with cumbersome siege operations, which were especially difficult in the extremely unfavorable weather conditions of that winter.[65] The regime of Aleppo used this interval to send urgent appeals to Sinan, the master of the Assassins in Masyaf, to the Crusader regent, Count Raymund III of Tripoli, as well as to Sayf al-Din Ghazi of Mosul.[66]

Saladin's retreat from Aleppo

Aleppo's diplomatic efforts produced the desired effects. The master of the Assassins accepted Aleppo's offer of lands and money in return for Saladin's assassination. Indeed, a group of Sinan's desperadoes did penetrate Saladin's camp, but before they could reach their intended victim they were recognized by Nasih al-Din Khumartigin, a feudal neighbor of theirs. When he questioned them, he was at once killed. But in the ensuing fracas the Assassins and several other men were killed, while Saladin himself escaped unscathed.[67]

The Crusaders, too, responded favorably to Gümüshtigin's appeal. They were fully aware of the grave strategic consequences Saladin's control of Syria would bring. To quote William of Tyre: "Any increase of Saladin's power was cause for suspicion in our eyes. . . . It seemed wiser to us to lend aid to the boy king . . . not for his own sake, but to encourage him as an adversary against Saladin." [68] In January 1175 Raymund carried out a dangerous raid in the direction of Homs where the citadel still held out against Saladin's besiegers. In spite of its mere diversionary nature, the Crusader attack was ingeniously devised to improve the strategic position of Aleppo. If allowed to continue, the Crusaders could easily entrap and annihilate the besiegers of Homs, in cooperation with the garrison of the citadel. The Crusaders would then be able to attack Saladin's main army while still embroiled with the tenacious defenders of Aleppo. Furthermore, a setback at Homs could imperil Saladin's communications lines with the south and encourage active resistance from his opponents in the area between Aleppo and Damascus. On the other hand, if Saladin decided to intercept the Crusader raid, he would have to give up the siege of Aleppo.

Saladin was too good a strategist to miss the implications of the Crusader attack. Obviously recognizing he had underestimated Aleppo's power of resistance and had left his rear unsecured, he suspended the siege operations and on 26 January 1175 led his army south to meet the Crusaders.[69] The humiliation of retreat, in addition to the assassination attempt, gave him a foretaste of difficulties he would meet if he persisted in his Syrian ambitions.

The Crusaders attacked Homs on 1 February, but the following day they learned that Saladin had reached Hamah and was closing in on al-Rastan. Shunning confrontation and having achieved their objective, the Christian forces speedily retreated. Saladin now decided to mop up any centers of potential resistance capable of obstructing future offensives against Aleppo. He also sent for reinforcements from Egypt. Although the full significance of this decision was not apparent at the time, it opened yet another phase in Saladin's use of Egyptian troops and resources. Instead of being totally committed to the struggle against the Crusaders, they were thereafter repeatedly deployed to support his private war with the Zangids.

Without waiting, however, for the reinforcements, Saladin captured the citadel of Homs on 17 March 1175 after several weeks of heavy fighting. Less than two weeks later, on 29 March, he forced Baalbek, the city of his childhood, to surrender. Thereupon he returned to Homs.[70]

Saladin's appeal to Baghdad

About that time Saladin shifted his diplomatic policy. Since respectful recognition of al-Salih's suzerainty had failed to assure his influence in the capital of northern Syria, he now asserted instead that his expedition was motivated by the plight of Shams al-Din and his brother, whom the ruling clique of Aleppo had imprisoned. But his appeal to al-Mustadi, the Abbasid caliph in Baghdad, actually proved more decisive.

The appeal was contained in a lengthy address written in elaborate diplomatic style by chancellor al-Qadi al-Fadil.[71] Its contents suggest Saladin's own notions about his earlier achievements as well as his ambitious aspirations. The letter opened with a section stressing Saladin's contributions to the holy war during Nur al-Din's lifetime, then listed his conquests of Egypt, Yemen, and the North African regions.[72] In describing the capture of Egypt, no reference was made to Nur al-Din or to Shirkuh; rather, the Egyptian appeals for help against the Franks were here addressed to Saladin.[73] After saving Egypt from external danger, he had successfully dealt with the internal opposition of the Sudanese and Armenian troops in Cairo; later on, he had defeated two dangerous Crusader attacks, one against Damietta, another against Bilbais—this claim having its source in "licentia diplomatica" rather than historical fact.[74] Particularly emphasized were Saladin's services to the Abbasid caliphate and the Islamic community, such as the restoration of Sunni supremacy in Egypt or his purportedly annual expeditions against the Crusaders. His capture of Ailah not only had eliminated a Crusader naval base but had reopened that sea to Muslim travelers. The conquest of Yemen had suppressed local Shiite sectarians and restored that area to pro-Abbasid allegiance. The letter also claimed that for the cause of Abbasid suzerainty Saladin had ordered military expeditions against North Africa where the Almohad dynasty had arrogantly usurped sovereign status.[75] All these triumphs made Cairo the object of visits by many ambassadors who sought diplomatic favors of Saladin.[76] Even Christian rulers, such as the master of Constantinople, had resumed diplomatic relations with Cairo. The attempt of the king of Sicily to seize Alexandria by naval invasion had been crushed. Other Christian maritime communities, such as Venice, Pisa, and Genoa, which had earlier mixed business with warfare in their relations with Egypt, were now compelled to establish commercial relations with Saladin and to supply him with war material needed for the struggle against the Infidels.[77] Only the death of Nur al-Din, Saladin insisted, had prevented him from launching a large-scale land and naval attack against the Crusaders. However, as soon as he had heard of the Frankish attack against Banyas, he had marched out with his army—only to be stopped by the news that the regime in Damascus had signed an armistice.[78]

After this long preamble, the letter went on to explain why Saladin had sent an embassy to Baghdad. Following Nur al-Din's death, Syria was politically fragmented and thus vulnerable to aggressive Crusader pressure. Saladin regarded it as his duty to bring Syrian political conditions to order, to watch over the interests of Nur al-Din's successor, and to free him from his greedy oppressors. Finally, the message asked the caliph to recognize formally Saladin's authority over all Egypt, the conquered North African regions, Yemen, Syria and other provinces which had belonged to Nur al-Din, as well as over all other lands he might succeed in conquering in the name of the Abbasid caliphate.[79]

All this eloquent and profuse recital of Saladin's record, with its emphasis on his dedication to the holy war had a crystal clear purpose. Having failed to capture all Syria in al-Salih's name, Saladin would try to do so under the auspices of the Abbasid caliph of Baghdad. Formal investiture from al-Mustadi would legalize his status for Syrian public opinion. The diplomatic prestige of the Abbasid caliphate ranked second to none, while at the same time, Baghdad was too distant and militarily impotent to interfere directly with Saladin's expansionist plans.

Even the ambassador to the Abbasid caliph was carefully chosen by Saladin, who selected Muhammad al-Baalbakki, reputedly the first preacher to invoke the pro-Abbasid *khutbah* in Egypt during Saladin's coup.

Counteroffensive of the Aleppo and Mosul forces

While Saladin was consolidating the gains he had made, Aleppo finally received military help from Mosul. Sayf al-Din Ghazi, concerned at the emergence of a new and powerful rival in Syria, declared his willingness to join in an alliance directed against Saladin. However, Sayf al-Din's hopes of an all-out effort were frustrated by the opposition of his brother, Imad al-Din, the master of Sinjar. The latter lived up to his diplomatic entente with Saladin, dating from the summer of 1174, and refused to support the planned expedition of the army of Mosul.[80] Saladin's diplomatic foresight had complicated the relief expedition and Sayf al-Din was compelled to divide his forces. One army, led by another brother, Izz al-Din Masud, and by a general known as Zulfandar, was dispatched against Saladin; the other marched under personal command of Sayf al-Din to Sinjar where, toward the end of March 1175, it began a protracted and ultimately futile siege.[81] The army Izz al-Din commanded arrived at Aleppo too late to engage Saladin, who was by that time at Baalbek. Izz al-Din and Gümüshtigin therefore decided to combine their armies and set out on an offensive directed against Hamah.[82]

That development caught Saladin at an inopportune moment. Four months of field operations in adverse climatic conditions had taken their toll. Saladin assigned a part of his army to garrison duties in the newly captured places and one contingent he dispatched to Sinjar to help Imad al-Din against his brother's attack.[83] The defection of Ibn al-Zafarani further reduced his army,[84] and only substantial reinforcements, expected to arrive from Egypt, could enable him to cope with the joint offensive of Aleppo and Mosul. Fortunately for the Ayyubid leader, the commander of the Mosul contingent hoped to end Saladin's intrusion by negotiations rather than by military showdown. This gained Saladin a little time while he awaited the arrival of the crucial Egyptian reinforcements. No wonder he replied positively to Izz al-Din's peace overtures and shortly afterwards received a delegation from the hostile camp, consisting of Ibn al-Ajami and Gümüshtigin himself.[85]

Peace terms, as offered by the two delegates, insisted on the recognition of Aleppo's supremacy. Saladin was also requested to give back Homs, Hamah, and Baalbeck, as well as other places captured during his military sweep north of Damascus. He could retain Damascus but only as a governor acting on behalf of the boy-king. This subordinate status would be confirmed by appropriate *khutbah* invocations and inscriptions on coins. Finally, Saladin would return all funds he had confiscated from the treasury of Damascus.[86]

Although these demands would wipe out all his gains, Saladin did not object to them. But the Aleppo representatives, observing Saladin's limited forces, rightly concluded that his apparent cooperativeness had its roots in military impotence.[87] It therefore seemed advantageous to them to provoke a breakdown in the negotiations and enforce a military solution instead. On the advice of Ibn al-Ajami, Gümüshtigin now insisted that Saladin must also renounce claims to Rahba.[88]

Small as it seemed, this condition had for Saladin certain specific political and family implications. Rahba with its surrounding territory had once belonged to Shirkuh's feudal holdings. During his absence in Egypt, Rahba had been controlled by his son, Nasir al-Din, until it was taken away by Nur al-Din who had wanted to curb the political ambitions of the Kurdish family.[89] Gümüshtigin's condition would force Saladin to recognize a decision of the late Sultan which had been specifically against his family interests and would therefore compromise him as the family leader. Furthermore, this demand would hurt Nasir al-Din, who had been one of the first Syrian military commanders to join Saladin during his expedition against Damascus. As Gümüshtigin hoped, Saladin was forced to reject the condition, thus ending the negotiations.[90]

Victory at the Horns of Hamah

The Aleppo delegates returned to camp, where they reported the result of their mission. They emphasized the weakness of the Damascus army and urged immediate resumption of their own offensive. Saladin also—undermanned as his army was—decided to march out, confident that his Egyptian reinforcements would catch up with him in time.[91] As the two armies closed upon one another, the reinforcements were still nowhere in sight, but Saladin did offset the disparity of numbers by gaining a superior position by the gorge of the Orontes River on the hills called the Horns of Hamah.[92] Trying to delay a head-on battle, he kept sending messages to the enemy camp; he even succeeded in establishing clandestine relations with some of the enemy officers, cooling their fighting zeal with bribes of money and gifts.[93]

In spite of these delaying tactics, on 13 April 1175 his small contingent had to accept a battle with the numerically superior enemy. Initiative in the battle belonged to Aleppo and Mosul, despite their military ineptness and the weakening effect of Saladin's tactics of subversion. Their initial attack gained considerable momentum once the troops perceived the numerical inferiority of the Damascus army. Saladin's situation rapidly deteriorated; his bid for Syrian supremacy appeared about to end, when the Egyptian reinforcements at last arrived. Led by Saladin's nephews Taqi al-Din Umar and Izz al-Din Farrukh-Shah, the relief expedition approached the Horns of Hamah without even realizing that a crucial battle was in progress. Their sudden arrival and immediate deployment for a furious counterattack turned imminent defeat into victory. The troops of Aleppo and Mosul beat a retreat without trying to resist. In no time their retreat changed into an ignominious and disorderly flight. Only specific orders from Saladin prevented the rout from becoming a carnage.[94]

The aftermath of the victory

The arrival of the Egyptian army allowed Saladin to regain the initiative in Syria. The victorious troops followed up their success with a push toward Aleppo. Faced with these unfavorable military developments, the Syrians around al-Salih were in no mood for yet another siege. They preferred to sue for peace. This time it was Saladin's turn to dictate a settlement. His terms proved rather moderate, especially considering the critical military position of Aleppo. He demanded recognition of the territorial status quo; in addition, he requested the surrender of al-Maarrah and Kafartab, the latter constituting his former feudal appanage. Furthermore, while allowing Gümüshtigin's clique to retain control over al-Salih, Saladin demanded that the army of Aleppo would join his forces against the Crusaders. Naturally enough, Saladin declared himself no longer bound to recognize the suzerainty of the successor of Nur al-Din. Finally, he ordered an immediate release of Shams al-Din ibn al-Dayah, of his brothers, of Jurdiq, and of other political prisoners held in Aleppo.[95]

Since the rulers in Aleppo did not dispute any of these terms, the signing of a formal agreement was accomplished without delay. On 6 May 1175 Saladin returned to Hamah, where an official delegation from Baghdad brought him a reply from the caliph. To a considerable degree Saladin's diplomatic appeal proved successful. The envoys formally invested Saladin with authority over Egypt, Syria, and the other areas stipulated in his application. Special diplomas, honorific robes, and the black banners of the Abbasids emphasized that Saladin's present exalted status had been recognized by the head of the Muslim world.[96]

Less than a year after the death of Nur al-Din, the Ayyubid conqueror had managed to establish himself formally as a powerful figure in Syria and jeopardize the position of the Nuriyah faction. Indeed, before the spring of 1175 was out, Saladin's name had been invoked in the mosques of Syria and Egypt, and the Cairo mint issued coins in his name: al-Malik al-Nasir Yusuf ibn Ayyub.[97]

Saladin's position in Syria following his first campaign against Aleppo

In spite of this splendid diplomatic accomplishment, Saladin's political and military position in Syria was not totally secure. Notwithstanding the welcome received in Damascus and his military gains against Aleppo, he had not eliminated opposition in Syria. Despite the debacle at the Horns of Hamah, the hostile establishment in Aleppo had not fared too badly in the armistice. While resigning themselves to the emancipation of Saladin from al-Salih's nominal control, they did not give up any territory—al-Maarrah and Kafartab excepted—that the army of Damascus had not conquered. Other than losing equipment and prestige, the army of Aleppo had suffered no extensive damage and after recuperating it could once again be deployed in the interests of the clique at al-Salih's court. This group was even formally recognized by Saladin. Although the armistice imposed military cooperation with Saladin on the rulers of Aleppo, it did not proscribe separate diplomatic connections with the court of Mosul, the Crusaders, the Assassins, or any other group hostile to the Egyptian sultan. That Aleppo did not scrupulously observe all its armistice pledges was immediately evident from the fact that despite specific provision, the regime of al-Salih had not released political prisoners.[98]

The moderate nature of the armistice agreement was related to Saladin's limited power in Syria. The victorious campaign of winter

1174–75 had not attained its main strategic objective. Saladin did not control all of Muslim Syria. The support received from local leaders proved neither adequate nor always dependable, as the defection of Ibn al-Zafarani demonstrated,[99] and only the timely arrival of the Egyptian army saved Saladin from catastrophic disaster.

This was an important strategic consideration; to pursue his expansionist policy in Syria Saladin had to depend on Egyptian troops, a condition which did not enhance Egypt's own security. The absence of a substantial tactical force from Egypt inevitably invited foreign aggression. In 1175, while the elite Egyptian troops were in Syria, the Normans of Sicily carried out a probing attack against the industrial center of Tinnis.[100] Obviously, despite failure of the attack against Alexandria, the Normans had not given up their aggressive designs on Egypt. Furthermore economic conditions in Syria could not support the expeditionary forces from Egypt, so Saladin had to consider sending them home.[101] In fact, Saladin's interests in Syria had to be financed at the expense of Egypt. The booty at the Horns of Hamah did not sate the Egyptians' appetites. Naturally, a lot would come from the capture of Aleppo, but if an assault were to degenerate into another difficult siege, Saladin would have found himself with dissatisfied troops in a famine-stricken Syria. But if he had sent his Egyptian troops home prior to coming to terms with Gümüshtigin, he might have exposed himself to another counteroffensive by Aleppo and Mosul, with a possible participation of the Crusaders and the Assassins. This, indeed, seems to explain why Saladin did not follow up his victory at the Horns of Hamah with an attack on Aleppo, and why he was willing to conclude a moderate armistice agreement. His blitzkrieg had not delivered all Muslim Syria to him, and consequently he needed time to stabilize his position in the conquered areas of Syria before resuming large-scale offensive operations.

Such an interpretation seems warranted in the light of Saladin's subsequent activities. In the second half of May 1175, he wound up his military drive in Northern Syria by marching to Barin to settle the score with Ibn al-Zafarani, who had defected during the conflict with Aleppo. Although it constituted a flagrant violation of the status quo as stipulated in the treaty, the Egyptian sultan subjected Barin to a heavy mangonel bombardment, forcing its garrison to surrender and its master to seek refuge in Mosul.[102] He then retaliated against the Assassins; a special army contingent conducted punitive raids on Assassin communities in Sarmin, Maarrat-Misrin, and Jabal as-Summaq, perpetrating wholesale massacres of their inhabitants.[103]

Such military measures he quickly reinforced with administrative ones. Anxious to place the key strategic fortresses between Damascus and Aleppo in trustworthy hands, Saladin assigned Hamah to his maternal uncle, Shihab al-Din al-Harimi, one of the chief promoters of the family's fortunes. His loyal cousin, Nasir al-Din, he entrusted with Homs. Finally, Baalbek was given to Ibn al-Muqaddam, perhaps as reward for the part that prominent Syrian commander played in Saladin's take-over in Damascus.[104]

At last, on 23 May 1175, Saladin returned to Damascus where he stayed until spring 1176. In the last days of July 1175 he received a mission from the Crusaders, who asked for a formal armistice agreement. Although one of Saladin's expressed reasons for intervention in Syria was that the rulers of Damascus had concluded a truce with the Christian foe,[105] and although relentless effort against the Crusaders constituted an important argument in his appeal to the Abbasid caliph for a formal, legal mandate to rule over Syria,[106] Saladin, having now established himself in Damascus, appeared once again to act according to his own immediate strategic needs. As in Cairo, the struggle against the Infidels did not top his list of political priorities. Thus in obvious disregard for his protestations in 1174 he did not hesitate to conclude a formal truce with the enemies of Islam.[107]

Saladin strengthens his authority over Egypt

Upon his return from the campaign against Aleppo, Saladin had to attend to pressing governmental responsibilities, although he did not refrain from indulging in hunting around Damascus.[108] One of his basic problems was the safeguarding of effective authority over Egypt. No one knew better how difficult Cairo was to control from Syria.

Since Syrian affairs necessitated his stay in Damascus, he had to take appropriate measures to keep Egypt not only loyal, but geared to sustain his political and military efforts in Syria. Although there was no reason for doubting the integrity of al-Adil, the brother he left in charge of Egypt, Saladin decided to bolster his authority and administrative efficiency by sending back to Cairo his trustworthy and experienced chancellor, al-Qadi al-Fadil.[109] Having demonstrated his dependability during the critical years of Saladin's rise to power, the chancellor could be expected to continue to protect the interests of his Ayyubid master in Egypt. The post of the chief secretary at Saladin's court in Syria was then assigned to Imad al-Din al-Isfahani.[110] From that time on, this famous historian and admirer of Saladin was able to participate personally and directly in most of the achievements of the great Muslim hero, whose story he so eagerly and colorfully recorded for posterity.

Another important decision pertained to the upkeep of the Egyptian expeditionary troops. Since the disastrous Syrian economic conditions made local maintenance impossible, it was imperative to release these troops to let them attend to harvesting in their feudal estates in Egypt. This measure did not apply, however, to Taqi al-Din Umar, one of the most outstanding leaders of the expeditionary contingent, for this nephew of Saladin was known to cherish political ambitions of his own.[111] Indeed, the successful expansionist drive into North Africa in 1173 had been carried out by his feudal contingent, under the leadership of his subordinate, Sharaf al-Din Qaragush. Beginning 1 August 1175 Qaragush embarked on another predatory raid against the rich provinces in the West, while his overlord, Taqi al-Din, was absent on the politically and economically unrewarding expedition to Syria. After conclusion of the campaign against Aleppo, Taqi al-Din was anxious to assume direct command over his forces raiding North Africa. To let Taqi al-Din return to Egypt under such circumstances would mean creating a potential source of trouble. The sultan decided that the expeditionary army should return to Egypt under the leadership of al-Qadi al-Fadil,[112] and that Taqi al-Din should stay behind in Damascus. To compensate Taqi al-Din, Saladin appointed him governor of Damascus in the fall of 1175, in place of Sayf al-Din Tughtigin.[113]

Political tension in Syria continues

In spite of the truce agreements with Aleppo and with the crusaders, Saladin's situation in Syria remained tense. This time Mosul generated the troubles. The master of Mosul was more insistent than the Aleppo establishment that Saladin's challenge be put to an end. Where the clique in Aleppo had to operate in al-Salih's name, Sayf al-Din Ghazi was himself a grandson of the famous Zangi, founder of the dynasty. Familiar with the formidable record of the ambitious Kurdish family, Sayf al-Din had every reason to fear that further tolerance of Saladin's presence in Syria might lead to a total extinction of the Zangid domination. Although his first intervention in the war between Saladin and al-Salih had ended in a failure, Sayf al-Din firmly believed that the combined forces of Mosul, Aleppo, and their feudal allies should be able to put an end to the arrogant claims of the Ayyubid upstart. Accordingly, he dispatched an ambassador to Aleppo to persuade its leaders into secret preparations for a major showdown with Saladin. At the same time, however, the ambassador was instructed to carry a letter to Damascus, in which Sayf al-Din—in an obvious attempt at deceitful appeasement—pledged his respect for the armistice concluded between Gümüshtigin and Saladin. Having successfully accomplished his mission at Aleppo, the ambassador proceeded to the court of Damascus. There, during an official audience with the Ayyubid sultan, instead of delivering Sayf al-Din's letter to Saladin, the ambassador handed over by mischance the written reply from Aleppo to Mosul expressing wholehearted approval of the proposed military alliance against the Ayyubid sultan.[114] Whether the secret really leaked out through the alleged ambassadorial error—which sounds too good to be believed—or whether it was revealed through more orthodox intelligence methods, Saladin had enough time to prepare for another military confrontation. This time he conceded that his Syrian units would be insufficient, and so he sent instructions to al-Adil that the Egyptian army should be ready to march for Syria by the end of February 1176.[115]

His enemies likewise were speeding diplomatic and military preparations. Sayf al-Din Ghazi levied troops among his vassals of Diyar Bakr and Jazirah, in whose company he crossed the Euphrates at Bira early in 1176, marching in the direction of Aleppo.[116] For its part, Aleppo tried to secure military cooperation from the Crusaders, to which purpose it released some prominent Frankish leaders from captivity, notably Count Jocelin of Courtenay and the notorious Reginald of Châtillon, the former regent of Antioch.[117] There was more than a touch of irony in Saladin's Syrian intervention bringing about Reginald's liberation. Upon his release, Reginald was appointed lord of Kerak and Shaubak, from which he terrorized caravan traffic in Transjordan for an entire decade. In 1183 he even staged a dangerous raid aimed at disrupting commercial and pilgrim traffic between Ailah and the Hejaz,[118] and in 1187 he provoked a showdown between the Crusaders and Saladin, which ultimately led to the Third Crusade.[119]

To underscore the spirit of political harmony prevailing in the anti-Saladin coalition, Gümüshtigin arranged a formal meeting between al-Salih and his powerful uncle from Mosul, at the court of Aleppo.[120] Inspired by this show of cooperation, various leaders loyal to al-Salih joined the forces of Sayf al-Din. By April 1175 this allied army counted 20,000 cavalry, in addition to infantry troops.[121] Once troop concentration was completed, Sayf al-Din set out for Damascus, leading not only mobile forces but their heavy equipment as well. The expedition did not seem in any haste to reach its objective, because it did not go beyond Tall as-Sultan,[122] only fifteen miles south of Aleppo. There the allied troops set up a sumptuous camp, passing time on frills rather than on improving their combat efficiency. Apparently their self-confidence made them forget the calibre of the enemy.

Saladin's victory at Tall as-Sultan

The army Saladin requested from Egypt arrived in time to allow him to march out of Damascus on 14 March 1176.[123] He first moved to Hamah, collecting local Syrian reinforcements. After maneuvering between Abu Qubais and Hamah for a few weeks, Saladin crossed the Orontes at Shaizar on 11 April 1176 and proceeded northwards.[124] In contrast to his enemy, the Ayyubid leader ordered all the heavy equipment sent back to Hamah to give his army more tactical mobility.[125] Even so, on the evening of 21 April when his mounted contingents approached Tall as-Sultan, they were too exhausted for combat deployment. This paralyzing fatigue was reported to Sayf al-Din by his cavalry scouts, but although his staff advisers urged him to exploit this unique opportunity, the master of Mosul refused to order an immediate assault. Instead he complacently and boastfully declared: "Why should we fight that outsider right now? Tomorrow morning we will get all of them anyhow!" [126]

On the morning of 22 April, however, victory in the great battle of Tall as-Sultan belonged to Saladin. Although early in the fight the allies scored a success against the left wing of the Damascus army, a furious cavalry charge, led personally by Saladin and highlighted by the bravery of his nephew Izz al-Din Farrukh, overpowered the lines of the Mosul army, throwing it into utter chaos. As at the Horns of Hamah, the impact of Saladin's cavalry defeated the allied expedition. Although Sayf al-Din Ghazi, his brother Izz al-Din, and some other generals managed to escape, several officers, including Abd al-Massih, a prominent Mosul politician, were captured. So was their lavish camp.[127]

According to most contemporary sources, that splendid victory was achieved by not more than 6,000 cavalrymen. Ibn al-Athir, however, maintained that Imad al-Din al-Isfahani had invented the modest figure to magnify the triumph of his idol over the 20,000 enemy troops.[128] Whatever the real size of the opposing armies, no one could minimize the significance of the battle. From that time on, Saladin held the initiative. Instead of pressing further military action, however, Saladin took time to reward his men with the rich trophies of the victory. Supposedly he showed the captured enemy camp, which looked "more like a tavern, with all its wines, guitars, lutes, bands, singers, and singing girls," [129] to his troops, and though he prayed that his own men might be preserved from such a degradation, he wasted no time distributing the loot, only withholding a share to finance his diplomatic activities.[130] The prisoners of war Saladin shrewdly decided to exploit for propaganda. Far from being vindictive, Saladin treated the captured enemy officers with courtesy and respect. After sending them to Hamah as evidence of his triumph, he set them free and allowed them to return to their homes.[131] Less respect was shown Sayf al-Din Ghazi. Saladin ordered the cages of doves, nightingales, and parrots found in the enemy canteen to be sent to their master, with a derisive message to amuse himself with them and keep out of military adventures in the future.[132]

Saladin's offensive in northern Syria

The situation following the great victory required more than psychological warfare alone. Allied units and refugees that had escaped annihilation in the battle of Tall as-Sultan flocked into Aleppo where the local regime started hectic preparations for an anticipated attack of the Ayyubid forces. However, the dejected leader of the Mosul camp was in no mood to continue hostilities, and after a brief stay in Aleppo, he retreated toward his own land, leaving his brother Izz al-Din behind. He stopped over in the Ismaili stronghold of Buzaah to allow his dispersed army to catch up with him and then resumed his inglorious withdrawal to Mosul.[133]

As for Saladin, he allowed his jubilant and lavishly rewarded troops a few days' rest and on 26 April 1176 marched in full strength to Aleppo. Contrary to his enemies' fears, the Ayyubid leader had no intentions of staging an all-out attack against the Nuriyah stronghold. Finding Aleppo's will to resist unbroken even by the disaster of Tall as-Sultan, Saladin preferred to avoid a repetition of the preceding year's abortive siege. Instead he initiated an ingenious and deceptive campaign aimed at strategic isolation of the indomitable city. On 1 May he left the area of Aleppo, leading his army to Buzaah, which only a few days earlier had sheltered the fleeing Sayf al-Din Ghazi. Buzaah capitulated on 4 May and was entrusted to Khushtarin the Kurd, the erstwhile defector from Shirkuh's army.[134] From there Saladin pushed northeast, to attack Manbij, located on the road leading to the Euphrates and to Mosul. In addition to strategic considerations, Saladin's move against Manbij appears to have been personally motivated. Manbij was held by Inal ibn Hasan, a persistent enemy of the Ayyubid sultan, who had indulged in derogatory remarks during his diplomatic mission to Damascus and been personally involved in effecting the Aleppo-Mosul alliance. Now came the chance to make the insolent Nuriyah commander regret his behavior, but Inal, by then, had abandoned his former cockiness. He quickly offered to surrender his fortress and his treasures in return for a safe-conduct. The prospect of gaining Manbij without bloodshed and waste of precious time appealed to Saladin, so he allowed Inal to proceed to Mosul, and on 11 May the Ayyubid leader took possession of the vacated fortress and its treasures.[135] The booty, consisting of gold and silver bullion, precious utensils and objects, with a total value of over two million dinars, proved very useful in sustaining the martial fervor of Saladin's army. While gloating over the spoils, the conqueror noticed the name of Yusuf inscribed on the bags with cash and on precious vessels. After asking for explanation, he was informed that Inal had a favorite son by that name, for whom all those treasures had been stored up. "Yusuf—that's me"—Saladin startled his perplexed entourage—"and I take over whatever has been reserved for me!" [136]

Saladin's victory at Tall as-Sultan and his penetration toward the Euphrates must have caused great concern at the court of Mosul. However, any fears of an offensive across the Euphrates proved unfounded. By securing Buzaah and Manbij, Saladin had interposed a block between Mosul and Aleppo, which was, after all, the strategic objective of his offensive.

There still remained the problem of the Crusaders, who were known to favor Aleppo over the invader from Egypt. Because the fortress of Azaz, situated between Aleppo in the south and a chain of Christian strongholds to the north, performed an important communication link, Saladin turned westward from Manbij, advancing on Azaz. Meanwhile, the leaders of Aleppo, conscious of Azaz's strategic importance, rushed reinforcements to strengthen its garrison.[137] When Saladin reached Azaz in the middle of May, he discovered that its garrison, far from intimidated by his fame, had no intention to surrender.

The siege of Azaz

Much to his chagrin Saladin was compelled to order a siege of Azaz, which dragged on for several weeks without any sign of surrender. The offensive campaign, losing its original momentum, had degenerated into a static and economically costly involvement. Moreover, it furnished the leaders of Aleppo with valuable time during which they were able to carry out all sorts of diplomatic and military countermeasures. Ultimately, on 21 June 1176, the heroic garrison capitulated but not before the besiegers themselves had experienced some surprise attacks from the outside.[138]

Shortly after the siege began, the overconfident troops of Saladin suffered a hit-and-run attack staged by a contingent from Aleppo. The raiders must have caught the besiegers napping, since they carried out their assault with ease and managed a successful withdrawal. Recovering from the shock, the Ayyubid forces staged a hot pursuit, but the raiders proved elusive in their retreat. The pursuers returned with only one enemy soldier captured. The losses endured in the raid and the disappointing result of the pursuit were too much for Saladin. Enraged, he ordered one hand of the captive cut off. Only the subtle and persuasive intercession of Imad al-Din al-Isfahani saved the prisoner from a mutilation which Muslim holy law reserves for thieves, never for prisoners of war.[139]

A few days later, Saladin again was the target of an Assassin attack. Possibly desirous of revenge for his punitive raid against the Assassin territories in May 1175 or perhaps in response to a new diplomatic approach of Gümüshtigin,[140] Sinan of Masyaf sent another suicide squad to hit the target which had eluded the previous year's assassination attempt. This time the desperadoes came much closer to achieving their deadly purpose. Not only did they infiltrate the Ayyubid troops, but they contrived to be enrolled in the sultan's bodyguard itself. On 22 May Saladin was resting in the tent, when suddenly a fanatic rushed in upon him and struck at his head with a knife, inflicting a superficial wound. A cap of mail saved the sultan for the moment, and he managed to grip the assassin's hand; but seated as he was, he could not prevent the killer stabbing at his throat. The dagger slashed the collar of the gambeson, but the armor rings kept it out of his neck. All this was the work of an instant, and in another, Sayf al-Din Yazkuj, one of Saladin's lieutenants, had grasped the knife and held it, though it sawed his fingers, until at last the desperado was killed, with the knife still clenched in his hand. By now Saladin's companions were alerted. Nasir al-Din Muhammad ibn Shirkuh felled one of the assailants with a deadly thrust to his abdomen; Ali ibn Abi al-Fawaris, who was seriously wounded in the struggle, killed another. Yet another commando escaped from Shihab al-Din al-Harimi, but was cut to pieces outside the tent. Though this assassination attempt failed, its immediate effects were horrifying. The tent was filled with the bodies of the Assassins and with mortally wounded Ayyubid men who had rushed in to save the life of their leader. The sultan himself, blood streaming from his forehead, mounted and rode to headquarters in a panic of fear.[141] No additional argument was needed to make him realize that his enemies would shun no means to prevent his conquering Syria. Indeed, after that gruesome experience Saladin adopted elaborate precautions, sleeping in a specially constructed wooden tower and allowing no one he did not know personally to approach him.[142]

Another confrontation and settlement with Aleppo and the Assassins

With the final surrender of Azaz Ayyubid forces sealed off the area north of Aleppo, between the Euphrates and the Afrin rivers, thus isolating Aleppo from Mosul. Only then did Saladin lead his army south against Aleppo itself.

At that stage of the war, Aleppo did not anticipate such a move. They thought that following the fall of Azaz, Saladin—as part of an obvious plan to encircle Aleppo—would reach south for Harim, strategically located between the northern capital and Antioch. To foil an Ayyubid attack in that sector, Gümüshtigin assumed personal command over the garrison of Harim. The leader of the Aleppo regime was further concerned about Harim which had been his personal possession since the overthrow of the Banu al-Dayah.[143] But Saladin decided to strike directly at Aleppo, so when on 25 July the Ayyubid army appeared in front of Aleppo, their principal leader was absent in Harim.[144]

Having experienced considerable difficulty overcoming Azaz, Saladin realized that Aleppo, with its powerful walls and impregnable citadel, could not be captured by frontal assaults. On the other hand, he was in an excellent position to starve them out, so after establishing his headquarters in Ras al-Yaruqiya, above Jabal Jawshan, he threw a tight military cordon around Aleppo, cutting off all traffic which at the same time put a severe economic squeeze on the surrounding population.[145]

This situation disturbed Gümüshtigin who, stranded as he was in Harim, feared that he might be left aside should peace talks between Saladin and Aleppo develop.[146] Therefore, seizing the diplomatic initiative, he approached Saladin and offered to help with mediation to seek a peaceful solution, provided he would be allowed to reenter Aleppo. He also managed to pass word to the court of al-Salih, asking them to approach Saladin with the same purpose. Apparently Saladin did not mind negotiating, because he let Gümüshtigin return to his capital. His pledge was not sufficient, however, for Aleppo insisted on an exchange of hostages. To this stipulation the sultan complied, sending as hostages his secretary Imad al-Din and Ibn Abi al-Mada. The two men quickly learned that their mission did not entitle them to diplomatic favors or immunity. After being brought into the presence of Ibn al-Ajami, they were confined to a chamber where, separated from their servants and deprived of any food and light, they passed their time in concern for their lives. When they were finally returned to their own camp, they told of their mistreatment,[147] which made it obvious that the offer of mediation was only a ploy by which Gümüshtigin had succeeded in reentering Aleppo to assume personal command over the beleaguered city.[148]

Abandoning positional warfare, the troops of the sultan switched to more aggressive operations, but Aleppo was strong enough to beat off all attacks. On 14 July the garrison staged a successful sortie, engaged the Ayyubid forces in a pitched battle, and inflicted heavy casualties.[149] The futility of continued hostilities became obvious to everybody.[150] Indeed, a few days after this bloody encounter, negotiations reopened which this time brought a quick termination of hostilities.

As in the preceding year, the new peace treaty was a compromise. Saladin officially accepted the fact that a rival regime existed in Aleppo, while al-Salih's clique resigned itself to a permanent establishment of the Ayyubid regime in Damascus. Nor did territorial provisions differ much from those adopted a year earlier. Saladin was conceded all territories in Muslim Syria, extending from Hamah in the north to the borders of Egypt in the south. Furthermore, the court of al-Salih solemnly undertook to furnish Saladin with military assistance, should he need it against the Crusaders. Finally, once again a special clause called for the release of political prisoners.[151]

Two important aspects of the new treaty distinguished it from the previous one. First, the new treaty was accepted and signed by parties besides al-Salih and Saladin, such as Izz al-Din, representing Mosul, and the princes of Hisn Kaifa and Mardin, who had participated in the war as vassals of Sayf al-Din Ghazi. Second, to insure the implementation of the treaty, all the parties swore to join together against any one of them who might break the agreement.[152]

According to most Arabic sources, the conclusion of peace furnished Saladin an opportunity for touching magnanimity. Lane-Poole says:

> When the treaty was concluded, there came to Saladin a young girl, the little sister of es-Salih [i.e., the daughter of Nur al-Din]. He received her with honour and asked her "What is thy wish?" "The castle of Azaz," she said. So he restored the castle to its old owners, loaded the princess with presents, and escorted her back to the gate of Aleppo at the head of his staff.[153]

Neither Arabic chroniclers nor modern authorities have cared to observe that Saladin could not easily garrison Azaz, which was isolated from the bulk of Ayyubid territories in the south, and more important, that Azaz belonged to the area retroceded to Aleppo in the peace agreement.[154]

By the end of July 1176 Saladin's troops had campaigned actively for nearly five months. Some showed battle fatigue, others were anxious to get home and enjoy the spoils of war. However, the Ayyubid sultan rightly considered that the peace treaty had left some areas of his security unattended. Consequently, despite the physical and psychological weariness of his troops, Saladin marched south on 19 July to attack Masyaf, the center of Assassin activities in Syria.[155] While his mangonels converged on the rocky fortress of Sinan, his troops spread out to prey on the population of the neighboring area. In spite of the critical situation, Sinan refused to capitulate.

The determination of the Assassins' master paid off. The siege was well advanced when Saladin received the news of a diversionary Crusader attack on the Biqa valley. Although Ibn al-Muqaddam of Baalbek [156] defeated the diversion in a counterattack, another Ayyubid contingent led by Shams al-Dawlah Turan Sahah (who had happened to return from Yemen), sustained some casualties.[157] This new factor, in addition to troop weariness and lack of decisive progress in the siege, induced Saladin to consider negotiations. Early in August 1176, through his maternal uncle Shihab al-Din al-Harimi, whose appointment to Hamah made him concerned with the neighboring Assassin lands, an agreement was reached. The actual terms of settlement between Saladin and the master of the Assassins remains shrouded in mystery. One thing is certain; despite his official anti-Ismaili stand, Saladin never afterward attacked the Assassins and they never again staged attempts against his life.[158]

Saladin's return from the campaign

Thus the Syrian campaign of 1176 was terminated. Saladin released his troops and set out for Damascus. On 10 August during a brief stay in Hamah, he experienced a joyful reunion with the valiant Shams al-Dawlah Turan Shah.[159] The latter, learning about the more attractive opportunities in his native Syria, had abandoned his dominions in south Arabia. The joy of their reunion was marred, however, by the death of the elderly Ibn Abi al-Mada, who had rendered such crucial diplomatic service to the Ayyubid cause.[160] Finally, on 25 August 1176 Saladin was back in Damascus.

Although the sultan remained there only twelve days, he made several important administrative and personal decisions. He appointed Shams al-Dawlah as the new governor of Damascus, in place of Taqi al-Din Umar,[161] and he also made several reassignments in the Damascus judiciary.[162] Of a more personal, if not entirely romantic nature, was Saladin's wedding on 6 September 1176 with a Damascus widow, Asimat al-Din, aged thirty-nine, at least.[163] This was by no means Saladin's first marital experience. Judging by references to his progeny, the sultan had married at least four women prior to 1176: Umm al-Afdal, the mother of his oldest son, al-Afdal (b. 1170); Umm al-Aziz, the mother of al-Aziz (b. 1171) and of al-Aazz (b. 1176); Umm al-Zahir, the mother of al-Zahir (b. 1173); and Umm al-Muizz, the mother of al-Muizz (b. 1174).[164] According to Imad al-Din al-Isfahani, the new union was precipitated by Saladin's noble intention to protect the "respectful status, chastity, and modesty" of the middle-aged lady.[165] However, a glance at her family connections suggests that the Ayyubid leader was not attracted by her character alone. His bride was the daughter of Muin al-Din Anar, former strong man in Damascus. More important, she was a widow of Nur al-Din himself, to whom she had been betrothed as early as 1147, when Saladin was scarcely nine years old.[166]

Quite appropriately, the marriage ceremony was presided over by Muin al-Din's son, Prince Saad al-Din Masud, who was one of the first Syrian princes to join Saladin's cause during the expedition against Damascus.[167] This marriage strengthened even more his bid for supremacy over Syria. In addition to the military power which his enemies had been taught to respect and the official blessing received from the Abbasid caliph, Saladin's marriage with Nur al-Din's widow constituted an important addition to his image as the best qualified contender for the legacy of the great Zangid sultan. Four days after the wedding Saladin left Damascus and on 22 September he made a triumphant entry into Cairo.[168]

The Ayyubid ruler of Egypt had good reason to be content with the results of the Syrian campaign. Less than two years had elapsed since his departure from Cairo, but during that short period he had acquired southern Syria, including Damascus, Baalbek, Homs, and Hamah, which extended his command over territories dangerously threatening the Crusader position. Although Saladin had not succeeded in taking over Nur al-Din's entire legacy, because of the stubborn opposition centered around al-Salih, his antagonists were compelled to acknowledge his authority in Damascus, as well as to pledge military cooperation. Any major threat from the Crusaders in the north appeared reduced by the delicate situation of the Crusaders of Antioch. Hitherto that area had depended on military and political support from the Byzantines, but on 17 September 1176, while Saladin was triumphantly returning to Egypt, the Byzantines under Emperor Manuel, suffered a crushing defeat by the Saljuqids of Iconium at Myriokephalon. Not long after, Constantinople began to withdraw from its Crusader involvements and even sought to conclude a formal treaty of cooperation with Saladin. Instead of receiving Byzantine assistance, the Crusaders of Antioch were left practically alone to continue their struggle against the Muslims.

All these propitious strategic developments in Syria, greatly improved Egypt's own security and with it her chances of economic expansion so important for the continuation of Saladin's ambitious policy.

8
Consolidation of power in Egypt & Syria

"My son . . . abstain from the shedding of blood; trust not to that; for blood that is spilt never slumbers."—Saladin to al-Zahir

New defense measures

Using the Nile Delta as his operational base, Saladin had expanded his influence over the southern and western approaches to Egypt, as well as over the Red Sea zone, including the Yemen. In addition to restoring internal stability, his successes spurred normal societal and economic developments in Egypt. Following the death of Nur al-Din, Saladin succeeded in spreading his authority over Muslim Syria: directly over its southern regions and indirectly over Aleppo and its northern dependencies. Although accomplished with Egyptian troops and Egypt's treasury, the expansion into Syria did not conflict with Egypt's interests. Traditionally, the foreign policy of the medieval Egyptian rulers was to maintain peace with the Byzantines, to neutralize northern Syria, and to control southern Syria. Typical Egyptian foreign policy could be seen in the Fatimid reaction towards the Crusader siege of Antioch in 1098. Mistaking the Crusaders for the Byzantines, the Fatimids proposed a diplomatic deal that would leave Antioch in the hands of the Christians but give Palestine to Egypt.[1] In this light, Saladin's moderation in respect to Aleppo and his eagerness to dominate southern Syria did not appear inconsistent with past objectives of Egyptian foreign policy. In implementing this policy Saladin followed, though in reverse form, the strategy of the great Nur al-Din. Nur al-Din had intervened in Egypt because of his genuine concern for Syria's safety; Saladin moved into Syria to strengthen the security of Egypt. Having ratified the peace treaty with his Syrian opponents[2] and made an armistice with the Crusaders, Saladin could again turn his attention to Egypt's internal policy.

The first problem to which he addressed himself concerned Egypt's military preparedness, particularly its static defense establishments. As far back as 1171 Saladin had instructed Baha al-Din Qaragush to reinforce the walls of Cairo.[3] Now in 1176 he ordered the same commander to undertake the construction of both a new belt of walls to encompass Cairo and Fustat and a mighty citadel on the Muqattam Mountain.[4] This gigantic undertaking, aimed at sheltering two hitherto separate areas behind one fortification system, took thirty years to complete. Obviously remembering the 1169 siege, Saladin wanted the whole capital area defensible as a single, logistically more economical, garrison. Naturally, this project necessitated a huge commitment of economic resources, even though the use of Christian prisoners of war scaled down the costs of labor. But Saladin regarded the security of the metropolitan area as an indispensable strategic condition.

Similar concern about fortifications was shown for Alexandria, which Saladin visited in the spring of 1177. On that occasion he issued instructions for a crash program to expand his fleet, to which purpose the sultan placed sufficient artisans, building materials, and naval equipment at the disposal of the Alexandrian shipyards. He earmarked special *iqta* assignments and other sources of revenue to finance the construction and maintenance of the expanded fleet, and he gave the commanding admiral full authority to recruit adequate men to enlarge the naval force.[5]

In this period Saladin's effective military units did not remain idle. Sharaf al-Din Qaragush, heading the feudal contingent of Taqi al-Din Umar, once again set out on a predatory raid in the direction of North Africa.[6] Other army units were deployed in the Fakus area in order to preserve their battle readiness.[7]

Finally, some naval elements engaged in successful attacks against Frankish shipping.[8]

Economic measures

Defense activities affected Egypt's economy in different ways. The new fortifications and swift expansion of the fleet called for heavy expenditures and a diversion of many mansons, shipwrights, and skilled and unskilled workers from other production sectors. Finally, the rapidly expanding need for recruits must have caused some trouble. But if this costly emphasis on military matters disturbed the civilian segments of Egyptian society, they must have been gratified that Saladin did channel some resources for peaceful purposes. In 1176 he provided funds for the construction and upkeep of another Shafiite college as well as a hospital in Cairo.[9] In the spring of 1177, during his stay in Alexandria, he decreed that the local jurists should be provided with funds obtained from the export duties imposed on Frankish merchants.[10] Furthermore, he promulgated a decree abolishing the toll charges, consisting of 7.5 dinars per capita, collected in Aidhab or Jidda from the pilgrims crossing the Red Sea on their way to Mecca. To compensate the authorities in Mecca for the loss of these monies, Saladin assumed the obligation of furnishing them annually with 2,000 dinars in cash and 1,000 *irdabb* of wheat. In addition, he assigned for their benefit some *iqta* estates in Upper Egypt and the Yemen, which were to make the yearly deliveries of 8,000 *irdabb* of wheat to Jidda.[11]

The implications of this fiscal gesture toward Mecca and its pilgrim traffic were more profound than the brief mention in the Arabic sources appears to suggest. First, the abolishment of the substantial toll charges—for 7.5 dinars one could normally buy over 6 *irdabb*, or about 15 bushels of wheat[12]—must have increased Saladin's popularity among the masses of pilgrims in Mecca, who thus became natural agents disseminating pro-Saladin propaganda all over the Muslim world. Second, Saladin's policy may have been aimed at boosting the pilgrim, or "tourist," traffic in Egypt.

By far the most interesting was the political implication of Saladin's offer to Mecca. In addition to his earlier establishment of military influence along the eastern coast of the Red Sea, Saladin now undertook to assume financial responsibility for Mecca. In other words, he reclaimed the patronage of the Muslim religious capital, a prestigious prerogative which Egypt had lost during the Fatimid decline.

Disastrous offensive against the Crusaders

Diplomatic and military activities of the Crusaders and their allies during 1177 justified Saladin's concern about Egyptian military preparedness. That summer a Sicilian fleet raided Tinnis,[13] and apparently more dangerous was the arrival in Palestine of Philip of Flanders, with a considerable retinue of knights. This by itself violated the armistice, which said that "if any king or great noble arrived they were free to give him assistance, and the armistice should be renewed on his withdrawal."[14] At the same time as Philip's arrival, Emperor Manuel—despite his defeat at Myriokephalon—sent a powerful fleet to Acre to fulfill obligations made previously with Amalric for a Latin-Byzantine expedition against Egypt. Fortunately for Saladin, Philip refused to participate and the projected allied offensive did not materialize. The Byzantine fleet sailed home, thus terminating the alliance between Constantinople and the Kingdom of the Crusaders.[15]

Whether or not Saladin was informed of the Christian plans to invade Egypt, he ordered mobilization of his troops and at the end of October 1177 led the bulk of the Egyptian army into southern Palestine.[16] So large was the mobilized army that its supply needs caused an immediate rise in food prices on the Egyptian markets.[17] The Crusaders for their part staged an attack against Hamah on 14 November 1177. In spite of the fatal illness of its master, Shihab al-Din al-Harimi, their attempt was foiled after four days of fighting by another renowned Kurdish commander, Ali ibn Ahmad al-Mashtub.[18] Consequently the Crusaders decided to lay siege to Harim, the feudal apanage of Gümüshtigin of Aleppo.[19] To relieve Crusader pressure in northern Syria was the reason Saladin thrust into the south. By 23 November his troops were raiding in the region of Ascalon and Gaza, spreading destruction, capturing substantial booty, and massacring Christian prisoners.[20] So confident and lighthearted were the plundering Egyptian troops that they let themselves be surprised at Tall al-Safiya, by a well-timed and vicious counterattack which the crusaders launched on 25 November under the leadership of Reginald of Châtillon. The Egyptians were completely routed. Only the heroism of individual soldiers and commanders, like Taqi al-Din Umar, saved the Egyptian army from annihilation. Saladin himself barely escaped, racing toward the desert where he was rescued by a searching party dispatched by al-Qadi al-Fadil. It was a stunning defeat. Many commanders, including Isa al-Hakkari, were taken prisoners. Many others, including a son of Taqi al-Din, perished on the battlefield. Lost was all the equipment and most of both mounts and pack animals. The remnants of the shattered army, short of water and food, straggled home as best they could, harassed by the Franks and the Bedouins.[21]

Grim, humiliating, and costly as the defeat at Tall al-Safiya had proved, Saladin was not demoralized. Sparing neither energy nor resources he proceeded to rebuild and reorganize his land forces. He stopped the pay of many of the Kurds accused of being responsible for the disaster.[22] He raised money to replace lost personnel, equipment, and animals.[23] Within four months, he had his army refitted and ready for another campaign in Syria. Once again, strength of character, relentless force, and Egypt's resources enabled Saladin to overcome a dangerous crisis.

Saladin's return to Damascus and his vengeance on the Crusaders

The year 1178 brought further complications in Syria. To begin with, Aleppo was undermined by growing economic difficulties and by an internal struggle for power. Assassins killed Vizir Ibn al-Ajami, possibly at the instigation of the jealous Gümüshtigin,[24] who in turn was tortured to death by the henchmen of al-Salih.[25] The internal weaknesses of Aleppo allowed the Crusaders to maintain their siege against Harim, whose garrison faced eventual starvation.

The Syrian developments called for Saladin's presence in Damascus where he arrived with fresh Egyptian troops on 22 March 1178. Much to his disappointment he found his brother Shams al-Dawlah had completely neglected his duties as governor and was on suspiciously good terms with al-Salih,[26] which must have alerted Saladin, who could hardly have forgotten Shams al-Dawlah's contacts with the pro-Fatimid conspirators in Egypt.[27] However, the very reappearance of the Ayyubid sultan in Syria and the threat of his intervention on behalf of Harim caused the Franks to abandon their siege and initiate negotiations with Aleppo. Coming to an understanding with al-Salih, the Crusaders retreated from Harim [28] and in late August 1178 turned against Saladin's forces by launching another attack against Hamah. Once again they were unsuccessful. Even without the help of Saladin's army, Nasir al-Din ibn Khumartigin, who commanded the garrison of Hamah after al-Harimi's death, repelled the assaulting Crusaders, whose leader along with many companions fell in that battle.[29] The prisoners of war were delivered to Saladin. If some of them expected magnanimity from the Muslim leader, they were in for tragic disappointment. Saladin still smarted from his last confrontation with the Crusaders; the prisoners furnished a convenient outlet for his vindictiveness. They were brought into his presence and summarily executed, one after another, by the members of his retinue. The preacher Diya al-Din al-Tabari began the bloodbath by personally decapitating a few of the defenceless captives. Another divine, Sulayman al-Maghribi, followed his example, then emir Aytghan ibn Yaruq and others did so. Only chancellor Imad al-Din al-Isfahani refused to join in the butchery.[30]

Conflict with Ibn al-Muqaddam and Qilij Arslan of Iconium

The year of his return to Syria Saladin did not seek actively to engage the Frankish enemy. One reason was his embroilment in an internal conflict at Damascus. Dissatisfied with the irresponsible performance of Shams al-Dawlah, Saladin appointed his nephew Farrukh-Shah as the new commandant.[31] Shams al-Dawlah now demanded the fief of Baalbek, where the Ayyubids originally came to power in Syria. Although he hardly deserved favors, Saladin granted the request. Unfortunately, Ibn al-Muqaddam, the feudal lord of Baalbek, who had played a key role installing Saladin in Damascus, refused to vacate the place. In the face of such defiance Saladin immediately committed his troops to a prolonged operation against Baalbek. Only after seven long months of siege and after being promised extensive fiefs in the north, did Ibn al-Muqaddam abandon his rebellious posture to resume service with the sultan.[32]

Saladin was also preoccupied with Qilij Arslan, the Saljuqid sultan of Iconium. Having fatally crippled the Byzantines in Asia Minor, Qilij Arslan turned towards the upper Euphrates region. Most of all he coveted Raban and Kabsun, which had been seized in 1160 by Nur al-Din. When Saladin returned to Damascus in 1177, an ambassador presented Qilij Arslan's claim to those places, which was that Nur al-Din had taken them from Iconium, but allegedly his son al-Salih of Aleppo retroceded them.[33] However, the sultan of Iconium apparently thought it appropriate to communicate his annexation plans to the new ruler in Damascus. Angered by the Saljuqid encroachment on Nur al-Din's legacy, Saladin rebuked the envoy and threatened his master with strong military measures.[34] Indeed, as soon as an army of Qilij Arslan laid siege to Raban, Saladin dispatched a contingent of 1,000 cavalry under Taqi al-Din Umar, which forced the Saljuqid aggressors to a speedy withdrawal.[35]

As with Ibn al-Muqaddam's defiance, the show of force against Iconium achieved the desired effect. But these successes were accomplished at cost to the Muslim population, since during that period the Crusaders carried out predatory raids against Muslim territories, including the eastern borderland of Egypt.[36] Moreover, at the insistence of the Templars, they succeeded in restoring a powerful strategic fortress at Jacob's Ford, the Bait al-Ahzan of the Arab sources, defending a passage over the Jordan, and commanding the approach to the plain of Banyas, the granary of Damascus.[37]

Offensive operations against the Crusaders

Saladin opened his campaign against the Crusaders in the spring of 1179. It was preceded with several command reassignments of his relatives. To fill the vacancy created by the death of Shihab al-Din al-Harimi, Saladin gave Hamah to his nephew Taqi al-Din. Nasir al-Din ibn Shirkuh was confirmed in his hold on Homs.[38] Farrukh-Shah took over Baalbek.[39] As for Shams al-Dawlah, the oldest of the Ayyubid brothers, he was "persuaded" to lead home the incapacitated and fatigued Egyptian warriors, who were restive under the privations of Syrian famine conditions.[40] They were replaced by 1,500 Egyptians picked by al-Adil, Saladin's younger brother.[41] Saladin assigned Shams al-Dawlah to Alexandria, away from Damascus, with no role in the government of Cairo.[42]

Early in April 1179 Farrukh-Shah and his Damascus regiment of *mamluk* (slave) troops, whom Saladin had ordered to shadow the movements of the Crusaders, found themselves engaged, almost by accident, in a battle near Belfort (Shaqif Arnun) and scored a brilliant victory.[43] Shortly afterwards Saladin invaded the Christian territories, dispatching both his regular units and auxiliary Arab tribal forces for retaliatory sweeps near Sidon and Beirut.[44] Then on 10 June 1179 the Ayyubid sultan achieved a success which must have erased any uneasiness caused by the defeat of Tall al-Safiya. Surprised in the plain of Marj Uyun (between the Leontes and the upper Jordan) by a large Crusader force that King Baldwin IV led and despite an initial reverse, Saladin managed to turn the battle into a notable victory. According to Imad al-Din, who drew up a register of the prisoners, there were over 270 knights, exclusive of lower ranks. Most were later ransomed for huge sums of gold—a much welcomed revenue to finance Saladin's war effort—and the release of Muslim prisoners, including Isa al-Hakkari.[45] But when Saladin proposed a ransom settlement to Odo, the master of the Templars, he was shown the uncompromising spirit for which the militant orders were known. "A Templar can give for his ransom naught but his belt and dagger," answered Odo, who was then sent to a Damascus jail from which he never returned alive. "He went from the prison to Hell," commented an Arab chronicler.[46]

These victories were coupled with successful offensive operations of the Egyptian fleet. By spring 1179 the Egyptian navy was ready for action. It amounted to eighty vessels, of which sixty were galleys, and twenty transports. It was apparently organized into two fleets of which one, numbering fifty ships, was to protect Egyptian shores and the other, about thirty ships, was to move against the Crusaders.

The Muslims sailed as far north as the Byzantine territories, either Cyprus, Crete, or the southern shores of Asia Minor. They made several landings on the Syrian coast, where they inflicted losses on the population as well as on coastal mercantile traffic. Moreover, on 10 June (the same day as the battle of Marj Uyun), they captured two enemy cargo ships. The fleet returned to Egypt bringing a great deal of spoil as well as about 1,000 prisoners. This was hailed as a great triumph and from then on Saladin's fleet was given the epithet, Victorious, by the enthusiastic Muslim chroniclers.[47]

After these victories Saladin felt ready to proceed against Bait al-Ahzan, the last element disturbing the territorial status quo which prevailed prior to the Crusader disruption of the armistice agreement. He first tried to obtain evacuation of the fortress in exchange for a monetary compensation.[48] When this offer was turned down, Saladin unleashed all the power and fury of his forces against the recalcitrant garrison. With large auxiliary groups of Turkomans and siege troops supplementing the Syrian regiments and the fresh Egyptian contingent, the attacking army ravaged the surrounding territory, and on 25 August 1179 began direct assaults against the fortress. Using relentless frontal attacks and mining operations, Saladin's troops penetrated the defense perimeter on the sixth day of the siege. The Crusaders' request for safe-conduct was ignored. The fortress, with all its stockpiles of weapons and supplies, fell to Saladin. As many as 700 defenders were led away into captivity, while many others were massacred on the spot, their bodies thrown into a cistern. The sultan was determined to render this place uninhabitable. In spite of the scorching heat, the stench of dead bodies, and an outbreak of epidemics which killed several of his commanders, Saladin remained at Bait al-Ahzan until the last stone of the wretched fortress had been razed.[49] Finally, after a series of forays in the vicinity of Tiberias, Tyre, and Beirut, the victorious sultan returned to Damascus[50] to learn of a daring raid the Egyptian fleet executed against Acre, the "Constantinople of the Syrian Crusaders."

Profiting by darkness the night of 14 October, the Egyptian ships penetrated the harbor of Acre, and before the surprised Christian garrison could organize resistance, the attackers took possession of all enemy ships. Keeping the defenders at a distance by volleys of arrows, the Egyptians held the harbor for two entire days. After causing a lot of destruction, the Muslims withdrew to return home in glory. This daring exploit, which cost the lives of three Muslim captains, constituted a real challenge to the hitherto unquestionable Crusader naval hegemony. No wonder that a Muslim chronicler describing this event says: "Our fleet once destroyed, became in turn the destroyer of the enemy. . . . Never a similar victory was achieved by a Muslim fleet, neither in the past centuries, nor even at the time of our naval supremacy and the weakness of our enemies." [51]

By the end of 1179, Saladin was once again in control of the situation in Syria. His blows inflicted on the Crusaders made the position of the Frankish Kingdom extremely vulnerable. The Crusaders had sustained heavy casualties, including many military leaders. Their unsuccessful ally, Philip of Flanders, had sailed home, and the Byzantines could no longer be expected to succor the Latin establishments in the Near East. To make matters worse, recurrent droughts in Syria created catastrophic food shortages.[52]

Saladin moves against his Moslem rivals

In 1180 despite his advantageous strategic position, Saladin did not press on with the war against the Crusaders. Among the reasons for this was the death, on 11 March 1180, of al-Mustadi, the Abbasid suzerain in Baghdad. He was succeeded by al-Nasir li-Din Allah, known not only for pro-Shiite leanings, but for unscrupulous political ambitions. Saladin hastened to dispatch a special emissary to Baghdad, expressing his submissiveness, in the expectation that the new caliph would reconfirm Saladin's authority over the lands in his possession and sanction any future conquests.[53]

Of a more immediate consequence was the death of Sayf al-Din Ghazi of Mosul on 28 June 1180. Aware of Saladin's political ambitions and expansionist tendencies, the establishment in Mosul quickly acclaimed Izz al-Din, the seasoned brother of the dead prince, as their new ruler. Immediately after his accession Izz al-Din sent a mission to Saladin to secure the latter's recognition of Mosul's authority over the Mesopotamian cities seized by Sayf al-Din Ghazi after Nur al-Din's death. Although such a recognition had been implied in the peace agreement of 1176, Saladin flatly refused to cooperate. These cities and provinces, argued Saladin, had been included in the general concession made to him by Caliph al-Mustadi; Sayf al-Din had only been allowed to control those areas in return for his promise to assist Saladin with Mesopotamian troops.[54] Concerned about public reaction to his rejection of Izz al-Din's request, Saladin hastened to dispatch a letter to al-Nasir in Baghdad, pointing out that he could not draw indefinitely on Egyptian forces for his campaigns against the Crusaders, that he needed the armies from the provinces claimed by Mosul, and that he expected the new caliph to reconfirm the original investiture.[55]

Less consequential was the death in June 1180 of the ambitious and politically restless Shams al-Dawlah, Saladin's oldest brother. Arab chroniclers have not furnished any details of his death, but their obituaries stress that Shams al-Dawlah enjoyed considerable prestige and influence in the army; that he coveted the kingdom of Syria; that Saladin had some misgivings about his political intentions; and, finally, that he was transferred to Alexandria to live out his time in frivolous pleasures.[56]

The situation in Mosul and Qilij Arslan's designs for the upper Euphrates area changed Saladin's political and military thinking. In 1180—though holding an upper hand over the anemic Kingdom of the Crusaders—Saladin once again made a deal with the enemy of Islam in order to secure freedom of action for his military moves against local rivals in the north of Syria.[57] He secured an armistice agreement with King Baldwin by negotiation and with the count of Tripoli by a show of naval force.[58]

His initial action was directed against Iconium. Early in 1180 a quarrel broke out on a domestic issue between Qilij Arslan and the Artukid prince of Hisn Kaifa, Nur al-Din. Although Nur al-Din was technically a vassal of Mosul, he appealed to Saladin, presumably invoking the Aleppo agreement of 1176. Saladin decided to intervene.[59]

He led a powerful army, which included an Aleppo contingent, as far north as Behesni, near the Sanja (Gök) River, a tributary of the upper Euphrates. There an ambassador of Qilij Arslan warned Saladin in threatening terms not to precipitate bloodshed between the two Muslim camps. But Saladin, scorning these attempts at intimidation, expressed his determination to launch an immediate offensive. The ambassador, impressed by the number and spirit of Saladin's troops, requested a personal audience with the sultan, during which he argued that a military engagement would only confirm suspicions many people had of the Ayyubid ruler—that he had cynically reached an accommodation with the Crusaders to promote his aggressive imperialist policy against his Muslim neighbors. Whatever the exact character of the negotiations, they did result in a settlement of the differences between Qilij Arslan and Saladin.[60] This new diplomatic agreement allowed the Ayyubid sultan to conduct a brief but vigorous campaign against Reuben, the Christian king of Little Armenia, on the pretext of his harsh treatment of Turcoman tribes. The impressive show of force induced Reuben, as well as other princes in that area, to seek an agreement aimed at pacification of the explosive northern area.[61] On 2 October 1180 a solemn pact was signed in which Saladin, the prince of Mosul, the sultan of Iconium, the king of Armenia, and several Artukid princes pledged to keep peace with one another for two years.[62]

By the end of 1180, Saladin had scored a major success, for he had imposed his political and military influence in the north of Syria. Considering that Constantinople had sent Saladin overtures of a formal alliance in that same year,[63] the Ayyubid ruler could easily risk a return to his Egyptian capital. During a stop-over in Damascus Saladin was provided with yet another reason for celebration. A delegation of high-ranking Baghdad officials brought him official investiture diplomas as solemn expression of Caliph al-Nasir's approval of Saladin's requests. Furthermore, the head of the delegation, the revered sheikh Sadr al-Din, indicated his desire to travel to Mecca by way of Egypt.[64] Nothing could have pleased Saladin more at that juncture, for he must have regarded this as public demonstration of Baghdad's satisfaction with Ayyubid accomplishments in the Red Sea zone. It had been a long time since a high religious Abbasid dignitary chose to journey to Mecca through the country of the Nile.

Saladin in Egypt, 1181–82

The period between 8 January 1181 and 11 May 1182 turned out to be Saladin's final stay in Egypt. He was preoccupied with feverish military and economic activities. In 1181 Saladin regularized the size of Egypt's standing army, fixing the number of the troops at 8,640, of whom 111 were amirs and 8,529 troopers of upper and lower rank. The regular army was supported by its feudal holdings whose proceeds were estimated at 3,670,500 dinars. The Egyptian economy also carried the burden of maintaining troops without fiefs, of Arab tribal units, of now sedentary Bedouin warriors, of the surviving Fatimid army contingents, and of various categories of noncombatant personnel; the total cost was some 1,000,000 dinars.[65]

Saladin also undertook a major fiscal and administrative reform of his navy. Hitherto he had maintained his predecessors' system of supporting the navy from the caliph's treasury. Since Saladin was not only a ruler but a field commander as well, he could not be burdened with administrative problems of the fleet, so he set up a special ministry of the fleet (*diwan al-ustul*). Several branches of Egyptian revenue were diverted to this new department.[66]

After his Euphrates expedition, Saladin could once again deploy his troops in areas more directly pertinent to Egypt's security and stability. In the eastern provinces some were used for punitive actions against the Bedouins accused of smuggling grain out to the Crusader kingdom.[67] Other troops had to man the fortified desert outposts scattered along the inland caravan trails connecting Egypt with Syria and exposed to harassment by Reginald of Châtillon. To neutralize his threat, Saladin ordered Farrukh-Shah, governor in Damascus, to put military pressure on the Christian establishment in southern Jordan. This precaution foiled Reginald's raid against Taima in northern Hejaz,[68] though it did not prevent him from capturing a caravan on its way from Damascus to Mecca.[69] In spite of all these defense measures, two Egyptian frontier towns, al-Arish and Tinnis, suffered in 1181 from Christian land and naval attacks respectively.[70]

While Saladin's troops proceeded to penetrate the North African provinces satisfactorily, the situation in the south Arabian dependencies left much to be desired. Shams al-Dawlah's successor as governor in the Yemen was recalled for administrative abuses and arrested upon his return to Cairo. Fortunately the government managed to recover the 80,000 dinars he had embezzled during his short stay in office. To restore order Saladin dispatched a new governor with a fresh contingent of 500 troops. Since their departure necessitated expensive replacement procedures, their maintenance costs had to be borne by the local payroll of the Yemen.[71] Eventually, in 1182, another brother of Saladin, Sayf al-Din Tughtigin, went to that area and established a strong Ayyubid regime which lasted for several decades.[72]

Finally, to consolidate the security of the Mediterranean coastline, Saladin ordered the strengthening of various fortifications in Tinnis, Damietta, and Alexandria.[73] Similar urgency characterized his building up the fortifications around the capital.[74]

In spite of the high costs, Saladin's defense budget had not yet overburdened Egypt's fiscal capacity. In fact, delinquent Muslim taxpayers in the area of Cairo, Fustat, Fayyum, and in Upper Egypt were treated with tolerance by the fiscal administration.[75] Furthermore, the government continued to finance various civilian public projects: a new canal, several bridges, hospices in the Delta, and a college and a hospital opened in Alexandria.[76]

The government of Saladin continued to promote internal and transit traffic across Egypt. That the Red Sea and India commerce must have recovered sufficiently is evident from the fact that in the summer of 1180 Saladin imposed on the so-called Karimi merchants, arriving from Aden, a charge amounting to a four-year tax levy.[77] On the other hand, all noncanonical charges collected from merchants and pilgrims in Qus were ordered discontinued.[78] Special military precautions were undertaken in Suez and Akhmim to secure undisturbed flow of alum from the mine districts in the south to the export centers on the Mediterranean coast.[79] This special concern for alum, as well as for natron, another mineral found in Egypt, was caused by their great demand among Christian merchants who supplied them to the north Italian textile industry. In turn, Egypt depended heavily on Italian deliveries of weapons and strategic raw materials such as lumber, iron, pitch, and oakum. Saladin's monopolistic control of alum and natron export permitted his government to reduce the outflow of gold coinage to Europe.

Despite all these urgent government preoccupations and tours of inspection, Saladin found time for worship, theological discussions, and for hunting and polo-playing.[80]

Diplomatic complications following the death of al-Salih

In the summer of 1181, Saladin received an ambassador from the court of Constantinople, who was gravely concerned by the aggressive mood of the Normans of Sicily.[81] The visit produced a formal treaty of alliance between Cairo and Constantinople, which constituted yet another instance of Saladin's adherence to traditional concepts of medieval Egyptian foreign policy. But towards the end of that year his attention became totally absorbed by serious developments in Aleppo. On 4 December 1181 al-Malik al-Salih, the son and successor of Nur al-Din in Syria, died. Shortly before his death he had prevailed upon his followers to give Aleppo to Izz al-Din of Mosul, as the only member of the Zangid family capable of safeguarding Syrian territories from Saladin's aggressiveness. The lord of Mosul did not need to be asked twice. On 29 December 1181 he entered Aleppo, seized its citadel and treasury, and—as if to match Saladin's accomplishments—married the mother of al-Salih, or another widow of the great Nur al-Din, thus strengthening his claims to northern Syria.[82]

The people in Aleppo insisted that the new ruler should exploit Saladin's absence to reconquer Damascus. Significantly even the people in Hamah staged an abortive uprising against their Ayyubid master, Taqi al-Din Umar.[83] However, Izz al-Din rejected these ideas, pointing out that he had been bound by the solemn treaty of 1179 to maintain peaceful relations with the Ayyubid sultan.[84] Moreover, he faced competition with his own brother Imad al-Din, the master of Sinjar and an erstwhile ally of Saladin. Imad al-Din showed an interest in al-Salih's legacy and threatened Izz al-Din that unless he would cede Aleppo to him, Sinjar would be offered to Saladin. This ultimatum prompted the lord of Mosul to close a deal with his brother. Imad al-Din was allowed to take possession of Aleppo, in exchange for Sinjar. Having resolved that conflict diplomatically, Izz al-Din returned to Mesopotamia, and Imad al-Din arrived in Aleppo on 20 May 1182.[85] By this time Saladin was already on the way to Syria.

9 Saladin's war against Mosul

"Saladin spent the revenues of Egypt to gain Syria, the revenues of Syria to gain Mesopotamia. . . ."
—al-Qadi al-Fadil

Saladin leaves Egypt for Syria

As soon as news of al-Salih's terminal illness reached Cairo, Saladin sent urgent orders to Farrukh-Shah at Damascus and to Taqi al-Din at Hamah to prevent the ruler of Mosul from taking Aleppo. This bellicose reaction—if translated into effective action—would have meant a blatant violation of the peace treaty of 1180, considering that Izz al-Din had not come to Syria as conqueror but by invitation of the recognized regime in Aleppo. As it happened, Saladin's preventive measures were not implemented because Farrukh-Shah was at that time countering moves of Reginald of Châtillon, and Taqi al-Din had to handle the pro-Zangid uprising in Hamah.[1] Having failed to prevent the Mesopotamian Zangids from reestablishing direct influence in Aleppo, Saladin regarded the Syrian balance of power so disturbed as to necessitate his personal intervention.

Saladin expressed his grave concern in a series of propaganda letters dispatched by his diplomatic service to the caliph's court in Baghdad. These letters claimed that the prince of Mosul had seized a province from Saladin, at a time when the sultan's troops had been busy protecting the city of the Prophet from the Infidels. Saladin further charged that the disputes between the Muslim princes were hindering the *jihad;* also, he accused his Mosul rivals of inciting the Crusaders and the Assassins against him; and finally, reasserting his claim to Aleppo on the basis of the rights conferred upon him by the Abbasid caliphate, he declared with an undertone of irritation that "if the Exalted Commands should ordain that the prince of Mosul be invested with the government of Aleppo, then it were better to invest him with all Syria and Egypt as well."[2]

On 11 May 1182 Saladin left Cairo for Syria. He was solemnly seen off by the chief officers and dignitaries of the court, who must have sensed the historic significance of the occasion.[3] Nor were they mistaken, for their great sultan, whom they had learned to admire during his fourteen years of political success at home and abroad, was not destined to come to Egypt again.

Between 1168 and 1182, Egypt was lifted from an abyss of political demoralization, economic decay, and military impotence to a position of real power influencing social, political, and ideological developments in the territories of the Fertile Crescent. In that phase Saladin's regime had restored stability in and around Egypt, creating favorable conditions for a revival of the agricultural, manufacturing, and commercial productivity of the Egyptian society.

The weakness of the Crusader Kingdom

Notwithstanding these propitious developments there had remained one area relating to Egyptian security which called for a determined effort: Egypt continued to be plagued by the existence of the Crusader establishments in Palestine and Jordan. The Crusaders continuously interfered with commercial and passenger traffic between Syria and Egypt; as late as 1181, they had launched damaging raids against the Egyptian towns of al-Arish and Tinnis. In that same year Reginald of Châtillon, Egypt's most aggressive Frankish neighbor, had made a thrust in the direction of Taima and captured a defenseless caravan heading for Mecca.[4]

Actually, this provocative activity by some Frankish leaders hardly reflected the real situation prevailing in the Crusader Kingdom.[5] Ever since Amalric's death in 1174, the political, military, diplomatic, and economic position of the Crusaders had rapidly deteriorated. In spite of military valor and remarkable ability, King Baldwin IV, afflicted by leprosy, had been turning executive control of the kingdom over to Guy of Lusignan, a relatively recent arriver in the holy land. Although influential at the royal court because of his marriage with Amalric's daughter Sibyl, Guy was extremely unpopular with the locally raised Crusader hierarchy. Court intrigues gave rise to factionalist tensions and disputes, virtually bringing the kingdom to the brink of civil war. The degree of moral corruption and political demoralization pervading Crusader ruling circles may best be illustrated by the fact that the count of Antioch's wife served as an obliging spy for Saladin.[6]

The military potential of the Crusaders had been further crippled by the blows sustained during their 1179 campaign against the forces of Saladin. The Crusaders were also vulnerable because they could no longer count on the steady support of their external Christian allies. Defeated by the Saljuqids of Iconium and attacked by the Normans of Sicily, the Byzantines had by then withdrawn their assistance and were seeking instead a diplomatic accommodation with Saladin. The Italian mercantile republics—meeting ever-increasing hostility and even bloody repressions in their operations in Constantinople—expanded their commercial relations with Egypt. France and England were opposed in a bitter diplomatic and military contest over the Plantagenet possessions on French territory. The potential of the Holy Roman Empire was strained to the utmost by the exhaustive struggle for supremacy in north Italy. As for the Holy See, the popes of that period, absorbed in reasserting papal influence in Europe, devoted little attention to the critical position of the Christian establishment in the Near East. The Third Lateran Council of 1179, hearing the pleas of the Eastern bishops, reacted by merely castigating those responsible for trading with the Muslims, especially in war materials.[7]

Naturally, indignant public opinion in Europe could not reverse the commercial trends prevailing in the eastern Mediterranean. Egyptian ports attracted European sea-merchants coming in search of alum, natron, and the traditional commodities and raw materials moving between the Indian Ocean and Mediterranean Egypt. Apart from strengthening Egypt militarily, this intensification of Egyptian international trade worked against the commercial interests of the Crusaders whose deteriorating economic situation was aggravated by the recurrent famine in Syria and by the devastating forays of Saladin's contingents.

In the light of all these adverse trends the Crusader Kingdom appeared doomed, unless some new dramatic events were to arouse Christian Europe to succor her outposts in the Near East.

Saladin reopens his campaign in Syria

It was against this background that Saladin marched into Syria with 4,000 horsemen, constituting one half of his regular Egyptian army, the other half having been left behind as a tactical reserve together with Arab tribal forces and other less disciplined units. After the Egyptian corps joined the contingents from Damascus, Homs, and Hamah, Saladin had some 6,500 regular cavalry under his command.[8] In addition, he could depend on the participation of the Turkoman auxiliaries. His Egyptian fleet was also ordered to join the campaign. With all these diverse tactical elements ready to launch an offensive under the leadership of an experienced warlord, the people of Egypt and Syria could expect a major breakthrough in the struggle against the Crusaders.

The offensive, begun in July 1182, Saladin directed against Beirut. The advantages of capturing that coastal fortress were obvious. Apart from driving a wedge in the coastal territory of the Crusaders, the possession of Beirut would also provide the Egyptian fleet with an excellent base in Syria. It would thus extend the operational perimeter of Egyptian ships which could replenish their provisions and supplies there instead of returning to Egypt. The plan of the attack was quite simple. Thirty Egyptian galleys were to launch a frontal attack from the sea while Saladin's troops were to assault the fortress on land.[9]

This projected operation ended in a fiasco. Delayed by an inconclusive encounter with the Crusaders near the fortress of Belfort, Saladin did not arrive in Beirut at the time of the naval attack. The Egyptian fleet failed to disembark in the harbor and was content with raiding the environs of Beirut. The element of surprise was lost, so when Saladin finally arrived in August 1182, all he could do was to establish a tight land and sea blockade of the fortress. After nearly a month of successful blockading, thirty-three Christian galleys suddenly appeared. The Egyptian fleet withdrew without battle, whereupon Saladin lifted the siege and retreated from the adamant fortress.

Why did this major operation fail? Obviously the land and sea attacks were not synchronized, which they had to be for effective action. The high morale of the besieged garrison and its stubborn resistance also influenced the course of events. But most of all, it is unquestionably true that Saladin withdrew from Beirut because the fleet failed in its mission. The fact that thirty Egyptian galleys dodged an encounter with an improvised Crusader fleet, consisting of thirty-three ships reassembled from various Christian ports, certainly did not attest to the fighting capabilities or courage of the Egyptians. They may have been adept at spreading destruction when taking their enemy by surprise, or by attacking inferior forces, but they seemed less than anxious for a full-scale naval battle even when both sides were more or less equal.[10]

Unsuccessful off Beirut, Saladin's naval units reported important gains in other sectors of the Mediterranean front. While still engaged in the siege of Beirut, Saladin received news that a large Christian cargo of Apulian provenience had been stranded off Damietta. The Muslims had taken about 1,700 prisoners, thus preventing them from reinforcing the Crusader ranks. The Egyptians also intercepted a ship full of Venetian refugees escaping from the anti-Latin riots in Constantinople of March 1182.[11] Although the Crusaders foiled Saladin's attack against Beirut, they could not but expect further blows to come from the Ayyubid sultan. Strategic advantages and tactical initiative rested firmly in his hands and his land forces were eager to engage the Christian enemy. Contrary to their expectations and much to the Crusaders' relief, Saladin decided to suspend the *jihad* and turned against his Muslim rivals instead.

Saladin's first expedition against Mosul

Although Aleppo had by then been taken over by a former ally, Imad al-Din, Saladin remained dissatisfied with the new situation in northern Syria. Consequently, after Beirut, he ordered Farrukh-Shah to withdraw into Damascus, while he himself proceeded to Aleppo with the main body of the army.[12] It was during his move north that the sultan received the visit of Muzaffar al-Din Gökböri, the governor of Harran. Being hostile to Mosul and aware of internal opposition to Mosul's parsimonious major domo, Qaymaz, Gökböri urged Saladin to undertake an expedition against the Zangid strongholds across the Euphrates. To this persuasion Saladin succumbed, and toward the end of September 1182, he led his army across the frontier river.[13] With this aggression the last vestiges of a tenuous peace, which since October 1180 had characterized relations between the Muslim leaders surrounding the Christian Kingdom of Jerusalem, gave way to a long war between the Ayyubid and Zangid forces. What a timely break for the beleaguered Crusaders.

On launching his expedition against northern Mesopotamia Saladin issued a proclamation pledging that "those who would surrender their cities to his authority would be allowed to remain in control of their places, provided that they join the army of the sultan, to follow him and to assist him in the war against the Infidels.[14] This propaganda won over many dissident amirs in Zangid territories, which facilitated Saladin's advance against Mosul. The master of al-Bira, who had a grudge against Mosul, assisted in the crossing of the Euphrates. Gökböri, who had been so instrumental in precipitating this invasion, and Nur al-Din of Hisn Kayfa, whom Saladin had earlier defended against Qilij Arslan, joined the Ayyubid leader and his army as soon as they showed up east of the Euphrates. Indeed, one after another, various cities of the Jazirah, or northern Mesopotamia, surrendered to Saladin. Only the castle of Nisibin staged some resistance but was overcome after a few days of fighting.[15]

At that point Saladin brought his swift campaign to a halt. Obviously, he found it necessary to take stock of the situation before deciding on his next move. Having convened his commanders, the sultan suggested that either Mosul, Sinjar, or Jazirat Ibn Umar should be selected as the next target. Gökböri insisted that they should aim straight at Mosul. "With Mosul in our hands no one will be able to resist us. Furthermore, if Izz al-Din and Qaymaz hear about our advance, they will evacuate the city and seek refuge in some obscure little mountain castle," argued the master of Harran.[16] Gökböri's view received the wholehearted support of Nasir al-Din Muhammad, Shir-kuh's son, who had earlier furnished a great deal of money to his cousin Saladin, in return for a promise that Mosul would be given to him as a fief. The arguments of Gökböri and Nasir al-Din prevailed and so Saladin ordered an advance on the capital of Izz al-Din.[17]

It was at that time that Saladin received news about the death of his nephew and deputy in Damascus, Farrukh-Shah. The vacancy was at once filled by the appointment of Ibn al-Muqaddam.[18] More disquieting news concerned the Crusaders. The Franks, emboldened by the sultan's absence and by his army's commitment to an invasion beyond the Euphrates, penetrated the territory of Damascus, plundering villages all the way to Darayya, a place only a few miles from the capital itself. Some people in Saladin's headquarters advised immediate return to protect Muslim lives and property, but as usual Saladin assessed the Frankish danger from the vantage point of his whole expansionist policy. "Let them," was his calm rejoinder. "While they knock down villages we are taking cities." [19]

Not that this acquisition of cities was accomplished without opposition. Contrary to Gökböri's optimistic prediction, Izz al-Din did not run away. Instead he more than adequately prepared his city's defenses to meet the oncoming challenge. When Saladin approached the Zangid capital the sight of the powerful bastion gave him disturbing pause. Within a few months he had led his warriors from the Nile, across the Euphrates to the Tigris, but now Mosul emerged as a real obstacle to further expansion and consolidation. To retreat meant conceding the field to Izz al-Din, which could in turn produce adverse psychological consequences for his prestige with his Mesopotamian allies. Bitterly critical of the ill-founded optimism of Gökböri and Nasir al-Din, Saladin had no choice but to order on 10 November the envelopment of the city. However, neither frontal attacks nor heavy mangonel bombardment could breach the city walls or break the spirit of the defenders.[20] Came December and Saladin's costly expeditionary army was still immobilized in front of Mosul.

Izz al-Din, for his part, engaged in hectic diplomatic efforts aimed at securing Saladin's withdrawal. He dispatched his secretary Baha al-Din Ibn Shaddad, who was later to become a close associate and biographer of Saladin, to Baghdad.[21] Another mission was dispatched to the Saljuqid sultan of Persia,[22] a well-calculated move considering how far Saladin's ambitious military activities had gone beyond the territories of Egypt and Syria. They had expanded dangerously close to Baghdad, becoming a potential source of complications in the political plans of the Abbasid caliph. Consequently, al-Nasir dispatched a high-ranking dignitary from his court to serve as mediator in the conflict over Mosul. Neither the mediation of the caliphate nor similar attempts by other neutral parties brought the hostile camps any closer to reconciliation. Saladin insisted that he be given Aleppo as a price for his withdrawal from Mosul, but Izz al-Din found the idea of selling out his brother absolutely unacceptable.[23]

With neither the siege nor negotiations leading anywhere, Saladin withdrew his army around the middle of December and marched three days to Sinjar. On his way there he completely routed a strong contingent from Mosul, dispatched to reinforce the garrison of Sinjar.[24] Even without reinforcements the master of the place, loyal to his Zangid overlord, refused to submit; but on 30 December 1182, after fifteen days of fighting, his resistance was overcome. The defenders must have given the Ayyubid army a lot of trouble, because once they entered the city, the population had to endure the wild excesses of Saladin's enraged soldiers, who broke all discipline in greed of plunder.[25] That Sinjar was captured during Ramadan demonstrated the lack of concern Saladin and his followers had about restrictive religious injunctions.

Following the important victory at Sinjar, Saladin marched to Harran. There, at long last, he sent home his contingents, exhausted by some seven months of strenuous campaigning.[26] However, neither he nor his army were to enjoy the rest for long. Mosul had no intention of tolerating the new situation created by the eastward penetration of Ayyubid influence. To oust the invader, Izz al-Din set up a coalition consisting of Mosul, Akhlat, Mardin, Bidlis, and Arzan.[27] News of these military preparations compelled Saladin to proceed with necessary countermeasures. On the diplomatic side he kept sending urgent messages to the chief ministers in Baghdad, reiterating his request to be recognized as suzerain of Mosul. All he received in reply was the caliph's diploma for Amida. It is significant that his claims regarding

Mosul were ignored.[28] However, undeterred by Baghdad's negative attitude, Saladin started preparations for another campaign against his Zangid enemy in Mesopotamia.

Crusader attack in the Red Sea

It was in that very period—January/February 1183—that the Muslim world was stunned by a daring Crusader attack against what had been thought the absolutely secure zone of the Red Sea and Hejaz. The man who had conceived that plan was the notorious Reginald of Châtillon, master of Kerak and Shaubak. Having obstructed the overland communications between Egypt and Syria, he decided to hit another sensitive spot by attacking the Red Sea traffic and hoping also to reach the heart of the Muslim world, namely Mecca. As early as summer 1181, Reginald carried out a raid aiming at Taima, situated on the important caravan trail leading to Mecca. Although frustrated on that occasion, Saladin left him unmolested long enough to conceive another predatory expedition against the Muslims. Saladin's Mesopotamian involvement provided a convenient opportunity; January 1183 was chosen as the time for the attack and Mecca as its target. The initial stages of this backdoor operation were quite successful. The Crusaders launched a flotilla near Ailah, leaving two ships there to besiege that fortress, and sailing with the remaining ones southwards, they destroyed at least sixteen Muslim ships and captured two others. However, in planning their operation, these twelfth-century precursors of the Portuguese overlooked two important factors about Egyptian naval organization. First, at the time of their attack, the Egyptian warships were not absent on cruises but lay at anchor in their winter bases. And second, there existed a special fleet whose purpose was the security of the country. As soon as news about the Crusader advance reached Cairo, special ships under the command of Husam al-Din Lulu were rushed to the trouble spot. They destroyed the two ships off Ailah and then engaged the main Christian flotilla off Aidhab. The Muslims carried out their attack with deadly effectiveness. They pursued, boarded, and destroyed all the Christian ships, one after another.

The Christian crews and soldiers managed to reach the shore only to be rounded up by Muslim pursuers.[29] Reginald escaped, but most of his men were killed on the spot. One hundred seventy others were captured and taken to the capital where Saladin specifically instructed that all be paraded in the major Egyptian cities and then decapitated.[30]

Reginald's surprise attack sent a thrill of consternation and horror around the Muslim world, but its rapid defeat by the Ayyubid forces from Egypt did as much as any other single event to increase Saladin's reputation as the defender of Islam against the Infidels.[31] But historical perspective makes it apparent that Saladin was to blame for allowing this dramatic incident to occur at all. To begin with, Saladin's pressure against Aleppo in 1174–76 had caused Reginald's release from Muslim captivity, from which he emerged to command the strategic Transjordanian territory. Second, Saladin's failure to suppress, or at least contain, Reginald's harassing tactics had allowed that arrogant *Raubritter* to undertake the deep naval thrust in the Red Sea. Third, it was Saladin's departure into distant north Mesopotamia which provided a convenient opportunity for the daring Crusader raid.

The furious Egyptian counterattack averted a major disaster on this occasion, but Saladin could not let it happen again. He was too concerned about the Red Sea commerce, always an important source of Egyptian revenue. Consequently, following the Christian naval raid, Saladin declared the Red Sea closed to non-Muslims.[32] Unfortunately in the long run this precautionary security measure produced adverse economic effects, because it eliminated Jewish and Coptic India merchants and their capital from direct participation in the Egyptian transit trade. As for immediate military measures, Saladin was too much obsessed by his rivalry with the Zangids to retaliate against the master of Kerak and Shaubak.

Saladin takes Amida and Aleppo

By the spring of 1183, Saladin's persistent military pressure in the north paid rich dividends. At his very approach the army of the Mosul alliance quickly dispersed.[33] Unopposed he moved north, without even waiting for the arrival of most of his contingents, to lay siege to the all-but-impregnable fortress of Amida in Diyar Bakr. Although the place was protected by a double belt of massive walls, iron gates, and a natural moat formed by the crescent bend of the Tigris, Saladin succeeded in capturing it on 6 May 1183 after three weeks of fighting.[34] This outstanding military feat, demonstrating the penetrating power of his assault troops and siege machines, further increased Saladin's reputation as a dynamic and irresistible conqueror.

Saladin's fame, as well as his undeniable expansionist tendencies, must have caused some misgivings at the court of Caliph al-Nasir. Nor were Saladin's impatient dispatches to Baghdad following the capture of Amida likely to allay these apprehensions. Why was the patent for Mosul still denied? This alone stood in the way of the union of Islam and the recovery of Jerusalem. Let the Commander of the Faithful compare the conduct of his clients and judge which of them had most faithfully served the cause of Islam. If Saladin insists on the inclusion of Mesopotamia and Mosul in his dominions, it is because "this little Jazirah [i.e., Mesopotamia] is the lever which will set in motion the great Jazirah [i.e., the whole Arab east]; set in its place in the chain of alliances, the whole armed might of Islam will be coordinated to engage the forces of unbelief." [35]

His difficulties with Baghdad notwithstanding, Saladin rode high in the wake of his impressive victory at Amida. The Artuqid princes of Maiyafariqin and Mardin abandoned the Zangid cause and joined the Ayyubid forces.[36] With his grip over the Euphrates provinces sufficiently secured, Saladin decided that the time was ripe for an outright action against Aleppo, and so, after capturing Tall Khalid and Aintab,[37] he descended south to lay siege on 21 May 1183 to the focal point of Nuriyah and Zangid opposition in Syria.[38] Once again the people of Aleppo refused to open their gates and in the course of fighting Saladin lost a brother, Taj al-Muluk Buri.[39] However, the new lord, Imad al-Din, proved amenable to a diplomatic arrangement. Following a series of secret negotiations, in which Izz al-Din Jurdiq had played an instrumental role,[40] an agreement was reached: Imad al-Din would surrender Aleppo to Saladin in exchange for his former possession of Sinjar and such other places in the Jazirah as al-Khabur, Nisibin, Raqqa and Saruj. In addition, Imad al-Din pledged to cooperate in the war against the Crusaders.[41]

At last on 11 June 1183 Saladin's yellow banners were hoisted on the citadel of Aleppo, while its last Zangid ruler headed for his eastern provinces. "We received dinars in exchange for dirhams," commented Chancellor al-Isfahani on the consummated agreement.[42] The finishing touch occurred on 22 June with the surrender of the fortress of Harim.[43] All Muslim Syria belonged now to Saladin.

The 1183–84 campaign against the Crusaders

A year earlier Saladin had suspended his offensive against the Crusaders because of Aleppo. In the winter of 1182 his insistence on acquiring either Aleppo or Mosul had ultimately deadlocked the negotiations. Now this objective was attained, his strategic position with regard to the Crusaders left little to be desired. From Egypt in the south to the Taurus Mountains in the north, the anemic Christian establishments faced lands united under the single command of the great Ayyubid sultan. With the addition of the Aleppo contingent and of various units from the Jazirah, the total size of Saladin's army amounted to 8,500 cavalry, numerous foot soldiers, Turkoman auxiliaries, and the over 4,000 strong reserve force of Egypt and her naval squadrons.[44] The navy continued operations aimed at blockading the Syrian coast. During a cruise in the spring of 1183, they captured a big transport whose 375 passengers consisted of knights with their armor and merchants with pockets full of money. That same year, the fleet intercepted yet another transport on its way to Acre with a cargo of lumber and a team of shipwrights; the Egyptian dockyards managed to use both the material and the men to the detriment of the Crusaders.[45]

The lull in the war against the Christian enemy, interrupted only by Reginald's attack in the Red Sea and limited Crusader raids against Damascus and Darum in southern Palestine,[46] was bound to end. Saladin consumed part of the summer, however, with organization of his administration in Aleppo and her dependencies.[47] Also in order to protect his new acquisition from the Crusaders of Antioch, Saladin concluded in July 1183, a truce agreement with their leader, Count Bohemund.[48] Incidentally, it was Bohemund's wife Sibyl who had rendered the valuable intelligence services to the Ayyubid cause mentioned above.[49]

Finally on 13 August 1183, after announcing to the caliph in Baghdad his decision to resume the *jihad* now that the alleged obstacles had been removed,[50] Saladin set out taking along the regular troops of Aleppo and the Jazirah, as well as the Turkoman cavalry and a large force of volunteers and auxiliaries.[51] Left in nominal charge of Aleppo, as if to emphasize the supremacy of the Ayyubids over the Zangids, was his ten-year-old son, al-Zahir.[52]

After a brief stay in Damascus (24 August–17 September 1183) Saladin assumed personal command over his concentrated army.[53] On 29 September he crossed the river Jordan, ravaged the country near Baisan, and sacked and burnt the town itself.[54] After a few more forays and skirmishes, he moved in the direction of Ain Jalut to meet the approaching Crusader army near al-Fulah.[55] Four years had elapsed since the disastrous Crusader losses sustained in the campaigns of 1179, so despite their internal disunity and debilitating intrigues, the Crusaders were able to field an army of 1,300 knights and over 15,000 well-armed infantry. In addition, their ranks were swelled by crowds of Italian merchants, Pisans, Lombards, Venetians, and Genoese, who had left their ships and hurried to join the army of the Cross. But even with all these enthusiastic if less than competent volunteers, Guy of Lusignan's Christian contingent was greatly inferior numerically to the army at Saladin's disposal.[56] And yet, in spite of his proclamations and acclaimed zeal for the holy struggle, Saladin failed to engage Guy's army in a battle. After facing the enemy for about a week, the sultan returned to Damascus on 13 October.[57] Thereafter he summoned al-Adil, his brother in charge of Egypt, to join him with Egyptian troops at Kerak which he attacked during November.[58] However, because of its elevated topographical setting, tremendously elaborated inner and outer defensive works, and Reginald's intrepid leadership, Kerak was virtually impregnable unless subjected to a long siege of attrition. An experienced leader of Saladin's caliber could not have been unaware of it. Predictably enough, after a few weeks of abortive operations, Saladin called off the siege, released his troops, and returned on 11 December 1183 to Damascus. His brother al-Adil, instead of returning to Egypt, was sent to take over Aleppo.[59]

Saladin launched a similar offensive in the summer of 1184. It had been preceded by a large-scale troop mobilization that spring. Egypt, for instance, had been ordered to furnish all available men, monies, weapons, and supplies.[60] Once all the contingents had collected, Saladin commanded the most powerful army that had yet operated in Syria, comprising the forces of Egypt, Damascus, Aleppo, the Jazirah and Sinjar, Hisn Kaifa, and Mardin.[61] But as in the preceding year, his new attack directed against Kerak in August 1184 ended in failure; Saladin dismissed the armies soon after a raiding expedition through Samaria and returned himself in the middle of September to Damascus.[62]

A question arises, of course, as to why Saladin's much-heralded war effort against the Crusaders really failed during the years of 1183–84. The ineffective offensive of 1183 could perhaps be attributed to the fatigue of the troops who had remained in the field for several months and had covered a territory from Amida in the north to Jordan in the south. But this argument could not apply in the spring of 1184. Was Saladin militarily incompetent? Or did he shun a major involvement with the Crusaders for some ulterior political motives? The latter alternative appears plausible in light of Saladin's earlier record. A decade before Saladin had shown little enthusiasm for Nur al-Din's efforts against Kerak and Shaubak, because the Ayyubid strategy of political and military build-up in Egypt dictated such restraint.[63] In 1183–84, when Egypt's safety called for eliminating the Frankish threat, when the strategic Red Sea zone and Mecca had experienced a shocking attack by the master of Kerak and Shaubak, Saladin had still failed to end the outrageous impunity of the Crusaders. One can conclude, therefore, that Saladin's campaigns of a few weeks were only sham offensives serving to reinforce his image as leader of the holy war. Actually, the Ayyubid sultan continued to focus on his rivalry with the Zangid ruler of Mosul.

Political preparations for a showdown with Mosul

Deteriorating conditions in Izz al-Din's domain seemed to invite outside intervention. In the winter of 1183–84 a bloodless coup d'etat in Mosul overthrew Qaymaz, the major domo.[64] But the men who succeeded him alienated various feudal lords, who began to secede openly or to establish clandestine relations with Saladin. The Zangid state became paralyzed by internal dissension, disunity, and secession. Izz al-Din, rightly suspecting Saladin sympathized with the dissidents, appealed to the caliph to exert a restraining influence on the Ayyubid sultan.[65] The caliph obliged—not without seizing Daquqa, a town under Mosul's jurisdiction [66]—by dispatching toward the end of February 1184, another embassy to Saladin.[67] Despite these envoys' urgent arguments, Saladin remained adamant in his support of the seceders. In fact, some of his exchanges with the chief mediator, the prestigious Sheikh al-Shuyukh Sadr al-Din, became angry threats implying far-reaching political and military consequences. In one instance when Sadr al-Din reiterated the basic demand that Saladin leave to Izz al-Din what duly belonged to him, or else "Pahlavan [the Saljuqid atabeg of Azerbaijan] and other Persian Princes will ally to march against you," Saladin replied ominously, "I'll march against you and once I am done with you I will move against Pahlavan." [68]

Because of Saladin's intransigence neither these negotiations nor similar ones, conducted in November of 1184, prevented further intensification of political and military tension in northern Mesopotamia.[69] In the spring of 1185, hearing that Izz al-Din and an army of 3,000 horsemen sent by Pahlavan menaced the master of Irbil, one of his Mesopotamian proteges, Saladin suspended his war against the Crusaders in order to launch one more expedition against Mosul.[70] To achieve security in the south, Saladin hastily concluded in early 1185 yet another truce with the Crusaders.[71]

Misgivings in Cairo about Saladin's attitude towards Egypt

Saladin's persistent commitment of military power and economic resources against Mosul provoked apprehensive concern in Cairo. Some of the people even protested directly to the sultan. During his latest stay in Damascus Saladin received a letter from Cairo, written by Zayn al-Din ibn Naja, the same theologian who had once conspired with Shirkuh against the Fatimids and later had proved so instrumental in the crushing of the pro-Ismaili plot of 1174.[72] His letter, couched in subtle oratorical terms, in essence complained about Saladin's protracted absence from Cairo;[73] the letter indicated that its author, a seasoned political observer, entertained doubts concerning the sincerity of Saladin's commitment to Egypt. Prior to his involvement in Syria, the Ayyubid sultan had concentrated on reinvigorating the political, military, and economic structure of Egypt, but now the focus of his political and military concern had plainly shifted to Syria. Saladin had succeeded in Syria thanks to crucial military and economic contributions from the reinvigorated Egypt, but by those very successes Egypt was slowly being relegated to the status of a colonial base, its resources dissipated by Ayyubid expansionist policies not always compatible with its basic interests. Zayn al-Din may well have feared the consequences such an exploitive policy would have on progress achieved in Egypt during the first decade of Saladin's administration.

Deterioration of the situation in Egypt

Several events in Egypt in 1184 appeared to warrant a criticism of Saladin's policy. Egypt's agricultural production was hit by a catastrophic flood of the Nile, the Judham Bedouins staged a revolt in the Eastern province, troops stationed in Egypt were afflicted by an outbreak of the plague,[74] and the mints of Egypt were having difficulty maintaining the regular high standard of their gold coins.[75] Yet Saladin insisted that all of Egypt's army and resources must be placed at his disposal in Syria. As noted above, the 1184 campaigns against the Crusaders did not further secure Egypt's eastern frontier. With the bulk of the Egyptian army in Damascus, there was much restive agitation in Cairo, Fustat, and Giza due to fear of Frankish attack.[76] In fact, news of a Crusader advance towards Fakus caused the inhabitants of Bilbais to evacuate their town in one single night, 18 September 1184.[77] Nor were their apprehensions unfounded. In the absence of the Egyptian army, which did not return until 30 November 1184, the Crusaders carried out a successful raid on the unlucky Bilbais.[78]

Gross extortionist practices of the customs officials toward foreign travelers, recorded as early as 1183, rapid changes in the high-level bureaucratic structure toward the end of 1184, and in June 1185 sailor riots in Alexandria—all may have signalled a social malaise following Saladin's final departure from Egypt.[79] Probably related to these developments was the decision in the fall of 1184 to chain up the imprisoned descendants and relatives of the last Fatimid caliph.[80]

But Zayn al-Din's plea on behalf of Egypt achieved nothing. Saladin's answer, though no less elegant and elaborate, reproached the religious official for transgressing his official authority. Otherwise most of Saladin's letter was filled with hyperbolic superlatives extolling the glory of the Syrian capital and leaving no doubt as to the real focus of his sentiments and political concern.[81]

"Egypt is like a whore. . . ."

A more articulate and sustained plea on Egypt's behalf was voiced by al-Qadi al-Fadil.[82] His attitude was the more significant because of his otherwise harmonious relationship with Saladin. Until then, this notable politician had remained absolutely committed to Saladin's regime, seeing in it the best guarantee of Egypt's political, economic, and social renaissance. Saladin, for his part, not only had been appreciative of al-Qadi al-Fadil's counsels and decisive constructive interventions, but had shown complete faith in the latter by entrusting him with the key administration of Egypt. If despite feelings of mutual respect, trust, and personal admiration al-Qadi al-Fadil found it necessary to criticize in his correspondence with Damascus, he did so out of growing concern about Egypt's role in Saladin's expansionist policy.

Not that Saladin had ever concealed his feelings about the issue. It had become obvious that he had never ceased to regard Syria as his fatherland and that the focus of his ambitious political career was to rule over Syria. Egypt was but a stepping stone toward his goals in Syria. In a letter to al-Qadi al-Fadil, Saladin likened the Egyptian phase of his career to an affair with a whore—"a whore [Egypt] who in vain had tried to part me from my faithful wife [Syria]." [83]

Such a denigrating reference to Egypt by the leader who had depended so much on its resources and support during his spectacular rise to power shocked and scandalized al-Qadi al-Fadil: "How could Saladin insult Egypt with such a word?" he wrote with deep indignation. "When the Infidels were threatening him with destruction it was Egypt which supplied him with aid." [84] Al-Qadi al-Fadil also deplored the change in Saladin's immediate entourage. "It pains me greatly that in spite of Egypt's will the High Command has become a Syrian Command!" [85]

Nor were these messages restricted solely to passive complaints. Saladin was warned not to demand too much because of Egypt's present economic difficulties. In comparison with the sufferings of Egypt, al-Qadi al-Fadil insisted, "those of Damascus are like a drop of water in the sea." [86] Furthermore, in at least one letter, al-Qadi al-Fadil served notice that any direct hostile move against Egypt might precipitate a crisis with the Ayyubid overlord. "If he [Saladin] throws one arrow against her [Egypt], I would raise my hand high enough [to repel it]." [87]

Whether for ethical and ideological reasons, or out of concern for Egyptian interests, al-Qadi al-Fadil did not condone Saladin's war against distant Mosul. Pleading with the sultan to stop fighting other Muslim rulers, the critical counselor went so far as to invoke divine intervention against the misuse of Ayyubid warriors: "May Allah wean the swords [of Saladin] from sucking the blood of other Muslims. . . ." [88]

Second campaign against Mosul and conclusion of the Zangid war

As it happened, neither Allah nor al-Qadi al-Fadil kept Saladin from his aggressive military policy against Muslims, for by spring 1185 he was again marching towards Mosul. Indeed, that final campaign against Izz al-Din revealed Saladin's aspiration to succeed Nur al-Din and establish the descendants of Ayyub as sole beneficiaries of the Zangid legacy.

The campaign opening was marred by serious trouble with Gökböri, the lord of Harran and Edessa, who had consistently prodded Saladin to reach after Mosul. He had even promised to contribute 50,000 dinars to the expedition costs. But when Saladin arrived in Harran in May 1185, he found these monies were unavailable, so he ordered Gökböri's immediate arrest. Rumor had it that Gökböri had swung over to Mosul, causing some of Saladin's associates to advise executing the allegedly disloyal prince. Saladin limited himself, however, to confiscating Harran and Edessa and allowing Gökböri to vindicate himself by continued service for the Ayyubid cause.[89]

This leniency produced immediate dividends. Saladin's army was joined by various dissident princes and defectors from Izz al-Din's state[90]—an interesting development considering that Izz al-Din had made some progress in setting up a defensive alliance with other eastern princes.[91] On the diplomatic front, the Ayyubid propaganda bureau dispatched a long letter to Baghdad, which accused Izz al-Din of beginning the *khutbah* invocations with Tughril, the Saljuqid sultan of Iraq and Persia, as well as striking coins in the name of that bitter enemy of the caliph, and of being in collusion with the Crusaders—this last a fairly hypocritical allegation considering Saladin was hardly inflexible or uncompromising toward the Christian foes. The letter further insisted that Saladin had not invaded to increase his kingdom but to force Izz al-Din's submission to the caliphate, as well as to protect those who were suffering from the expansionist arrogance of the master of Mosul.[92]

On 9 June 1185, when Saladin's expeditionary army reached Mosul, its master once again refused to surrender. The oppressive summer heat ruled out any extensive siege operations and forced Saladin to consider some drastic measures. One possibility he entertained was to divert the course of the Tigris, forcing Mosul to submit by cutting off their main water supply.[93] However, even before this ambitious plan was decided upon, Saladin's attention had been diverted by a new complication arising from the death of the prince of Akhlat in Armenia. Pahlavan, the Saljuqid atabeg of Azerbaijan, had set out to lay his hands on Akhlat,[94] so Saladin had to leave a part of his forces in front of Mosul and on 30 July 1185 led the rest of his army northwards. Spearheading his advance were Nasir al-Din Muhammad ibn

Shirkuh and the veteran diplomat, Isa al-Hakkari. Whether Saladin did this to protect his northern flank, to control the important strategic area of Lake Van, or perhaps through some atavistic leaning towards the lands of his Kurdish ancestors, it constituted the northernmost extension of the Sultan's expansionist drive. It is quite unlikely that any Egyptian politicians who had once supported the ambitious commander's bid for power in Cairo could have imagined that a little over one decade later the resources of Egypt would be spent on a militaristic adventure in distant Armenia.

Contrary to his hopes, Saladin was unable to assert control over Akhlat because the people in charge preferred to submit to Pahlavan.[95] Frustrated in that sector, Saladin made up for it by capturing Maiyafariqin in August 1185 after a brief siege.[96] By November Saladin again stood before the walls of Mosul, determined to continue the siege in winter.

With no effective military assistance from the Saljuqid allies in sight, and faced with Saladin's grim determination to prosecute the war irrespective of costs or diplomatic reverberations, Izz al-Din once again tried to negotiate. He even sent out his wife, a daughter of the great Nur al-Din, accompanied by other Zangid princesses, to plead with the great Saladin. But their intercession failed to move the Ayyubid warlord. All Saladin would accept was the mediation of Imad al-Din, the brother of Izz al-Din and a former ally of Saladin.[97]

Any hopes Saladin had of personally entering Mosul were denied to him by fate. That same winter of 1185, he fell seriously ill and on 25 December he left Mosul for Harran, ordering the withdrawal of his troops to Nisibin. With his health steadily deteriorating, he turned his attention towards working out political arrangements which in the event of his death would preserve all the acquired territories for descendants of Ayyub.[98]

His anxiety was not unwarranted. While clever diplomatic maneuvers and successful military campaigns had carried him to the point of a final victory over the Zangid opposition, the record of his achievements against the Crusaders—a very important gauge of political acceptability in twelfth century Syria and Egypt—could hardly compare with the glorious accomplishments of Zangi and Nur al-Din. Beginning with the capture of Edessa in 1144 and culminating twenty years later in the march to Egypt, the Zangid heroes had led Islam to a position of such strategic superiority that total destruction of the Crusader kingdom had finally become a realistic possibility. But following the illusory extension of Nur al-Din's authority over Egypt, and especially after his death in 1174, the struggle against the Crusaders lost much of its earlier impetus. Indeed, during the entire decade following Nur al-Din's death, the Latin Kingdom of Jerusalem —whose military resiliency had been crippled by internal conflicts and dissensions—had hardly lost an inch of territory to Islam.

Responsibility for this rested mainly with Saladin. Driven by his obsession to win political supremacy for the Ayyubid family he had committed all available military and economic resources to the task of suppressing internal opposition in the Islamic camp. A few successes in the rare confrontations with the Crusaders—grossly exaggerated by Saladin's propagandists—could fool or even excite the populace but not his political and military peers. Indeed, the overly long and bloody conflict in the Muslim camp had been caused, not by Saladin's ambition to build a united front against the Crusaders, but by his opponents' realistic refusal to recognize his claims for other than they were: an adventurous and unscrupulous policy of personal and territorial aggrandizement. In view of Saladin's stern determination, unquestionable war experience, and military strength, various weak leaders and inept princes were left little choice of action; they could either join the dynamic Ayyubid contender in the hope of being duly rewarded, or to offer resistance and face the prospect of quick and violent extermination.

The eleven years following the acquisition of Damascus in 1174 saw Saladin annex all of Muslim Syria. However, while his political dexterity and military might undeniably kept his Syro-Egyptian dominions together, they never achieved an ideological unity. This absence of any cohesive principle, of a higher moral or ideological order, constituted a serious weakness in the nascent Ayyubid state, should it be deprived of Saladin's authoritative leadership.

The vulnerable character of the Ayyubid establishment was plainly revealed during Saladin's serious illness. His first cousin and brother-in-law, Nasir al-Din Muhammad ibn Shirkuh, who had heretofore loyally assisted Saladin in his rise to power in Syria, and who had been promised Mosul as a prize for faithful services, began to insist on his right to take over the legacy of the sultan. His claims were not limited to rhetoric. Since al-Adil had rushed from Aleppo to assist his ailing brother in Harran, Nasir al-Din moved south to Syria to hatch a conspiracy that would promote his seizing power. In Aleppo he secured the cooperation of a group of the city militia (*ahdath*) and, after entering his feudal center of Homs, he established contact with some people in Damascus, obtaining their promise to deliver the capital to him in the event of Saladin's death.[99]

These circumstances made prompt termination of the conflict with Izz al-Din a dire necessity. Toward the end of February 1186, Saladin —his serious condition notwithstanding—received Baha al-Din ibn Shaddad, the envoy of Mosul, to settle the peace terms. Disregarding his early pledge to Shirkuh's son, Saladin offered to recognize the rights of Izz al-Din and even restored to him the small district of Baina-n-Nahrain, between Nisibin and the Tigris. In return the Zangid leader promised to substitute Saladin's name in the *khutbah* invocations and in the coin inscriptions for that of the Saljuqid sultan —acts tantamount to official acknowledgement of Ayyubid suzerainty. The peace formula proved acceptable to both sides, and so on 3 March 1186 the treaty-signing allied the whole of northern Mesopotamia and part of Kurdistan with Saladin's forces and placed the army of Mosul at the disposal of the Ayyubid sultan.[100]

By then Saladin's health had sufficiently improved to permit him the enjoyment of these events. A different fate befell his cousin Nasir al-Din Muhammad. Unsuccessful in his expectations concerning Mosul, as well as in his recent bid for power in Syria, the son of Shirkuh was found dead in the morning of 4 March 1186.[101] Most sources attribute his death to overindulgence in wine, "like father, like son"—except that certain Arab chroniclers also raised the possibility that Saladin had ordered him poisoned.[102]

Upon receiving the news of Nasir al-Din's sudden death, Saladin publicly expressed his grief and sorrow and hastened to confirm Asad al-Din Shirkuh, the twelve-year-old son of the deceased, as the new master of Homs and its dependencies. The great sultan even made a personal trip to Homs to supervise distribution of Nasir al-Din's rich legacy. On that occasion he met Asad al-Din Shirkuh and was reported greatly impressed by his sagacity. When asked about how far he had gone in learning the Quran, the precocious boy is said to have replied: "As far as the place where it is written, '*As to those who swallow up the goods of orphans unjustly, verily they shall swallow down fire into their bellies and burn at the blaze.*'"[103] [Lane-Poole's italics.]

Finally, on 23 May 1186, Saladin returned to Damascus.[104] Although by then his authority extended over vast regions spreading from Egypt to Kurdistan, the incident with Nasir al-Din ibn Shirkuh cast a shadow on the solidity of the nascent Ayyubid establishment. Nor was it the only instance of rebellious tendencies within the ruling elite. There are indications that al-Qadi al-Fadil himself—frustrated by the futility of the military campaign against Mosul—had engaged in secret peace negotiations with Izz al-Din behind Saladin's back.[105] Furthermore, when later that summer of 1186 Saladin decided to switch important commands by assigning al-Adil to Egypt in place of Taqi al-Din Umar, his impetuous nephew became so infuriated that he seriously contemplated defying the sultan's authority by rallying other malcontents in Egypt and leaving for North Africa where his own feudal contingent had continued their rewarding military forays. Unlike the tension between Nur al-Din and Saladin in the early 1170s, Taqi al-Din did not remain obstinate. Relinquishing his arrogant stance and turning away from his rebellious supporters, he returned to Damascus to place his military talents at the sultan's disposal.[106]

In spite of this undeniable triumph over several Moslem rivals, Saladin could hardly indulge in political and military complacency. The forceful manner in which he had realized his political ambitions and the volatile disposition of his relatives, allies, and recently subjugated foes were not conducive to the future stability of his regime. One practical way of increasing his prestige and promoting the ideological cohesion of his forces would be by committing all his manpower and resources to a cause attractive to Muslim leaders and masses alike. This cause, of course, was the *jihad* or holy war aimed at destroying the moribund kingdom of the Crusaders. A total victory over the Christian enemy would bring tremendous advantages; strategically, it would eliminate a foreign and hostile body embedded in the middle of Saladin's dominions; and a feat of such magnitude would certainly dispel any skepticism concerning his widely publicized claims of wholehearted dedication to the cause of Islam.

10 The showdown with the Crusaders

"As for the claim of the Caliph that I've conquered Jerusalem with his army and under his banners—where were his banners and his army at the time? By God! I conquered Jerusalem with my own troops and under my own banners!"— Saladin to Caliph al-Nasir

Traditional treatment of Saladin's career is open to question

To modern western readers Saladin is best known for his military battles with the Crusaders between 1187 and 1192. This is understandable in view of the dramatic character of that struggle and the fact that it involved formidable naval and land forces and prominent leaders from Europe. The interest aroused by that brief climactic phase in Saladin's career is reflected in the arrangement of Lane-Poole's biography. The initial section of his book, entitled "Egypt" and covering the period from Saladin's birth to Nur al-Din's death (1138–74), is surveyed in sixty-three pages of rather diluted narrative. The second part, called "Empire" and dealing with the years of 1174–86, requires sixty-five pages. But to the third part, "The Holy War," covering 1187 to the signing of the peace agreement in 1192, Lane-Poole allocated one hundred sixty pages.

Does this traditional focus on Saladin's showdown with the Crusaders enable one to understand the real significance of his personality and the effects of his ambitions and accomplishments in history? According to Lane-Poole, "The Holy War had long been a fixed resolve with Saladin," so that following a series of provocations on the part of the notorious master of Kerak and Shaubak, the sultan "resolved to try no more half-measures, but to wage a war of extermination of the whole Christian kingdom." [1]

From the viewpoint of the history of the Crusades, Saladin's career is highly relevant to the story of European militaristic and economic penetration of the Near East during the Middle Ages. And that has been the main reason Saladin's personality and achievements have produced such an impact on the imagination of European writers from the Middle Ages down to modern times.

However, despite the dramatic and seemingly romantic nature of the "European" aspect of Saladin's career, both the Crusaders and, above all, Saladin himself belong integrally to Near Eastern history.

The history of the Crusades did not begin or end with Saladin, nor was the range of his historical accomplishments limited to his involvement with the Crusaders.

The validity of viewing Saladin's career solely in terms of his struggle with the Crusaders has been challenged by H. A. R. Gibb. In his article, "The Achievement of Saladin," Gibb proposed a new thesis concerning the ideological motivations and, consequently, the real historical role of the Ayyubid sultan.

The immediate task to which he found himself called was to drive the Franks out of Palestine and Syria. This was the part that his contemporaries saw, and that later generations assumed to have been his whole purpose. It is natural, when a man accomplishes some great work, to imagine that this was what he had set as his goal. In reality, it is more often the case that what a man achieves is only a part of what he sets out to achieve; and perhaps it is only because his eyes are fixed on some more distant goal that he succeeds in doing as much as he does.

This was, in my view eminently true of Saladin. His wider design was one which only a man of unbounded ambition or of unbounded simplicity would have entertained. In a certain sense, Saladin was both, but his ambition arose out of the simplicity of his character and the directness of his vision. He saw clearly that the weakness of the Muslim body politic, which had permitted the establishment and continued to permit the survival of the crusading states, was the result of political demoralization. It was against this that he revolted. There was only one way to end it: to restore and revive the political fabric of Islam as a single united empire, not under his own rule, but by restoring the rule of the revealed law, under the direction of the Abbasid Caliphate. The theory of the Caliph's disposal of provinces by diploma, to the other princes of the time a convenient fiction, was to him a positive and necessary reality. He saw himself as simply the adjutant and commander of the armies of the Abbasids, as he had become for a brief time the wazir and commander of the armies of the Fatimid Caliphs. That he was called Sultan was simply the title he had inherited as wazir of the Fatimids; it had nothing to do with the theory of claims of the Seljuk Sultanate, and it never appears in his protocol or on his coins. Imad al-Din relates an incident during the siege of Acre, which is particularly instructive because it is one of the occasions on which the secretary reproaches Saladin for his simplicity. At the request of an envoy from the Caliphate, he had consented to transfer the region of Shahrazur in Kurdistan to the Caliph's possession; when faced with the anger and scorn of his amirs at his decision, he replied: "The Caliph is the lord of mankind and the repository of the True Faith; if he were to join us here I should give him all these lands—so what of Shahrazur?" [2]

If one considers that the total range of Crusader activities, even at their most expansive phase, affected a very limited area of the Near East, and, on the other hand, if one realizes that Saladin's alleged ideals aimed at reviving the political fabric of Islam under the auspices of the caliphate, then Gibb's thesis dramatically upgrades the significance of the great sultan in Near Eastern history.

For my part, I am happy neither with focusing on Saladin's Crusader struggle nor with attributing to him lofty devotion to "the true faith," which I am afraid are not borne out by the whole factual record. Historical phenomena are not finally assessed by the ideals of human protagonists, but by the effects these ideals or their implementation produce on society. The old saying that "the road to hell is paved with good intentions" is a handy maxim in drawing up the balance sheet of historical figures.

With Saladin one cannot be too certain concerning his real intentions at any stage of his colorful career, one can only assess his actual activities and accomplishments.

Saladin's diplomatic arrangements with the Crusaders and the Byzantines

Although the conflict with Mosul was ended by 1186, Saladin showed no eagerness to prepare immediately for resumption of the Crusader war. His passivity may have been motivated by the fact that, even without his direct pressure, the Christian kingdom was moving toward self-destruction. The crowning of the unpopular Guy of Lusignan as King of Jerusalem, following the death of Baldwin IV in 1185 and Baldwin V in late summer 1186, resulted in a rebellious challenge from Count Raymund of Tripoli. The new king, advised by the master of the Templars, decided to correct this defiance by drastic military measures. But Raymund refused to be intimidated and to strengthen his own position requested assistance from Saladin. The Muslim sultan replied by sending him a number of troops and a promise of more.[3] By supplying fuel Saladin undoubtedly hoped to further the rapid disintegration of the Crusader kingdom, thus sparing himself the trouble of mobilizing troops and economic resources upon the expiration of his own truce.

At about that time Saladin concluded a formal treaty of alliance with the Christian Empire of Constantinople.[4] The policy of rapprochement between the Byzantines and Saladin, initiated by the last Comneni emperors, had been continued by their successors of the Angeli dynasty. Such a development was nothing new in the international politics of the eastern Mediterranean. Independent (Fatimids) and semi-independent (Tulunids and Ikhshidids) rulers of Islamic Egypt had engaged in diplomatic cooperation with Constantinople, even if such policy hurt both the interests of other Muslim leaders and the prestige of the Baghdad caliphate. In the last quarter of the twelfth century the Byzantines and the Ayyubids were drawn together by opposition to the same enemies. The Normans of Sicily were as dangerous to Egypt as to the Byzantines; the Saljuqids of Iconium had emerged from Myriokephalon as the strongest power in Asia Minor, capturing many Byzantine provinces and threatening Saladin's interests in the north; Cyprus, which had rebelled against Constantinople, was a possible adherent of the Crusaders; and finally, the Crusaders and their potential allies from Western Europe constituted a bloc as hostile to the Byzantines as to the Ayyubids.

There is no doubt that the last factor primarily induced Saladin to cooperate with Constantinople, though he may have been somewhat influenced by two Angeli princes, Alexius and Isaac, who stayed as guests at his court. Indeed, Alexius was still there when Isaac was raised to the Byzantine throne in September 1185.[5]

The first Greek embassy proposing a formal alliance had reached Saladin in the summer of 1185. However, the terms proved unacceptable to Saladin because Constantinople, besides arrogating to itself a suzerain status in respect of the Muslim warlord, claimed too many territorial concessions in Palestine, including Jerusalem and various maritime cities.[6]

Saladin proposed his own terms, rejecting the Byzantine claim to suzerainty, but offering to convert the existing Latin churches in the Holy Land to the Greek rite—a clever move, bound to promote pro-Ayyubid feelings among the Greek Christians in the Crusader kingdom. Saladin's counterproposals were favorably received by the Byzantines. With the Normans threatening the capital itself, Emperor Isaac II Angelus confirmed the revised version of the treaty and summoned his brother Alexius back from Saladin's court.[7]

Predictably, rumors of the Byzantine-Muslim alliance reached the Crusaders, so when Alexius Angelus was passing through Acre on his way to Constantinople, the Count of Tripoli seized and imprisoned him. Learning of that outrage, Isaac wrote to Saladin prodding him to attack the Crusaders in order to secure Alexius' release.[8] By then Saladin's relations with the Kingdom of Jerusalem had been brought to an explosive point of Reginald of Châtillon's blatant violation of the armistice. Early in 1187 Reginald attacked an important caravan passing between Cairo and Damascus, carried off considerable booty, and imprisoned its military escort. Breaking the truce was a serious matter, as even Reginald's friends realized. Saladin still tried negotiations to avert hostilities, but Reginald flatly refused to comply with the categorical requests of King Guy and ignored the Ayyubid ultimatum.[9] A showdown between the Muslim forces of the Ayyubids and the

Crusaders could not be avoided.[10] Saladin proclaimed a *jihad*, to which the Muslim population in the areas affected by Reginald's recurrent bloody provocations responded with enthusiasm.[11] In addition to planning an all-out war against the Christians, Saladin vowed to take personal vengeance on Reginald.[12]

War with the Crusaders and victory at Hattin

At the end of May 1187 Saladin's contingents completed their concentration. His cavalry alone reached an impressive total of 12,000 with possibly as many auxiliary troops and irregulars. Though they had come from different regions of his dominions—from Egypt and Syria, from al-Jazirah and Diyar Bakr, from Damascus, Aleppo, and Mosul—the warriors of the Ayyubid sultan were united by the idea of fighting the Frankish Infidels.[13] In spite of total mobilization of the fleet, however, the warships did not participate in the decisive expedition. Possibly the fiasco at Beirut caused Saladin to doubt the effectiveness of his fleet under real battle conditions. Or perhaps his decision was motivated by the knowledge that earlier in the spring the Byzantines had sent a fleet to attack Cyprus. Indeed, the Crusaders had interpreted the appearance of the Byzantine armada in Syrian waters as naval support for Saladin's offensive.[14] On Friday, 26 June 1187, Saladin set out for Palestine to start the momentous struggle [15] which was not terminated until five years later.

Aware of the all-out character of Saladin's new offensive, the Crusaders succeeded in collecting an army which numerically more or less equalled the Muslim force. The defeat of the Byzantine fleet off Cyprus by the Normans and the absence of the Egyptian navy allowed the Christian coastal fortresses to release all their fighting men for the main army. But they were internally disunited, they lacked confidence in Guy's leadership, and their tactics were greatly inferior to those of the experienced Ayyubid warlord. Although Raymund of Tripoli had insisted they should follow defensive tactics by using their castles, King Guy and some hawks in his entourage decided to march north to meet the Muslim army in open field. There they were outmaneuvered by Saladin, and after a few preliminary and costly skirmishes they had to accept battle under most unfavorable conditions on the plain of Hattin, overlooking the Lake of Tiberias. The Crusader army, exhausted by the summer heat and Muslim harassment, found access to the lake barred by fresh and confident contingents of Saladin.[16] There on 4 July 1187 occurred one of the most decisive military confrontations between the forces of Islam and the Latin Kingdom of Jerusalem. It was a battle which the Crusaders need not have fought at all and certainly should not have lost.[17] However, because of Saladin's superior tactics and especially because of renewed wrangling among the Christians on the eve of the battle, the Muslim forces won a smashing victory. It was Saladin's victory, it was Saladin's great day, from which he acquired the image of *jihad* leader *par excellence,* the Allah-inspired nemesis of the Frankish Infidels.

The emotions Saladin experienced during the battle were dramatically reported by his son al-Afdal:

"It was my first set battle," said al-Afdal, at that time but sixteen-years old, "and I was at my father's side. When the King of the Franks had retired to the hill, his knights made a gallant charge, and drove the Moslems back upon my Father. I watched him, and I saw his dismay; he changed color, tugged at his beard, and rushed forward, shouting 'Give the devil the lie!' So the Moslems fell upon the enemy, who retreated up the hill. When I saw the Franks flying and the Moslems pursuing, I cried in my glee, 'We have routed them!' But the Franks charged again and drove our men back once more to where my Father was. Again he urged them forward, and they drove the enemy up the hill. Again I shouted, 'We have routed them!' But Father turned to me and said: 'Hold thy peace! We have *not* beaten them so long as that tent stands there.' At that instant the royal tent was overturned. Then the Sultan dismounted, and bowed himself to the earth, giving thanks to God, with tears of joy." [18]

It was indeed the end. In one single day Saladin routed virtually all local Christian forces capable of defending the Crusader establishment in the Near East. Only a small group led by Raymund of Tripoli managed to escape annihilation. Other Crusader leaders not killed in the battle were taken prisoner, including King Guy himself. Knights fared better than the foot soldiers, not only in escaping the bloodiest carnage but in receiving better care as captives. No code of chivalry or hope of ransom protected the lowly born. For Reginald of Châtillon Saladin reserved a special treatment.

Saladin exacts bloody vengeance

As soon as Saladin's tent had been pitched on the battlefield, he had the prisoners brought before him. He made King Guy sit down near himself, with Reginald next to him. Seeing the Christian king burning with thirst, the sultan ordered a cooling drink served to the royal prisoner. Guy drank and passed the cup to the lord of Kerak. At this, Saladin ominously remarked to Guy: "It is you who served him water. I, certainly, gave no water to him." [19] Saladin had never shown mercy to traitors or perjurers, Muslim and Christian alike. Reginald, who for over a decade had harassed the borders of Egypt and Arabia, who had dared to launch an expedition against Mecca, and who had caused the outbreak of war, the sultan had sworn to slay personally. [20] The prisoners were taken outside—all except Reginald. Saladin then proffered him the adoption of Islam, but the proud knight refused. Thereupon Saladin drew his scimitar and felled the defenseless prisoner with a blow that split his shoulder wide open. A coup de grace was then administered by a guard in attendance. Seeing Reginald's body dragged out of the tent, King Guy believed his own turn was coming. But Saladin reassured him: "It is not the custom of kings to slay kings; but that man had transgressed all bounds, so what happened— happened." [21]

Saladin's thirst for blood, however, had not been quenched by killing Reginald. He next ordered the execution of all captive Templar and Hospitaler knights, offering a reward of fifty dinars for every one brought to headquarters. In no time 200 prospective victims were led to the place of execution. [22] As on a similar occasion in 1178, Saladin personally watched the slaughter, with rows of soldiers sitting in front of him. His immediate entourage consisted of divines, jurists, and members of Muslim mystical orders. They asked the sultan to let each of them kill a prisoner of his choice. When permission was granted, they drew their swords and joined in the killing, though not all proved up to the grim task. "There were some whose strength gave out, so they backed out and were excused; there were others who did not hit strong enough and were laughed at by the crowds and had to be replaced by others; but there were some who revealed their noble descent in administering their blows." [23]

Triumphant blitzkrieg and a strategic dilemma: Tyre or Jerusalem

So total and decisive was the victory at Hattin that Saladin followed it up immediately with a multipronged offensive against various Crusader cities and fortresses depleted of defenders. On 5 July he secured the capitulation of Tiberias, and on 9 July he received the surrender of Acre where, incidentally, he set free the Byzantine emperor's imprisoned brother.[24] After Acre the blitzkrieg gained such momentum that less than two months after Hattin all the major ports south of Tripoli, with the exception of Tyre and Ascalon, were in Muslim hands. In addition, virtually all the inland towns and castles south of Tiberias, except Shaubak and Kerak in Transjordan, capitulated. Only these two southern strongholds, and a few formidable castles in the north, such as Belvoir (Kaukab), Safad, and Belfort, managed to hold out.

It was to Tyre that Raymund of Tripoli had escaped from the battlefield of Hattin. And it was to Tyre that European reinforcements, led by the renowned Conrad of Montferrat, came following the fall of Acre. However, instead of attacking Tyre forthwith, Saladin marched south to Ascalon, the last Crusader outpost obstructing the direct coastal route between Egypt and Syria. This operation ended successfully on 5 September 1187 when Ascalon surrendered in exchange for the release of King Guy from captivity.[25]

Now Tyre, the last Crusader coastal fortress in that area, acquired great strategic significance. If it could repulse Saladin's troops, Tyre could become the rallying point for Crusader refugees and stragglers, military and civilian alike. Moreover, if it held out long enough, Tyre could serve as a beachhead for European reinforcements.

That chance Saladin provided himself. After the victory at Ascalon, he marched not against Tyre but against Jerusalem. This proved to be a strategic blunder which ultimately wiped out all the advantages achieved by the victory of Hattin. Experienced warlord as he was, Saladin must have realized the strategic implications of leaving Tyre alone. Certainly his troops, his miners, his naval contingents could have overpowered Tyre, animated as they were by an aggressive, dynamic mood. During his military career, Saladin had conquered many a difficult fortress, Ailah in 1171, Bait al-Ahzan in 1179, Amida in 1183, and all the coastal establishments captured that same summer of 1187.

On the other hand, Jerusalem, with but a handful of able-bodied defenders, completely cut off from both Crusader support and the coast itself and containing Greek inhabitants eager to shake off the Latin regime, presented neither a threat nor even a major military problem to Saladin. By then restoration of the holy city to Islam was merely a question of time, to be selected by the victorious sultan. And yet despite the strategic importance of Tyre, Saladin chose Jerusalem. What made him commit this grave strategic error? The answer seems to be that Saladin hoped to collect tremendous propaganda dividends from an easy occupation of the holy city.[26] He had already established his popularity as suppressor of the Shiite caliphate in Egypt; he had also been acclaimed as protector of the city of the Prophet. Now he could achieve a glory which in Islam's long and heroic history had been enjoyed only by Umar ibn al-Khattab, companion of Muhammad himself and chief architect of the seventh century Islamic ascendancy. And if some people were still skeptical about the real motivations behind his incessant campaigns, behind his staggering drive for power, behind his unrestricted investment of economic resources in military expenditure, their doubts must be dispelled by the reconquest of Jerusalem. Saladin's name had already been invoked in the *khutbah* all over Egypt, in North African regions, in Syria, in Jazirah, and in Mosul. Why should it not resound from the mosques of the liberated holy city? Ayyubid prestige would certainly be well served, even if failure to capture Tyre immediately risked inviting a new European invasion.

Recapture of Jerusalem: the crowning achievement of Saladin's career

Predictably enough, Saladin had no trouble in forcing the garrison of Jerusalem into surrender. On 2 October 1197 the yellow banners of the Ayyubid conqueror appeared on the walls of the holy city which after eighty-eight years was finally returned to the fold of Islam. With this achievement the great sultan reached the apex of his political and military career. News of the dramatic event, stressing Saladin's role, spread quickly over the Muslim and Christian worlds. Jubilant letters were sent by his chancery to the caliph of Baghdad, to various Muslim princes and notables,[27] as well as to the Byzantine emperor.[28] When word of Jerusalem's fall reached Western Europe, it produced shock and grief—and calls for revenge.

Official celebrations honoring the liberation and purification of Jerusalem took place on Friday, 9 October 1187. An immense congregation assembled to pray with Saladin in the sanctuary of al-Aqsa. The chief qadi of Aleppo, Muhyi al-Din ibn al-Zaki, preached the main sermon. He praised God for the triumph of the faith and the cleansing of his holy house; he declared the pure creed of the Quran, and pronounced the blessings upon the Prophet and the caliphs, in the prescribed form of the Sunni bidding-prayer. He invoked the name of the reigning caliph, al-Nasir li-Din Allah. Finally, concluding his peroration, he declared:

> And prolong, O Almighty God, the reign of thy servant, humbly reverent, for thy favor thankful, grateful for thy gifts, thy sharp sword and shining torch, the champion of thy faith and defender of thy holy land, the firmly resisting, the great al-Malik al-Nasir, the unifier of the true religion, the vanquisher of the worshippers of the Cross, Salah al-Dunya wa al-Din. Saladin, Sultan of Islam and of the Moslems, purifier of the holy temple,

Abu al-Muzaffar Yusuf, Son of Ayyub, reviver of the empire of the Commander of the Faithful. Grant, O God, that his empire may spread all over the earth, and that the angels may ever surround his standards, preserve him for the good of Islam; protect him for the profit of the Faith; and extend his dominion over the regions of the East and of the West. . . ." [29]

Saladin's calamitous failure at Tyre

Saladin's very belated action against Tyre proved disastrous. Only on 1 November 1187 did he dispatch an army against it. Twelve days later he arrived there to assume personal command.[30] One hundred nineteen days had elapsed since the battle of Hattin and fifty-six since the capture of Ascalon. During that crucial period the number of defenders in Tyre had been increased by refugees from all the places that had capitulated that summer. Conrad of Montferrat had worked intensively on strengthening fortifications, encouraging the defenders, and "directing them with superior ability." He had deepened and extended the moats till Tyre became "like a hand spread upon the sea, attached only by the wrist," an island approached by so narrow a spit that it would be easily defended by a small force, as well as covered by crossbows on the shielded Christian barges.[31] The Crusader garrison, knowing the momentous significance of the impending confrontation, was ready to resist or die.

The same was not true of Saladin's army. For nearly a month they had been celebrating their recapture of Jerusalem, proclaimed all over the Muslim world as the supreme and sacred objective of the *jihad*. And now, instead of being allowed to return home, covered with glory and rich in booty, they were being deployed against a spirited and tenacious Frankish garrison, well sheltered behind the strong defensive works of Tyre.

This imbalance in morale was the main reason that Saladin could neither intimidate nor overrun the Crusaders of Conrad of Montferrat. Saladin's attack against Tyre degenerated into a protracted siege in which the Egyptian fleet assumed an important function. Its duty was to blockade the port and deprive the defenders of relief by sea.[32] In December 1187 rain and snow converted the besiegers' camp into a sea of mud, and damp and cold bred sickness among the soldiers and horses. Exhausted by the strain of the siege some of Saladin's commanders voiced their pessimism regarding the outcome.[33]

To a large extent their doubts were caused by economic factors. Operating within the strictly defined feudal structure of military obligations and rights to regular compensation, Saladin's warriors had expected to return home, once their regular periodic campaign service was over, to collect the proceeds of their fiefs. One way of securing their extended participation in the campaign, beyond the prescribed duration, would be direct cash compensation from the coffers of the sultan. Unfortunately Saladin did not possess adequate monies. The long years of heavy military expenditure and of gold drain caused by extensive purchases of war material from Europeans had resulted in an acute cash crisis which his victories in Syria and Mesopotamia failed to alleviate.

Had Saladin been able to inspire his troops, had he been able to sustain the original enthusiasm for war which Reginald's outrageous provocations had generated and which the victories of Hattin, Acre, and Jerusalem later magnified, then the besieging generals and soldiers might have endured the extraordinary sacrifices required for the continuation of the siege. But Saladin was hardly the man to demand of his followers blind devotion to the holy war. After all, whatever his popular image among the Muslim masses, Saladin's personal and political conduct hardly served as an inspiring example of self-denial for the *jihad*.

Toward the very end of 1187, when Saladin experienced difficulties in maintaining discipline in his army, the Egyptian fleet suffered a humiliating setback. The Muslim ships blockading Tyre let themselves be taken by surprise—they were boarded during the night of 30 December by Christian raiders who succeeded in capturing five ships, together with their crews and the two top men in command. Saladin immediately ordered the remaining five ships to lift the blockade and proceed to their nearest base in Beirut. When the port of Tyre was thus opened, some Christian galleys, hitherto bottled up in the harbor, pursued the withdrawing Egyptian ships, whose crews had neither the courage to resist nor determination to bring the ships safely to Beirut. They simply abandoned the ships, jumping overboard and trying to save themselves by swimming ashore.[34]

This naval humiliation increased Saladin's trouble with his land forces. In spite of support from old associates such as Isa al-Hakkari and Izz al-Din Jurdiq, the sultan found it impossible to control the defeatist feelings pervading his camp. On 1 January 1188, he ordered a general retreat, dejectedly leaving all heavy equipment and armament behind.[35]

Lane-Poole rightly regards the ignominious retreat from Tyre as the "turning-point in Saladin's career of victory."[36] He also states that:

> Whatever the difficulties of the siege, *Delenda est Tyrus* should have been his immutable resolve. He should have built a new fleet, destroyed the Tyrian galleys, filled the moats, breached the walls, if he lost half his army in so doing. The only answer is that Saladin knew his men, and felt that he could not count upon their endurance. But even this does not explain his neglect to blockade the city by sea and land, to keep off reinforcements, and to starve its crowded population. However we look at it, Saladin's measures against Tyre appear neither soldierly nor statesmanlike. Tyre became the rallying point from which the Crusaders recovered part of their lost power and prestige along the coast of Palestine; and had this one city not held out, it is a question whether the Third Crusade would ever have been heard of at Acre.[37]

To this accurate assessment of Saladin's failure at Tyre one may add that not only did the sultan know his men, but his men, especially various military commanders, some of them his former rivals, were quite familiar with his previous record. They had recognized Saladin's consistent moves to strengthen and expand his own power, and they were aware of his political ambitions for the Ayyubid family. The disastrous siege of Tyre demonstrated that even the glorious reconquest of Jerusalem had not dispelled their doubts regarding Saladin's devotion to the holy war.

Serious deterioration of relations with Caliph al-Nasir

The caliph of Baghdad also expressed skepticism about Saladin's political ideals during the difficult siege of Tyre. Unlike other congratulatory messages Saladin received from different quarters of the Muslim world, as well as from Constantinople, al-Nasir's letter contained nothing but sarcastic, insinuative questions and reproaches. Why had Saladin granted asylum to several political refugees from Baghdad? How dared he assume the honorific title of al-Nasir which was the official name of the Abbasid suzerain? And finally: "As to your jubilation over the capture of Jerusalem—had she not been conquered by the troops of the Caliph, under the banners of the Caliph?" [38]

Obviously the caliph had become deeply troubled by Saladin's staggering successes, especially the extension of his authority to northern Mesopotamia. There were people in Baghdad who accused Saladin of planning to finish off the Abbasids as he had the Fatimids.[39] The caliph's message was a warning; it was also an attempt to undermine the prestige of the sultan by refusing to recognize the mandate Saladin claimed destiny had entrusted to him to wage the holy war. The caliph's letter greatly shocked Saladin, who had been expecting expressions of thanks for his great accomplishments. He was not repentant. In talking to the envoy from Baghdad he rejected one after another of the caliph's points.

The refugee knights who join my camp do it because a refugee is happy even with an old hut in the desert as long as it protects him from death. As for the alleged usurpation of the Caliph's honorific name—By God! I did neither choose it nor usurp it. It was given to me by Caliph al-Mustadi after I had destroyed the two-hundred-year-old regime of his Ismaili enemies.[40] This matter had been settled in a letter from Baghdad to Nur al-Din, before thine accession to the throne. I would not object if ten thousand Turkomans and Kurds in my army were called Saladin. As for the claim of the Caliph that I conquered Jerusalem with his army and under his banners—where were his banners and his army at the time? By God! I conquered Jerusalem with my own troops and under my own banners.[41]

Although Saladin refrained from public manifestion of his bitterness, al-Nasir's letter opened a rift between the two men. The caliph's first reprimand was followed by a much harsher lesson. An occasion was furnished when the official Syrian and Iraqi pilgrim caravans met at Arafat near Mecca on 9 February 1188, during a traditional celebration of the sacred pilgrimage month. The Iraqi caravan and its military guard was led by Tashtigin, a prominent member of the Baghdad court. The caravan from Damascus was headed by Ibn al-Muqaddam, a man well known for his close political relations with Saladin. That year the Syrian caravan was unusually large, because it included crowds of pilgrims from Iraq, Mosul, Jazirah, Akhlat, Anatolia, and other regions, who had flocked to visit Jerusalem and other holy sites Saladin had newly liberated. The Ayyubid conqueror's popularity must have been at its highest point in the Hejaz and greater than that of other contemporary leaders. Perhaps for that very reason Ibn al-Muqaddam wanted his caravan to lead the procession of the pilgrims from Arafa to Mecca. This Tashtigin vigorously contested and when the leader from Damascus refused to yield, the caliph's representative signalled his men to attack. In the ensuing melee the Syrian caravan was ignominiously dispersed and its prominent leader bludgeoned to death.[42]

Relations between Saladin and the Abbasid caliph became colder than ever.

Shortcomings of Saladin's leadership

Despite his popular image following the great victory of Hattin and the glorious recovery of Jerusalem, Saladin's position as leader of the Muslim forces fighting the Crusaders was not too comfortable. As early as 1186, incidents with Nasir al-Din ibn Shirkuh and Taqi al-Din Umar had indicated that Saladin could not even trust his own relatives.[43] Events at Tyre in 1187 had revealed that the rank and file was not overwhelmingly inspired by the *jihad* ideal which Saladin publicly embraced, and this self-asserted mandate itself had been repudiated in no uncertain terms by the caliph of Baghdad. Nor did Saladin's successes evoke any enthusiasm from the powerful Almohad rulers of North Africa and Spain. This was because of the Ayyubid raids against their territories, which, however, the vigorous countermeasures of the great Yaqub al-Mansur [44] had ended in 1187.

It seems that Saladin's persistent expansionist policies in Egypt, Arabia, North Africa, Syria, and northern Mesopotamia had eroded confidence in the sincerity of his proclaimed devotion to the war against the Infidels. With his moral leadership open to doubts, Saladin might perhaps have impressed his followers with monetary inducements, but unfortunately his economic position precluded such a solution. Having earlier committed Egyptian resources to finance the relentless campaigns against his Muslim rivals, Saladin was now without substantial cash reserves. This proved an essential cause of failure in the attack against Tyre. It was also bound to create further complications if the war against the Crusaders escalated.

Saladin's alliance with the Byzantine Empire

On 6 January 1188—only a few days after his withdrawal from Tyre —Saladin received in Acre a Byzantine embassy bringing Emperor Isaac's thanks for the liberation of his brother and congratulations on the Muslim sultan's reconquest of Jerusalem. The Byzantine envoys also informed Saladin that a new Crusade was being summoned in the West to retrieve the holy sepulchre from the Muslims.[45]

Shocked by Saladin's capture of the holy city, Europeans reacted by mobilizing tremendous military and economic resources to reconquer Jerusalem. This mobilization produced numerous multinational armies and naval contingents ready to challenge Saladin's claim to supremacy in the holy land. In addition to a great many princes, barons, and prominent noblemen, the new Crusade included three mighty European sovereigns: Philip Augustus of France, Richard the

Lionhearted of England, and the Holy Roman Emperor Frederick I Barbarossa.

The new European expedition was as disquieting to Saladin as to Isaac Angelus and dictated a tightening of military ties between the two rulers. Therefore, Saladin sent his own ambassadors back with the Byzantine embassy to negotiate an active military alliance to counter the invasion. Among the fabulous gifts dispatched to Isaac were two items attesting to Saladin's military imagination: a huge silver jar of poisoned wine and great quantities of poisoned flour and grain. These deadly foods (one whiff of the wine was said to have slain a Latin prisoner on whom it was tested) were apparently supplied for chemical warfare against the Crusaders passing through Byzantine lands; indeed, the chronicles of Frederick Barbarossa's Crusade contain a number of stories concerning Byzantine attempts to destroy the Germans by such means.[46]

Although the Ayyubid sultan and the Greek emperor firmly concluded an alliance in 1188 or 1189 and sustained it by regular exchanges of embassies, it proved of no essential military or political consequence. Apart from keeping Saladin informed about Crusader movements, Isaac proved incapable of helping Saladin during the Third Crusade. Frederick Barbarossa traversed Greek territory without meeting any serious Byzantine opposition. Only his accidental drowning in the Saleph River on 10 June 1190 prevented Frederick from reaching the holy land. As for Philip Augustus and Richard the Lionhearted, they elected to go to Acre by sea.

Disappointing though it was in military terms, the alliance with the Byzantines produced a significant diplomatic success: the emperor conferred on Saladin responsibility for the personnel and ritual activities in the mosque of Constantinople, an honor hitherto reserved for the Saljuqid sultans.[47] This act was tantamount to a formal recognition of Saladin as the official, legitimate champion of Sunni Islam.

The beginning of the Third Crusade

Following Saladin's victory of Hattin, the failure to capture Tyre was not his only strategic blunder. In 1188 he refrained from assaulting

Tripoli, and that same year, instead of attacking Antioch, he concluded on 1 October an eight-month truce with its master, Bohemund.[48] No matter how impressive his numerous conquests in 1188–89, three crucial fortresses on the Syrian littoral remained in enemy hands. Not only had they survived the Muslim deluge, they now served as vital bases for renewed Frankish resistance which fresh troops from Europe gradually reinforced. Finally in August 1189 King Guy felt confident enough to lead his revitalized army, supported by a Pisan squadron, on an expedition against Acre.

In anticipation of the Crusader attack Saladin had ordered the fortifications of Acre strengthened and had committed to its defense his elite troops with abundant arms, food, and other supplies.[49] Finding Acre well prepared to meet a direct attack, King Guy's army was compelled to lay siege during which it in turn was surrounded on land by Muslim relief contingents which Saladin led. The action at Acre, where a Muslim garrison was first besieged by Crusader naval and land forces, which were in turn encompassed by Ayyubid land troops, gradually escalated into one of the most dramatic military confrontations between Islam and Christianity—the famous Third Crusade. As a result of Saladin's ultimate failure to crush this new wave of European aggressors, the Crusader Kingdom in the Near East won a new lease on life which lasted for yet another century.

Saladin's lack of authority over his principal commanders

The battle of Acre lasted almost two years, 1189–91, during which the Crusaders, besieging and besieged, had to conduct difficult military operations, often under most adverse climatic, logistic, economic, and sanitary conditions. The situation in the Crusader camp became quite critical in the winter which rendered them more vulnerable to Muslim attacks. However, having survived the desperate winter of 1190–91, Crusader strength reached its peak in the spring of 1191 with the arrival of King Philip of France and King Richard of England and their forces.

The tremendous power the combined naval and land forces of the

Third Crusade unleashed proved too much for the garrison of Acre, by then completely exhausted and cut off from any supplies. On 12 July 1191 the heroic defenders capitulated, having lost faith in Saladin's capacity to defeat the Crusaders. In addition to loss of the elite troops and huge quantities of war material, the fall of Acre was a terrible strategic and propaganda blow to Saladin, which threatened to wipe out all the advantages gained by the victory of Hattin.

A fundamental reason for Saladin's failure to defeat the Third Crusade, particularly in its initial winter stage, was his inability to sustain a rigorous campaign against the Europeans. On 4 October 1189 Saladin inflicted a bloody defeat on the Crusaders, but he was unable to follow it up, because his commanders insisted their troops deserved the rest to which they were formally entitled after fifty days of uninterrupted campaigning.[50] A year later, with the approach of winter, the Crusader situation had become so desperate that some prospects existed for an advantageous armistice agreement. However, Saladin's impatient regional commanders frustrated his plans by insisting on going home immediately. The Zangid prince of Sinjar, Imad al-Din, pressed the Ayyubid sultan to dismiss all troops for the winter. Another Zangid vassal, Sinjar of al-Jazirat al-Umar, attempted to lead his contingent home without even receiving permission. Finally, beginning mid-November 1190, Saladin gave in, and different contingents, preceded by the Zangid units, began to depart, leaving the sultan with only a few dedicated commanders and his own guard.[51]

Saladin's lack of a more forceful hold over his troops could be partly attributed to his deteriorating health. During the two-year siege of Acre, the sultan, who was over fifty, suffered violent attacks of what the Arab chroniclers called "colic," more probably the malignant Syrian fever.[52] This affliction handicapped his capacity to command undiminished loyalty of all his followers and especially the attachment of his Zangid vassals.

As Lane-Poole remarked, "It was not to be expected that the vanquished descendants of Zengy should show much enthusiasm in their supplanter's service."[53] Nor was this deplorable lack of enthusiasm limited to his Zangid vassals. In 1191 Taqi al-Din Umar, Saladin's nephew, failed to show up at the battle for Islam, because he was busy asserting his authority in his feudal possessions. This in turn caused the troops from Diyar Bakr to delay arrival, because their leaders had to protect their interests which Taqi al-Din imperiled. During the same spring, Izz al-Din of Mosul laid siege to al-Jazirat al-Umar, accusing its master, Sinjar Shah, of aiding his domestic enemies. This prevented Sinjar Shah from joining the battle of Acre. "This is the work of satan!" exclaimed Saladin when he learned about this shocking disobedience of his troop concentration orders.[54]

In June 1191 some of Saladin's men mutinied; they refused to attack the Christians and accused him of "ruining Islam."[55] Succumbing to defeatism, three leading amirs in the garrison of Acre deserted their posts in panic,[56] and finally, the garrison itself disobeyed the sultan's orders and surrendered to the Crusaders.[57]

Muslim rulers indifferent to Saladin's struggle

In his efforts to protect Palestine from the Crusaders Saladin appealed in all directions for military and economic assistance. Swallowing his pride he kept sending urgent messages to the caliph of Baghdad,[58] to his own brother in the Yemen,[59] even to the Almohad sultan, Yaqub al-Mansur. In this last instance Saladin, cynically disavowing any responsibility for Qaragush's raids against North Africa, hoped that cooperation of the Moroccan fleet would slow down Christian shipping between the West and Acre.[60] But Saladin's anti-Crusader cause evoked little active support outside his own dominions. The caliph responded with two loads of naftah (a kind of twelfth century napalm), five specialists in the use of flame-throwers, and a promissory note of 20,000 dinars. This token aid so affronted Saladin that he returned the monetary portion.[61] Instead of receiving assistance from Yaqub al-Mansur, Saladin learned that North African ports had extended hospitality to the Genoese sailing to support the Crusaders at Acre.[62] One of the Saljuqid princes of Persia, instead of furnishing troops, asked for help against his own rivals.[63] Another Saljuqid prince, the master of Malatya, came to Saladin in 1191 and asked for support against his father and brothers in Anatolia.[64] Saladin's correspondence at the time of the battle of Acre contains many references to the caliph's indifference and the lack of outside assistance in his lonely struggle against the enemies of Islam. Obviously, Saladin's prestige as the champion of Islam did not rate high at the various Muslim courts. After all, had he not appealed to the same ideal during the entire period of 1174–86, while grabbing the lands of his Muslim neighbors? Furthermore, did not his earlier diplomatic arrangements with the Crusaders and his alliance with the Christian emperor of Constantinople darken his image as idealistic leader implacably dedicated to the *jihad?*

The successes of Richard the Lionhearted and the conclusion of the Third Crusade

In spite of their triumph at Acre the Crusaders did not pursue their original intention of liberating Jerusalem. Most of them, including the king of France, immediately returned home. Responsibility for continuing the war against Saladin was assumed by the intrepid king of England. Despite the small number of his troops and obvious logistic limitations, Richard maintained the strategic and tactical initiative. Skillfully exploiting available Christian naval support, he extended the Crusader beachhead southward: on 6 September 1191 Arsuf was captured; three days later—Jaffa; and on 20 January 1192 the Crusaders entered Ascalon. The acquisition of that gateway to Egypt allowed Richard to harass Saladin's communications lines with his main base of supply. Indeed, on 20 June Richard's troops intercepted a great caravan laden with supplies en route from Egypt to Saladin's camp in Jerusalem. According to an Arab chronicler, the Crusaders captured 3,000 camels, 3,000 horses, 500 prisoners, and a large amount of supplies.[65] Naturally, the presence of an aggressive Christian king in Ascalon brought back painful memories of Amalric and his Egyptian campaigns.

While inflicting humiliating reverses on the Muslim enemy, the English king did not rule out a negotiated end to the conflict. Following a series of diplomatic exchanges the belligerents agreed to suspend hostilities, and on 2 September 1192 they signed a three-year truce. The Crusaders were to hold a strip of coastal territory from Tyre to Jaffa; Ascalon was restored to Saladin, but its fortifications were to be demolished, so that it would cease function as a military base; finally, both Christians and Muslims were to have free passage through the whole of Palestine, which meant that Christian pilgrims could visit the holy sepulchre and other venerable sites in Jerusalem and elsewhere.[66]

Because Christian Europe had intervened, the kingdom of the Crusaders, which only five years earlier was threatened with total extinction, reestablished itself on the Syro-Palestinian littoral to serve as a focal point of aggressive plans against the Muslims for another century.

Saladin's leadership crisis

Modern accounts of the Third Crusade concentrate on the dramatic battle of Acre; and when discussing personalities, they emphasize both the bravery of Richard the Lionhearted and the chivalrous deportment of Saladin towards the Christian enemy, particularly in the last year of the historic confrontation.

Much less publicized is the shocking failure of the Muslim resistance. Although for two years the Crusaders were confined to a beachhead outside the walls of Acre, Muslim warriors proved incapable of crushing the aggressors or even effectively supporting the besieged garrison.

Later, after most of the Crusaders departed, the forces of Islam suffered further humiliations from a handful of Christians commanded by King Richard. In spite of overwhelming odds in their favor, the Muslims could neither outfight the Christian contingent nor simultaneously protect Ascalon and Jerusalem. Considering the military organization and defense-oriented economy of the Muslim countries and in view of the strategic advantages they secured in 1187-89, the terms of the 1192 armistice must be regarded as a humiliating concession the Christian invaders imposed on Islam.

This grievous failure of Islam during the Third Crusade must be attributed to lack of enthusiasm for the holy war. As at Acre, the

Muslim leadership crisis was much in evidence during the 1191–92 campaign against Richard. The confidence Saladin originally enjoyed reached its low point in the final stage of the Third Crusade. Even one of Saladin's bravest and most experienced commanders, his impetuous nephew Taqi al-Din Umar, practically deserted the Sultan's cause. While his uncle was facing King Richard, Taqi al-Din was advancing into Armenia. His aim was the town of Akhlat on Lake Van; he succeeded in defeating the master of Akhlat, Sayf al-Din Bektumir, and seized much of his territory. Thereupon Bektumir appealed to Caliph al-Nasir who hastened to send a bitter letter to Saladin, reprimanding him for Taqi al-Din's attack. Moreover, the caliph requested that Saladin send to Baghdad al-Qadi al-Fadil, his experienced adviser and loyal friend. Predictably enough, Saladin paid little attention to his Abbasid suzerain. "Taqi al-Din went north," stated Saladin, "to collect troops, and he will return to participate in the *Jihad*. . . . As for al-Qadi al-Fadil, unfortunately he suffers from numerous physical indispositions and his lack of strength precludes a strenuous journey to Iraq." [67]

The callous pursuit of selfish territorial interests by Saladin's nephew came to an end when he died on the night of 9 October 1191 during his siege of Manzikert.[68] This gave rise to a dispute over his legacy between al-Afdal, Saladin's oldest son and al-Adil, Saladin's famous brother. At first the sultan conferred the disputed territories on his son, so on 19 February 1192 al-Afdal left the exposed area of Jerusalem with special diplomas and 20,000 dinars to help him get established. However, al-Adil put enough pressure on Saladin to cause him to rescind the earlier decision, which meant that al-Adil left Jerusalem to replace al-Afdal. News of his recall made al-Afdal so angry that upon his return to Damascus in May he refused to rejoin Saladin's service. Only the sultan's special persuasion made his defiant heir apparent return to action against the Crusaders.[69]

In addition to lack of family cooperation, Saladin ran into difficulties with his rank-and-file troops. It was their cowardice which forced him to give up defense of Ascalon.[70] Their defeatist feelings even caused them to doubt whether Jerusalem should be defended at all against Richard the Lionhearted.[71]

The most flagrant defiance of Saladin's authority on the battlefield occurred 5 August 1192, following the Muslim recapture of Jaffa. Doubting their chance of repelling the attack, the Crusader garrison had asked for terms and Saladin agreed to allow the Christians to leave the city with their goods, in exchange for money ransom. But the sultan could not control his troops, who had broken into the town, so the Christian garrison retired to the citadel while the Turks and Kurds pillaged. The angry sultan ordered his *mamluks* to stand at the city gates and take the booty away from the plunderers.[72]

Speeding to the rescue of Jaffa, Richard established his camp outside the city walls. As the Crusader relief contingent arrived by sea, the knights had no horses and could only fight as spearmen or bowmen. When Saladin realized the enemy's vulnerability, he decided to finish them off by a surprise night attack, which would avenge earlier humiliations and recover his prestige.

After dark on 5 August squadrons of Muslim cavalry moved against the Christian camp. But their movement had been detected and Richard warned. He drew up his little troop in battle array. When Saladin's warriors saw the solid line of the Crusaders, they lost all interest in battle. True, the *mamluks* made a few mounted charges, suffering heavily from the crossbow volleys, but the rest of the troops simply refused to attack. Saladin's famous biographer, Baha al-Din, who had become the sultan's secretary in June 1188, admitted the dismal performance of the Muslim soldiers. They were supposedly embittered by Saladin's protecting the Christians of Jaffa. Some of his troopers, observed Baha al-Din, had even taunted the sultan: "Make your own *mamluks* charge who beat off our people on the day we took Jaffa!" [73]

Whatever the cause, Saladin could not get his men to attack. To add insult to injury, Richard publicly exposed this total disobedience by riding along the whole front of Saladin's men, lance at rest, mocking them, and not a soldier attempted to touch him.[74] Saladin at last left the field in a fury and the next day was in Jerusalem ordering fresh fortifications.[75] A few weeks later, on 2 September, a formal armistice proclamation ended his long war against the Crusaders.

Certain developments in Damascus and Aleppo during that final stage of the war hinted at the rise of the antiestablishment sentiments on the homefront. In 1191 Saladin had to dismiss Muhammad ibn

Abd Allah ibn Abi Asrun from his position as judge of Damascus, because of his harmful contacts and influence with the military. Nominated in his place was Muhyi al-Din ibn al-Zaki, the preacher who had delivered the famous sermon after the liberation of Jerusalem.[76]

Aleppo became the scene of the activities of al-Suhrawardi, one of the greatest mystics in the history of Islamic religious philosophy. The popularity which his unorthodox ideas began to enjoy with the traditionally liberal-minded population of Aleppo could not be tolerated by the Ayyubid regime. Saladin ordered this teacher of ideological deviation put to death; so on 29 July 1191, to the roll of Muslim mystic martyrs was added al-Suhrawarti.[77]

Egypt and Saladin's war against the Crusaders

If despite so many difficulties with his army and the apathy of various Muslim princes, Saladin succeeded in preventing the Third Crusade from reconquering Palestine, this was mainly due to the steady military and economic support received from Egypt. Egypt had once enabled Saladin to get established as a strong and independent ruler. Again, during his early bid in Syria, the troops based in Egypt had saved Saladin from imminent destruction. The Egyptian troops and resources had proved instrumental in annexing Aleppo and Mosul. And Egypt it was which supported Saladin's desperate struggle against the Third Crusade.

Besides providing him with means to maintain his own regiment of *mamluk* guards, Egypt supplied Saladin with about 4,000 cavalry for the offensive of 1187. As soon as he captured Acre in 1187, the sultan ordered al-Adil in Cairo to furnish more troops and to dispatch the Egyptian fleet. The opening of a direct coastal route between Egypt and Palestine had facilitated, of course, the movement of troops and supplies.

Still during the summer of 1187 when Saladin decided to transform Acre into an operational base for the war, he turned to Cairo to find personnel and money for that purpose. Baha al-Din Qaragush was recalled from overseeing the defense constructions in the Egyptian capital and came to Acre with architects, tools, and a prisoner-of-war labor force to fortify that town. The impressive results the Egyptian architects achieved allowed Saladin to conceive the strategy of containing the main forces of the Third Crusade on the beaches of Acre. He provided the fortress itself with experienced troops, equipment, and supplies, all of which Egypt furnished.

During the two-year battle of Acre, al-Adil or al-Qadi al-Fadil continued to send fresh troops and naval units from Egypt, either to supply the besieged garrison by breaking through the Frankish blockade or to join Saladin's army in the field. Beyond a doubt, Saladin's stand at Acre was made possible only because of Egypt's gigantic war effort. Later, during the struggle against the English king, Egyptian contributions in men, equipment, money, and naval support likewise sustained Saladin's operations. As a result of Egypt's essential support, most of the Europeans lost their crusading fervor following the capture of Acre, and Richard the Lionhearted's offensive operations fell short of the intended liberation of Jerusalem.

But the price Egypt had to pay was staggering. Besides the casualties suffered by units operating outside, the Egyptian land forces sustained their greatest losses from the fall of Acre. The surrender meant the loss of both experienced commanders such as Baha al-Din Qaragush and al-Mashtub and a great many Egyptian warriors, as well as large quantities of war material. Some of the commanders, including al-Mashtub, were later ransomed, but the king of England massacred the bulk of the rank and file.

The fall of Acre meant a disastrous blow to Egyptian naval power. During the siege of the city the superior naval forces of the Crusaders either captured or sunk many ships. Some of the Egyptian units had succeeded in breaking the blockade and penetrating the harbor, however, one of the surrender terms was that the Crusaders were to take all ships anchored in the harbor. Consequently the fall of Acre cost almost total loss of the Egyptian navy.[78]

Because of these disastrous naval developments, Saladin had to reckon with a possible invasion of Egypt. During the battle of Acre he had undertaken measures to prevent various towns in Palestine and the Lebanon from serving as fortified bases for the Crusaders in case they launched an inland offensive. In 1190 the sultan had ordered the walls destroyed at Tiberias, Jaffa, Arsuf, Caesarea, Sidon, and Jubail.[79] Following the loss of Acre, Ascalon once again emerged as the key to Egypt's safety. But Saladin's discouraged staff insisted that it would be impossible to defend Egypt and Palestine at the same time, so Saladin—placing the interests of the Holy Land above those of Egypt —ordered Ascalon abandoned and its walls dismantled, hoping to render it useless for a Christian invasion of the Delta.[80] This concern was not unwarranted, for Richard pushed as far south as Darum which had once served as a staging place for Amalric's invasion of Egypt.[81]

Saladin undertook other emergency measures in Egypt itself. He instructed his brother al-Adil to assume personal responsibility over the ministry of the fleet.[82] Fortifications of Damietta were refitted, while all women were ordered to leave. Tinnis was completely evacuated of its civil population—a measure which spelt the end of that once-flourishing urban center.[83]

Egypt's war effort also entailed considerable economic sacrifices. The need to produce costly replacements in personnel, equipment, and animals, as well as Saladin's recurrent demands for cash, strained to the utmost Egypt's financial resources. Saladin's administration in Cairo had traditionally been plagued with a gold shortage and its detrimental effect on the quality of the Egyptian dinars. In 1187—the year of the great triumph over the Crusaders—Saladin ordered a major monetary reform probably aimed at removing debased coins from circulation.[84] But the effects of that reform proved shortlived. During the critical struggle against the Third Crusade, production at the Egyptian mints decreased and their coins suffered from debasement.[85]

To finance the Third Crusade the faithful in Western Europe were called upon to pay a special tax, called Saladin's tithe.[86] For his part, Saladin—lacking economic and military support from other Muslim rulers—imposed special taxes on the Egyptian population. Among other levies, al-Adil proposed an income tax of 1 percent, but Saladin found this absolutely inadequate considering the costs of the war.[87] Taxes on non-Muslim Egyptian minorities were also expanded.[88] In general, the Egyptian population suffered as more and more of its resources were absorbed. Egyptian ports witnessed a gradual increase of Turkish slaves, imported either to replace casualties or to beef up the regular cavalry units in anticipation of a Crusader attack against Egypt.

Large-scale government purchases of foodstuffs caused prices of commodities to skyrocket, especially in the metropolitan area where the price of beans in 1192 increased by 100 percent.[89] Social malaise, if not outright discontent with developments in Egypt, found its expression in rumors and agitations affecting the life of Cairo and Fustat and even in a revival of Ismaili and pro-Fatimid propaganda. The first pro-Ismaili riots in Ayyubid Cairo occurred as early as 1188.[90] In 1192 a Fatimid pretender, supported by some surviving members of Shawar's family, staged an abortive revolt in Cairo. The administration found it necessary to remove the imprisoned members and followers of the Fatimid dynasty to a secure place from which they could neither engage in nor even inspire subversive activities.[91]

One of the lasting effects of Egyptian involvement in the Third Crusade was that the Christian leadership came to recognize Egypt as the key objective in efforts to recover the holy city. "The keys to Jerusalem are found in Cairo"[92] became the principle of Crusader strategy following the confrontation with Saladin. Continuous military pressure and two dangerous invasions by the Franks and their European allies, in 1218 and 1249, led to ever-increasing Egyptian defense efforts. Imports of costly slaves for the *mamluk* regiments had to be stepped up, and to finance this expansion it became necessary to expand governmental control over various areas of the Egyptian economy, including the transit and export trade. Egyptian political and economic systems underwent a process of militarization, which culminated in the middle of the thirteenth century, when a ruthless militaristic regime of the Mamluks took power. By then the delicate balance between Egypt's security needs and economic capacity had been decisively disturbed with prolonged and ruinous consequences for its society.

One of the main reasons precipitating that disastrous development in medieval Egypt was the costly expansionist policy of Saladin, his procrastination in launching a total war against the Crusaders, and his catastrophic failure to eliminate the Christian kingdom from Palestine.

11 The final six months

"Have care, son of Ayyub, what sort of end you will come to—you who are helped to mount by a Saljuqid prince and a descendant of Atabag Zangi."—A Mosul officer to Saladin

Saladin's unfulfilled wish to perform a pilgrimage to Mecca

The great war against the Crusaders was over. Richard the Lion-hearted, that most puissant and persevering of the Christian invaders, had returned to Europe. Both leaders and people in the opposing camps were exhausted by the long struggle and looked forward to a much needed respite secured by the armistice. Throngs of Christians and Muslims, soldiers and civilians alike, hastened to honor the occasion by visiting peacefully the city of Jerusalem. Saladin, too, returned to the holy city on 11 September 1192 to pass there the month of Ramadan and to take care of administration details. He was eager to reward those of his followers who had stayed with him loyally during the critical moments of the war. He placed Izz al-Din Jurdiq in charge of the district of Jerusalem [1] and appointed Baha al-Din professor in a Shafiite college he reopened and funded.[2] In addition, he gave Baha al-Din charge of charitable foundations and of judicial matters.[3]

As the holy month of the pilgrimage was approaching (December 1192–January 1193) Saladin expressed a wish to fulfill the solemn Muslim obligation of performing a pilgrimage to Mecca. He even sent appropriate letters to Egypt and to his brother Sayf al-Din, the master of the Yemen, requesting ships, supplies, and other items required for a trip to the Hejaz. However, his plans of leaving Syria ran into opposition from his staff.[4]

One argument against the journey was the problem of the sultan's relations with the caliph of Baghdad. The caliph had for a long time been jealous of Saladin's popularity as the true champion of Islam.

Saladin's recognition as such by Constantinople must have added to Baghdad's uneasiness. And since on an earlier confrontation of pilgrims from Syria with those from Iraq had resulted in a bloody incident,[5] repetition of such scandal should be avoided. As a matter of fact, the caliph's court seemed inclined to improve relations with Saladin. Baghdad contacted al-Adil and asked him to urge his brother to resolve the conflict.[6] Some of Saladin's advisers urged Saladin to write the caliph, explaining the intention and itinerary of his proposed pilgrimage lest the trip, as innocent as it appeared, be misinterpreted by Baghdad.[7]

Another argument put forward to dissuade Saladin was the desolate state of his dominions. How could he leave the country in such disorder? Was not the task of defending the frontier fortresses his primary obligation? His advisers maintained that he should have no illusions concerning the solidarity of the peace. The Franks were but waiting for an opportunity to perpetrate another act of treachery, as they had in the past.[8] The prominent al-Qadi al-Fadil was most articulate in his protests stressing the need for immediate elimination of economic and social ills:

> In the district of Damascus the abuses oppressing the farmers are so outrageous that one wonders whether the rain still waters their fields; oppression of the *iqta* holders towards their tenants exceeds all imagination. At Wadi Barada and at al-Zabadani disorder reigns permanently, the sword causes streams of blood, and nothing appears to stop the excesses. Frontier towns of Islam need to be fortified and supplied. It is further imperative to promote collection of taxes and to adjust expenditure accordingly, for expenses without revenue—as any enterprise without solid grounds —are nothing but absurdity. All these issues have been discussed on earlier occasions, but other critical problems have diverted the attention of our Lord, and in consequence these affairs follow a precipitous course. Even if many of our misfortunes have ended— may God prevent their recurrence—an empty treasury may as yet prove the greatest catastrophe of all.[9]

The weight of such arguments is said to have changed Saladin's mind and postponed his intended pilgrimage to Mecca. As it turned out, his wish remained unfulfilled.

To what extent should one accept these explanations? Does it, for example, not sound strange that his closest associates, particularly al-Qadi al-Fadil should have so insisted on Saladin's presence in Syria? After all, the Hejaz was not that distant. By February 1193, some of the people participating in the pilgrimage had already returned to Damascus. Would Saladin's absence from Syria for two to three months really have jeopardized the return of normal economic, administrative, and defense conditions in his dominions? Indeed, one wonders whether the whole story about Saladin's pilgrimage intentions was not concocted by his biographers to absolve their hero from his failure to fulfill the sacred obligation incumbent on every able-bodied and economically capable Muslim. On the other hand, the sultan might have been dissuaded from carrying out his pilgrimage of piety, because his political position at home was not thought too secure.

Saladin returns to Damascus

On 4 November 1192, after four difficult years spent fighting the Crusaders, the Ayyubid sultan reentered Damascus.[10] What were his thoughts on that occasion? Did he reflect on his achievements of the last few years? Or did he perhaps ponder the dramatic developments which had taken place since his first departure with Shirkuh's army to save Egypt from political, economic, and military disaster? Those twenty-eight years, from 1164 to 1192 witnessed his victories in Egypt, Syria, and Mesopotamia, his conquests and frustrations in the struggle with the Crusaders. Had he attained the aims he had hoped to? Did his thoughts turn to the memory of those who had contributed so much to his rise to power?

His father, Ayyub, and uncle Shirkuh had died in the earliest stage of his career in Egypt. His uncle Shihab al-Din al-Harimi and his brothers Shams al-Dawlah, Farrukh-Shah, and Taj al-Muluk, as well as his cousin Nasir al-Din Muhammad ibn Shirkuh, had met their deaths during the struggle for domination in Syria. His impetuous nephew Taqi al-Din Umar had perished during his expedition against Akhlat in 1191. His loyal and diplomatic supporter Isa al-Hakkari had died on the battlefields of Acre. Another commander, al-

Mashtub, so essential in bringing about Saladin's election as commander of the Syrian expeditionary corps in Egypt in 1169, died on the very day of Saladin's return to Damascus.

Did Saladin give a thought to the people he had eliminated during his career? The shrewd Shawar, the brilliant poet Umarah, the great religious philosopher al-Suhrawardi . . . ? Did he recall the bloody vengeance exacted from the vanquished Frankish prisoners, massacred wholesale or individually, like Reginald of Châtillon or like that unlucky common Christian soldier whom the sultan had slain when he noticed a minor facial scratch his son al-Afdal sustained in the battle of Arsuf.[11]

Perhaps in that moment the mighty sultan was wondering how much executive power he still enjoyed. Or how to resist the ambitions and claims of the new Ayyubid generation.

Once in Damascus, Saladin mixed business with pleasure. He enjoyed staying with his little children, and he was eager to do gazelle hunting in the plains outside Damascus. But the people seen in his company suggested that he tended to the affairs of state. Al-Afdal, Saladin's oldest son and prospective successor, popular with Syrian amirs and commanders, appeared to be playing a prominent part in court activities. Chancellor al-Fadil, the real brains of Saladin's state machinery and a consistent advocate of Egyptian interests, was also in Damascus. Emissaries from Count Bohemund of Antioch successfully negotiated terms for Saladin's protection,[12] and the quarreling Saljuqid princes appealed to his arbitration.[13] The ambitious al-Adil, placed by the sultan in charge of the Eastern regions of the Ayyubid state, came to visit with his brother on 25 November. Saladin met him outside the capital whereupon the two brothers spent four days hunting before returning to Damascus. In January 1193, on another hunting expedition, they spent over two weeks in isolation. Once they parted they were not destined to see each other again.[14]

Yet another trustworthy official and biographer of Saladin, Judge Baha al-Din, arrived in Damascus on 17 February. When he came to the palace he was struck by the sultan's absence from the audience hall, in which the court elite surrounded Prince al-Afdal. Notified about the arrival of Baha al-Din, Saladin let him come to his private quarters. By then no one was admitted without the sultan's specific permission. Although their separation had lasted hardly four months, Saladin was unusually moved on this occasion. He got up from his seat made a few steps forward and with tears streaming from his eyes embraced his friendly guest.[15]

The presence of Baha al-Din was requested on the following day. When he appeared, Saladin asked him about the people gathered in the audience hall. Baha al-Din reported having seen Prince al-Afdal and his supporters in attendance, whereupon the sultan cancelled his public appearance.[16]

On 19 February Saladin received Frankish envoys in his palace garden pavilion in the presence of his little children and Baha al-Din. When one of the youngsters began to cry, the sultan abruptly dismissed his foreign visitors before they even started their address. When a meal was served he showed no appetite. He complained about the heaviness of his body movements. Digestive functions were also giving him trouble. In spite of that discomfort he expressed a desire to meet the caravan of pilgrims returning from Mecca. So on the following day, Friday 20 February, Saladin set out on his last ride on a horse. All the satisfaction and excitement notwithstanding, the long day spent welcoming the returning pilgrims did not help his bodily resistance. To make matters worse, he had neglected to wear his quilted gambeson. Before the night was over, the fatal illness had struck. When the sultan woke up on Saturday morning he was suffering from fever.[17]

The fatal illness [18]

While the general public of Damascus remained uninformed, anxiety about the sultan's condition dominated court life. Having visited the patient, Baha al-Din and Chancellor al-Fadil were invited to dinner by al-Afdal. Al-Qadi al-Fadil declined the invitation outright. Baha al-Din left during the meal, because he could not suppress his grief on seeing al-Afdal occupy the sultan's usual seat. Saladin's two loyal friends and collaborators kept returning to the castle to inquire about his condition, now steadily deteriorating.

The fourth day of the illness was decisive. By then the fever had affected his mind. Doctor al-Rahbi, a court physician who had once loyally served Nur al-Din, administered bloodletting. He did it over the unanimous opposition of all other doctors in attendance. According to one prominent chronicler, this treatment caused Saladin's death. Al-Rahbi had to be whisked away by some women to be sheltered from the wrath of the people.[19]

As for the patient, increased dehydration was inexorable, bringing him to the limits of exhaustion. It was more and more difficult to ease his discomfort. On the sixth day of his illness, Saladin rejected one drink as too hot, another as too cold, complaining: "By the glory of God, can no one prepare for me the right kind of water?"[20]

During the sixth, seventh, and eighth days his condition further deteriorated and his mind began to give way. On the ninth day he went into convulsions. By that time the news of his grave illness had spread over all Damascus. Overwhelmed by anxiety and concern for the great sultan, many waited outside the castle to hear the reports from people returning from the court.

On Sunday, the tenth day of the illness, enema treatment produced slight relief. The patient drank a good draught of barley water and broke into perspiration. Unfortunately, the perspiration was so intense and profuse that his dehydration passed the limits of endurance. By Monday morning Saladin had sunk into a coma.

While the physicians attended to the patient, al-Afdal decided to take care of political matters. Having assured himself of his father's hopeless condition, he proceeded with the swearing-in ceremony establishing himself as the new sultan. The ceremonies lasted all day long and were interrupted only by an official evening reception. One after another, the Syrian commanders pledged allegiance to al-Afdal. Not a single dignitary from Egypt joined in the proceedings.[21]

Saladin's final agony lasted about forty-eight hours. At daybreak on Wednesday, 4 March 1193, a preacher, called Abu Jafar, was reciting the confession of faith and reading the Quran to the unconscious patient. The hour of morning prayer was over. Chancellor al-Fadil hurriedly appeared in the room. The preacher recited: "He is God, besides whom there is no other God,—who knoweth the unseen and the seen—the Compassionate, the Merciful."

"True," whispered Saladin, momentarily returning to consciousness.

The preacher continued: "There is no God but He, in him do I trust!"

The dying man smiled, his face lighted up, and the great sultan was no more.[22]

12 Saladin in historical perspective: a dissenting view

"Our people alone bore most of the sufferings of the Crusades, out of which they emerged poor, destitute and exhausted. In their exhaustion they were simultaneously destined by circumstances to submit to and suffer further indignity under the hoofs of the Mongol and Caucasian tyrants. They came to Egypt as slaves, murdered their masters and became masters themselves. They were driven into Egypt as Mamelukes, i.e., owned, but shortly they became kings in our good and peaceful land.

"Tyranny, oppression and ruin characterized their rule in Egypt, which continued for many dark centuries."—President Gamal abd al-Nasir of Egypt.

The degree to which an individual, endowed with natural intellectual and physical powers and exploiting inherited or self-gained social, political, and economic advantages, plays an influential role in the process of historical change—generating it, controlling or merely reacting to it, or converting its results either to the benefit or the detriment of his society—constitutes a valid criterion of the real significance of history's identifiable heroes.

Saladin's intellectual and physical endowments, his prominent family background, his court education and professional military training, all qualified him to respond to the call of history. It was because of the high caliber of his leadership that the Kurdish faction of the Syrian troops asked him to succeed Shirkuh in Egypt and that experienced Egyptian politicians saw in his elevation to the vizirate a chance to revive the moribund Fatimid state. It was because of his initial military exploits, his cool tactical maneuver in the battle of al-Babain, his heroic stand in Alexandria, his victory in the siege of Damietta, and his reconquest of Ailah, that early in his independent career he could claim it as his destiny to utterly destroy the Kingdom of the Crusaders. These hopes, though not entirely ill-founded, remained to the last unfulfilled.

Popular though the story of Saladin's war against the Crusaders has always been, it constitutes but one aspect of his political and military career. To obtain a full understanding of that glamorous historical career, one has to consider both his role in the foundation of the Ayyubid regime and his policy towards Egypt, as well as his commitment against the Crusaders.

Saladin lived up to the hopes vested in him by his immediate family; at the end of his career the descendants of Ayyub ruled over Egypt, most of Syria, and Yemen. But the way in which this domination was accomplished hardly helped lay effective foundations for a cohesive and united regime. Saladin's ruthless policy of military suppression—to cite only the Fatimids and Zangids as its most prominent victims—did realize his immediate personal ambitions, but the lack of a sincere moral or ideological motivation prevented consolidation and preservation of his dynastic heritage. His authority over the leading members of his family was at best rather tenuous. After Saladin's death the absence of any profound loyalty and respect for him became apparent when his sons and legitimate successors were quickly pushed aside by his equally ambitious brother and nephews. Continuous warfare among various Ayyubid contenders, waged against a background of new Crusader aggressions and the Mongol invasion, undermined the position of that militaristic establishment. By the middle of the thirteenth century—only fifty-six years after Saladin's death—the Ayyubid domination in Egypt and Syria came to an abrupt end with the brutal seizure of power by the Mamluk commanders in Egypt.

Viewed as a whole, Saladin's policy towards Egypt is a depressing record of callous exploitation for the furthering of his own selfish political ambitions. This is not to deny his role in bringing about major changes which decisively affected Egypt's history. It was Saladin who suppressed the Fatimid caliphate. It was Saladin who restored the official domination of the Sunni Islam in Egypt. It was Saladin who installed a new Ayyubid regime in Cairo and its dependencies. Even

so, the motivation behind all these impressive changes bears consideration. For instance, at the outset of his vizirate Saladin did not show
any hostility to the Fatimid sovereign; furthermore, he resisted Nur
al-Din's pressure to end immediately the whole Ismaili political superstructure. This restraint seems to have been a calculated desire to avoid
at any cost—material or religious—steps which could weaken his delicate position in Egypt. Once he had abolished the caliphate, Saladin
instituted an Ismaili purge in Egypt—a rather insignificant move considering that the Ismaili creed had never grown deep roots in that
country and by the time of the Ayyubids it was on the verge of natural
extinction. At that time the only dangerous, fanatically heterodox
Muslim sectarians were the Assassins. With them Saladin—the acclaimed Sunni protagonist—secured an expedient diplomatic accommodation.

Much more significant is the fact that in the long run Saladin failed
to meet the needs of the Egyptian society. Quite obviously Saladin
subordinated Egypt's interests to his expansionist dynastic ambitions
in Syria. His Syrian policy reduced Egypt to a quasi colony with the
usual adverse consequences: economic exploitation, increased taxation,
interference with freedom of trade, promotion of European commercial interests in Egypt, and a disastrous increase in military expenditure. But Saladin's greatest blunder in respect to Egypt was his procrastination and ultimate failure to free her from the spectre of the
Crusaders. Quite the reverse, his transformation of Egypt into a potent
militaristic establishment compelled the Crusaders to concentrate their
offensive strategy on Egypt; in the first half of the thirteenth century,
Egypt became their primary target. The persistent military crisis,
which Saladin should have eliminated, decisively contributed to a
further expansion of the *mamluk* forces, which increased the prestige
of their leaders. Ultimately, this failure of Saladin led to the establishment of the Mamluk sultanate—a long and bitter experience in Egypt's
history.

But of course it was neither Saladin's dynastic pursuits nor his
Egyptian involvements which won him a lasting international reputation. Rather the dramatic struggle against the Crusaders, the spectacular victory at Hattin, and recapture of Jerusalem far outshone his
other activities and secured him an illustrious place in history.

Were his accomplishments against the Crusaders really so impressive? It is true that during his early career Saladin successfully fought off a number of Amalric's attacks on Egypt, that he thwarted the Norman assault against Alexandria, and that he recaptured Ailah. But he utterly failed to exploit the crisis in the Crusader kingdom following Amalric's death by launching total war against the Christian dominions. The record shows that he almost always chose whatever political or economic advantages he might gain from resisting or attacking other Muslim princes over prosecuting a vigorous campaign against the Christian enemies of Islam. As early as 1174 Saladin had attained a favorable strategic position because he had united the forces of Cairo and Damascus and because of Amalric's death, but thirteen long years elapsed before a major confrontation finally took place on the battlefield of Hattin. Even then the actual battle was precipitated not so much by Saladin's premeditated resolve as by Reginald's shocking provocative act.

Fundamental tactical errors of the Crusaders permitted Saladin to achieve the great victory of Hattin. Destruction of almost the entire Christian army made it possible for him to conduct a relatively easy campaign against places held by the Crusaders and to win the most celebrated prize of all—Jerusalem. But despite the enthusiasm Jerusalem's return generated, despite the momentum and popularity which his *jihad* enjoyed following the victories of 1187, and despite a tremendous military, psychological, and logistical superiority, Saladin did not eliminate the Crusaders. His incredible indolence in handling Tyre led to the hardening of Christian resistance. His inability to hold his commanders in the field long enough to crush the early contingents of the Third Crusade led to the disaster of 1191, the humiliations at the hands of Richard the Lionhearted, and the armistice of 1192. To be sure Islam retained Jerusalem, but Acre and almost the entire Syrian littoral remained in Christian possession.

Thus the *jihad*, which had received such a boost in 1144 when Zangi recovered Edessa and which appeared to be reaching a successful climax as a result of Nur al-Din's relentless efforts, suffered a major setback because of the shortcomings of Saladin's policy. His failure gave a new lease of life to the Crusader kingdom, which continued for another century to aggravate the political and economic difficulties of Egypt and Syria.

Let us assume, for the sake of argument, that Saladin had died from his serious illness of 1185–86. Would his historical legacy have been more than a record of unscrupulous schemes and campaigns aimed at personal and family aggrandizement—a theme too common in Near Eastern history to elicit any unusual treatment from medieval chroniclers and modern historians? And the great "Saladin might have remained plain Salah-ed-din of Damascus with a name too obscure to be Europeanized." [1]

As it happened—whether tardily or not, whether through his own efforts or because of Crusader blunders—Saladin did liberate Jerusalem. That action alone established him as a glorious hero whose career not only deserved immortalization, but was a useful model to edify and inspire Muslim princes and rulers. [2]

His principal biographer, Baha al-Din ibn Shaddad, used such an approach to portray his hero Saladin. The very arrangement of his *Biography of Saladin* [3] indicates the main emphasis. In depicting the various stages of Saladin's career Baha al-Din devoted nearly three-quarters of his book to the events of 1187–93 and only one-sixth to the earlier phases of the sultan's life. Moreover, the book is provided with a lengthy introduction extolling various praiseworthy personal attributes of Saladin, exemplified with many episodes from his life. However, a glance at any standard Islamic instructive manual for princes (Islamic *Fürstenspiegel*) raises doubts as to the credibility of this part of Baha al-Din's contribution. "The Ruler must observe faithfully the daily worship," prescribed an early medieval Arabic moraliser. [4] "As for the canonic prayers, he [Saladin] performed them assiduously, . . ." echoed Baha al-Din. [5] "The Ruler must observe faithfully the Religious Law," [6] insisted the former. "[Saladin] venerated deeply the laws of the Faith," reassured his biographer. [7] "Do not let wealth accumulate in your treasury, but expend it on the people's welfare," exhorted the moraliser. [8] "Saladin's generosity was too widespread to be recorded here and too well known to need mention: I shall restrict myself to one significant fact; that he, ruler of all those lands, died leaving forty-seven Nasirite *drachmas* of silver in his treasury and a single piece of Tyrian gold, . . ." eulogized Baha al-Din. [9]

If one were to assume that the popularized image of Saladin's exemplary personality is based on reality, what would be its actual historical relevance? Assuredly, Saladin's generation of Syrians and

Egyptians included some holy, pious, virtuous, magnanimous, charitable, and righteous personalities, and yet their careers have left absolutely no record in human history. As for Saladin, his alleged moral and religious attributes influenced neither the course of his public endeavours nor the conduct of his contemporaries. Political egoism and materialistic selfishness were at the root of Muslim setbacks during the Third Crusade. As for his successors, their lack of true commitment to the *jihad* prolonged the Crusader danger in the Near East. And finally, a cool, political calculation on the part of al-Kamil, Saladin's nephew, led in 1228–29 to the surrender of Jerusalem—the sacred symbol of the bloody issue between Islam and Christendom—to Frederick II and his Crusaders.

Most of Saladin's significant historical accomplishments should be attributed to his military and governmental experience, to his ruthless persecution and execution of political opponents and dissenters, to his vindictive belligerence and calculated opportunism, and to his readiness to compromise religious ideals to political expediency.

Because medieval Arab writers were concerned with the humiliations Islam endured at the hands of the Crusaders, they glorified the victory of Hattin and recovery of Jerusalem as Saladin's main achievements. The splendor of that triumph reduced all other aspects of his colorful career to relative insignificance. To them the war of 1187–92 was the decisive action for determining Saladin's place in history. Thanks to the literary talent of Imad al-Din al-Isfahani, the skillful pen of Baha al-Din ibn Shaddad, and the prevailing anti-Crusader mood in the Fertile Crescent, Saladin's posthumous reputation rose to the level of legendary grandeur and sanctified irreproachability.

It is this dominating emotional attitude which has influenced modern historiography. Rather than the alleged attractiveness of his romantic personality, it was the potent spell of his tendentious biographers which has clouded the perceptions of most modern writers retelling the story of the great sultan. It is hoped that this study may in some measure serve as an antidote to the still prevalent vulgarization of Saladin's career, returning to him the true historical interest he so richly deserves.

Notes

Abbreviations

"The Achievement of Saladin":
H. A. R. Gibb, "The Achieve-
ment of Saladin," in Stanford J.
Shaw and William R. Polk, eds.,
*Studies of the Civilization of
Islam* (Boston: Beacon Press,
1962) pp. 91–107.

"The Armies of Saladin": H. A. R.
Gibb, "The Armies of Saladin,"
in Stanford J. Shaw and Wil-
liam R. Polk, eds., *Studies on the
Civilization of Islam* (Boston:
Beacon Press, 1962), pp. 74–90.

ASh: Abū Shāmah, *Kitāb al-
rawḍatayn* (Cairo, 1956).

ASh, *RHC, HO:* Abū Shāmah, *op.
cit.,* in *Recueil des Historiens des
Croisades, Historiens Orientaux*
(Paris, 1872–1906).

Ashtor: E. Ashtor, *Histoire des Prix
et des Salaires dans l'Orient
Médiéval* (Paris, 1969).

BJ: Claude Cahen, "Une Chronique
Syrienne du VIe/XIIe siècle: Le
'Bustān al-Jāmiʿ,'" *Bulletin
d'Études Orientales* 7–8 (1937–
38): 113–158.

EI: The Encyclopaedia of Islam,
2nd ed. (Leiden: E. J. Brill,
1960–).

Elisséeff: N. Elisséeff, *Nur al-Din*
(Damascus, 1967).

Grousset: René Grousset, *Histoire
des Croisades et du Royaume
Franc de Jérusalem* (Paris, 1934–
1936).

IA, *al-Atābakīyah:* Ibn al-Athīr,
*al-Taʾrīkh al-bāhir fi al-Dawlah
al-Atābakīyah* (Cairo, 1963).

IA: Ibn al-Athīr, *Taʾrīkh al-kāmil*
(Cairo, 1884).

IS: Bahāʾ al-Dīn Ibn Shaddād, *al-
Nawādir al-sulṭānīyah* (Cairo,
1964).

Itt.: Aḥmad ibn ʿAlī al-Maqrīzī,
Ittiʿāz al-ḥunafāʾ, MS. AS 3013,
Istanbul, Top Kapu Sarayi
Library.

IW: Ibn Wāṣil, *Mufarrij al-Kurūb*
(*Cairo,* 1953–60).

Labib: Subhi Y. Labib,
*Handelsgeschichte Ägyptens im
Spätmittelalter (1171–1517)*
(Wiesbaden, 1965).

al-Nuzum al-Mālīyah: H. M. Rabīʿ,
*al-Nuzum al-Mālīyah fi Miṣr
zaman al-Ayyūbīyīn* (Cairo,
1964).

"The Place of Saladin": Andrew S. Ehrenkreutz, "The Place of Saladin in the Naval History of the Mediterranean Sea in the Middle Ages," *Journal of the American Oriental Society* 75 (1955): 100–116.

Prawer: J. Prawer, *Histoire du Royaume Latin de Jérusalem* (Paris, 1969–70).

"The Rise of Saladin": H. A. R. Gibb, "The Rise of Saladin, 1169–1181," in Marshall W. Baldwin, Robert Lee Wolff, and Henry W. Hazard, eds., *A History of the Crusades,* 2 vols. (Philadelphia: University of Pennsylvania Press, 1958–1962), 1:563–589.

Saladin: Stanley Lane-Poole, *Saladin and the Fall of the Kingdom of Jerusalem* (London, 1906).

Sibt: Sibt ibn al-Jawzī, *Mirʾāt al-zamān,* VIII/1 (Haydarabad, 1951).

Sulūk: Aḥmad ibn ʿAlī al-Maqrīzī, *Kitāb al-sulūk,* vol. 1, pt. 1, ed. by M. M. Ziyādah (Cairo, 1956).

TD: Ibn al-Khazrajī, *Taʾrīkh Dawlat al-Akrād wa al-Atrāk,* Ms, Hekimoǧlu Ali Paşa 695.

Introduction

1. See "Recent monographs and articles (1946–71)" in Bibliography, p. 263 below.

2. E.g., Abū Shāmah, *Kitāb al-rawḍatayn,* vol. 1, pts. 1, 2 (Cairo, 1956–62); Bahāʾ al-Dīn ibn Shaddād, *Sīrat Ṣalāḥ al-Dīn* (Cairo, 1964); Claude Cahen, "Une Chronique Syrienne du VIe/XIIe siècle: Le *'Bustān al-jāmiʿ,' " Bulletin d'Études Orientales* 7–8 (1937–38): 113–158; ʿIzz al-Dīn ibn al-Athīr, *Al-Kāmil fī al-taʾrīkh* (Beirut, 1965–66); idem, *Al-Taʾrīkh al-bāhir fī al-Dawlah al-Atābakīyah* (Cairo, 1963); Abū al-Ḥusayn Muḥammad ibn Aḥmad ibn al-Jubayr, *The Travels of Ibn Jubayr,* translated by R. J. C. Broadhurst (London, 1952); Ibn al-Qalānisī, *Dhayl Taʾrīkh Dimashq* (Leiden, 1908); Ibn Ḥammād, *Histoire des Rois Obaidides* (Algiers and Paris, 1927); Ibn Mammātī, *Kitāb qawānīn al-dawāwīn* (Cairo, 1943); Abū al-Maḥāsin Yūsuf ibn Taghrī Birdī, *Al-Nujūm al-Zāhirah* (Cairo, 1939); Ibn Wāṣil, *Mufarrij al-Kurūb* (Cairo, 1953–60); ʿImād al-Dīn, al-Iṣfahānī, *Al-Fatḥ al-qussī fī al-fatḥ al-qudsī* (Cairo, 1965); idem, "Al-Barq al-Shāmī: The History of Saladin by the Kātib ʿImād al-Dīn al-Iṣfahānī," *Wiener Zeitschrift für die Kunde des Morgenlandes* 52:93–115; Aḥmad ibn ʿAlī al-Maqrīzī, *Kitāb al-sulūk* (Cairo, 1936–); Murḍa ibn ʿAlī al-Ṭarsūsī, "Tabṣirat arbāb al-albāb," *Bulletin d'Études Orientales* 12 (1947–48); 103–163; Sibṭ ibn al-Jawzī, *Mirʾat al-zamān,*

vol, 8, pt. 1 (Hydarabad, 1951); cf. Francesco Gabrieli, *Arab Historians of the Crusades* (Berkeley and Los Angeles, 1969); also S. D. Goitein, *A Mediterranean Society: The Jewish Communities of the Arab World as Portrayed in the Documents of the Cairo Geniza* (Berkeley and Los Angeles, 1967).

3. Cf. M. Hilmy M. Ahmad, "Some Notes on Arabic Historiography during the Zengid and Ayyūbid Periods (521/1127— 648/1250)," in *Historians of the Middle East* (London, 1962), p. 81.

4. *Saladin,* p. 370.

5. Ibid., pp. 367–368.

6. J. Hartmann, *Die Persön-lichkeit des Sultans Saladin im Urteil der abendländischen Quellen* (Berlin, 1933), p. 120.

7. *Saladin,* pp. 368–369.

8. "The Achievement of Saladin," p. 99.

9. Charles J. Rosebault, *Saladin, Prince of Chivalry* (New York, 1930), pp. 63–64.

10. Vladimir Minorsky, *Studies in Caucasian History* (London, 1953), p. 136.

11. Gertrude Slaughter, *Saladin (1138–1193),* New York, [1955].

12. *EI,* 1:797.

13. Zoe Oldenbourg, *The Crusades,* translated from the French by Anne Carter (New York, 1966), pp. 379, 380.

14. Ibid., p. 381.

15. J. Prawer, *Histoire du Royaume Latin de Jérusalem* (Paris, 1969–70), 1:627 (my translation).

16. Ibid., 1:539–540 (my translation).

17. Ibid., 1:540, n. 1 (my translation).

18. *Saladin,* p. iii.

Chapter 1

1. Cf. Bernard Lewis, "The Ismailites and the Assassins," in *A History of the Crusades,* edited by Robert Lee Wolff and Henry W. Hazard, 2 vols. (Philadelphia, 1958–62), 1:106–107.

2. Hasan Ibrāhīm Hasan, *Taʾrīkh ul-Dawlah al-Fāṭimīyah* (Cairo, 1964), p. 177.

3. Ibid., p. 184.

4. Ibid., p. 313.

5. Cf. s.v. "Fāṭimids" (by M. Canard), *EI,* 2:857–858.

6. Cf. p. 70 below.

7. A. Schaube, *Handelsgeschichte der romanischen Völker des Mittelmeergebiets bis zum Ende der Kreuzzüge* (Munich, 1906), p. 36.

8. Gaston Wiet, *Précis de l'histoire d'Égypte,* in G. Hanotaux, *Histoire de la nation égyptienne* (Paris, 1937), 4:278), 286 (*Précis* in later references).

9. Ibid., p. 288.

10. H. Wieruszowski, "The Norman Kingdom of Sicily and the Crusades," in *A History of the Crusades,* 2:30.

11. "The Place of Saladin," p. 102.

12. Ibid.

13. Ibid.

14. Wiet, *Précis*, 4:280, 288, 291–292.

15. Ibid., p. 276.

16. ASh, vol. 1, pt. 1, p. 207.

17. Aḥmad ibn ʿAlī al-Maqrīzī, *Ighāthat al-ummah* (Cairo, 1940), p. 28; Gaston Wiet, *Le traité des famines de Maqrizi* (Leiden, 1962), p. 29.

18. Rāshid al-Barrāwī, *Ḥalat Miṣr al-iqtiṣādiyah fī ʿahd al-Fāṭimīyīn* (Cairo, 1948), p. 338 (*Ḥalat* in later references).

19. H. Derenbourg, *ʿOumâra du Yemen* (Paris, 1897), 1:53.

20. See p. 101 below.

21. Al-Barrāwī, *Ḥalat*, p. 353; Stanley Lane-Poole, *A History of Egypt* (London, 1901), p. 175.

22. Andrew S. Ehrenkreutz, "Arab dīnārs struck by the Crusaders: a case of ignorance or of economic subversion," *Journal of the Economic and Social History of the Orient* 7 (1964): 167–182.

23. Robin Fedden and John Thomson, *Crusader Castles* (London, 1957), pp. 24–27.

24. "The Place of Saladin," p. 102.

25. Ibid.

26. Wiet, *Précis*, p. 287.

27. Ibid., p. 288.

28. Lane-Poole, *A History of Egypt*, p. 175; *Itt.*, fol. 150r. This and subsequent data from *Ittiʿāẓ al-ḥunafāʾ* have been derived from the final and unpublished fragment of a unique manuscript (cf. *Revue des Études Islamiques* 10 [1936]: 343–344, 352) containing a complete version of the interesting treatise of al-Maqrīzī, and held in the Topkapu Palace Archives. Another incomplete manuscript, *Kitāb Itti ʿāẓ*, from the Gotha Library (MS. 1652), was edited by Hugo Bunz (Leipzig, 1909) and by Dr. Gamal al-Dīn al-Shayyāl (Cairo, 1948). In 1967 the latter undertook to prepare a revised version of the *Itti ʿāẓ*, based on the Gotha and the Istanbul manuscripts (cf. *Itti ʿāẓ*, Cairo, 1967), but his death prevented the final fragment from appearing in print. Some of the information from the unpublished manuscript was included in Shayyāl's *Aʿlām al-Iskandarīyah fī ʿaṣr al-Islām* (Cairo, 1965).

29. Lane-Poole, *History of Egypt*, p. 176.

30. See above, pp. 16–17.

31. ASh, vol. 1, pt. 2, p. 416.

32. Ibid.

33. See p. 47 below.

34. A. H. Helbig, *al-Qāḍī al-Fāḍil, der Wezir Saladins* (Leipzig, 1908), p. 13.

35. ASh, vol. 1, pt. 2, p. 420.

36. Ibid., p. 417.

37. Ibid.

38. Ibid.

39. Lane-Poole, *A History of Egypt*, p. 177.

40. ASh, vol. 1, pt. 2, p. 417.

41. Ibid., p. 332.

42. See above, p. 20.
43. ASh, vol. 1, pt. 2, p. 418.
44. Ibid.
45. Ibid.

Chapter 2

1. "The Achievement of Saladin," p. 99.
2. *Saladin,* pp. 66–67.
3. Ibid., pp. 72–73.
4. Ibid., p. 76.
5. Ibid., p. 73.
6. Ibid., p. 4.
7. Vladimir Minorsky, "Prehistory of Saladin," in Vladimir Minorsky, *Studies in Caucasian History* (London, 1953), p. 133.
8. Ibid., p. 136.
9. IW, 1:8.
10. ASh, vol. 1, pt. 1, p. 369.
11. Ibn al-Qalānisī, *Dhayl taʾrīkh Dimashq* (Leiden, 1908), p. 270.
12. Elisséeff, 2:469.
13. ASh, vol. 1, pt. 1, p. 210.
14. Ibid., p. 250; IW, 1:268–269.
15. Elisséeff, 3:917, 926.
16. IW, 1:268.
17. *Saladin,* p. 75.
18. IA, 11:95; IW, 1:130–131.
19. Elisséeff, 2:531–533.
20. Ibid., pp. 518–519. However Elisséeff believes that the incident reported by Ibn al-Athīr took place during the earlier illness of Nūr al-Dīn.
21. Ibn Taghrī Birdī, *al-Nujūm al-zāhirah* (Cairo, 1935), 6:69.

22. ASh, vol. 1, pt. 1, p. 210.
23. Ibid., pp. 250–251.
24. Ibid., p. 251.
25. Ibid., p. 252.
26. Ibid., p. 268.
27. Abū Shāmah (*Rawḍatayn,* vol. 1, pt. 2, p. 395) places Saladin's house *bi-ḥarat Qutāmish jiwār qaysāriyat al-qiṣāʿ wa ilayhā yajrī al-māʾ min ḥamām Nūr al-Dīn* . . . This information is confusing. Should *qaysāriyat al-qiṣāʿ* be related to *darb al-qaṣṣāʿ-in* (cf. N. Elisséeff, *La Description de Damas d'Ibn ʿAsākir* [Damascus, 1959], p. 85), then the house of Saladin would be situated too far from the bathhouse of Nūr al-Dīn to draw water from it (cf. Elisséeff, p. 278).
28. ASh, vol. 1, pt. 1, p. 252; ibid., vol. 1, pt. 2, pp. 378, 382.
29. See below, pp. 169, 228.
30. ASh, vol. 1, pt. 2, p. 440; *Saladin,* p. 99.
31. Sibt, p. 227.
32. ASh, vol. 1, pt. 1, p. 311.
33. Elisséeff, 2:558–559.

Chapter 3

1. *Itt.,* fol. 155 v.
2. Ibid.
3. *Itt.,* fol. 155 v; ASh, vol. 1, pt. 2, p. 420.
4. ASh, vol. 1, pt. 2, p. 421.
5. To the north of al-Tāj, *Itt.,* fol. 155 v.

6. Cf. *Jacut's Geographisches Wörterbuch* (Leipzig, 1867), 2:79.

7. Ibid.; cf. ASh, vol. 1, pt. 2, p. 421.

8. *Itt.*, fol. 155 v.

9. Details of the entire battle at Kawm al-Rīsh and in Cairo, recorded by Ibn Abī Ṭayyi, are found in *Itt.*, fol. 155 v.–156 r.

10. *Saladin*, p. 83.

11. Sibṭ, p. 252.

12. See above, pp. 31–32.

13. ASh, vol. 1, pt. 2, p. 671; Sibṭ, p. 327.

14. *Itt.* fol. 156 r.

15. Ibid.

16. ASh, vol. 1, pt. 2, p. 400.

17. Ibid., p. 424; *Itt.* fol. 156 r.

18. ASh, vol. 1, pt. 2, p. 425; *Itt.*, fol. 156 v.

19. Ibid.

20. Ibid.

21. ASh, vol. 1, pt. 2, p. 60.

22. Ibid., p. 425.

23. For a description of the ceremony see, *Saladin*, pp. 87–88.

24. ASh, vol. 1, pt. 2, p. 526; *Itt.*, fol. 157 r.

25. See above, p. 41.

26. ASh, vol. 1, pt. 2, p. 527; *Itt.*, fol. 157 r.

27. Ibid.

28. *Itt.* fol. 157 r.

29. ASh, vol. 1, pt. 2, p. 370, 427; *Itt.* fol. 157 r.

30. *Itt.* fol. 157 r; *BJ*, p. 137.

31. *Itt.* fol. 157 r; cf. *Saladin*, p. 91.

32. ASh, vol. 1, pt. 2, p. 428.

33. *Itt.* fol. 157 r.

34. ASh, vol. 1, pt. 2, p. 428; *Itt.* fol. 157 v.

35. ASh, vol. 1, pt. 2, p. 383.

36. Idem, p. 381, 382.

37. Idem, p. 372.

38. Idem, p. 366; *Itt.* fol. 157 v.

39. Ibid.

40. Ibid.

41. ASh, vol. 1, pt. 2, p. 431; *Itt.* fol. 158 r; *BJ*, p. 138.

42. ASh, vol. 1, pt. 2, p. 401; *Itt.* fol. 157 v.

43. ASh, vol. 1, pt. 2, p. 375; *Itt.* fol. 157 v–158 r.

44. ASh, vol. 1, pt. 2, p. 428; *Itt.* fol. 157 v.

45. *Itt.*, fol. 159 r.

46. ASh, vol. 1, pt. 2, p. 390.

47. Ibid., p. 430; *Itt.*, fol. 158 r.

48. ASh, vol. 1, pt. 2, pp. 430–431; *Itt.*, fol. 158 r.

49. Ibid.

50. ASh, vol. 1, pt. 2, p. 431.

51. Ibid.; *Itt.*, fol. 158 r–158 v; *Saladin*, p. 92.

52. ASh, vol. 1, pt. 2, p. 431; *Itt.*, fol. 159 r.

53. ASh, vol. 1, pt. 2, p. 431; *Itt.*, fol. 158 v.

54. *Itt.*, fol. 158 v.

55. Ibid., ASh, vol. 1, pt. 2, p. 432.

56. ASh, vol. 1, pt. 2, p. 433; *Itt.*, fol. 159 r.

57. Ibid.

58. ASh, vol. 1, pt. 2, p. 432; *Itt.*, fol. 158 v.

59. *Itt.*, fol. 158 v.

60. Ibid.

61. Ibid.

62. ASh, vol. 1, pt. 2, p. 393.

63. Ibid., p. 394; IW, 1:159.

64. Ibid.

65. Ibid.

66. Ibid.

67. "The Armies of Saladin," p. 74.

68. ASh, vol. 1, pt. 2, p. 393; IW, 1:160; *Itt.,* fol. 158 v.

69. "The Armies of Saladin," p. 74.

70. ASh, vol. 1, pt. 2, p. 449.

71. See above, p. 47.

72. ASh, vol. 1, pt. 2, p. 432; *Itt.,* fol. 158 v.

73. ASh, vol. 1, pt. 2, p. 433; *Itt.,* fol. 159 r–159 v.

74. *Itt.,* fol. 159 v.

75. ASh, vol. 1, pt. 2, p. 433.

76. Ibid., p. 434; *Itt.* fol. 159 r.

77. Ibid.

78. ASh, vol. 1, pt. 2, p. 435.

79. Ibid., pp. 398, 435.

80. Ibid., pp. 396–397, 435; *Itt.,* fol. 160 r. According to Cahen, *EJ,* p. 138, Shirkūh was warned by al-ʿĀdid himself.

81. ASh, vol. 1, pt. 2, p. 397; *Itt.,* fol. 160 r.

82. IW, 2:443–454.

83. *Itt.,* fol. 160 v.

84. Ibid.

85. Sibṭ, pp. 277–278.

86. *Saladin,* pp. 95–96.

87. ASh, vol. 1, pt. 2, p. 455; *Itt.,* fol. 160 r.

88. *Itt.* fol. 159 v.

89. ASh, vol. 1, pt. 2, p. 403.

90. *Itt.,* fol. 160 v.

91. ASh, vol. 1, pt. 2, p. 402.

92. *Itt.,* fol. 160 v.

93. Ibid.

94. ASh, vol. 1, pt. 2, p. 437; *Itt.* fol. 160 v–161 r.

95. ASh, vol. 1, pt. 2, p. 437; *Itt.* fol. 161 r.

96. ASh, vol. 1, pt. 2, pp. 406, 441.

97. ASh, vol. 1, pt. 2, p. 403.

Chapter 4

1. *Saladin,* p. 98–99.

2. IW, 1:168; Sibṭ, p. 278.

3. Since the Nūrīyah commanders were the only ones to refuse joining the pro-Saladin block it implies that Bahāʾ al-Dīn must have supported Saladin, cf. *Itt.,* fol. 161 v.

4. IW, 1:169.

5. Ibid.

6. Ibid.

7. IW, 1:170.

8. ASh, vol. 1, pt. 2, p. 407; IW, 1:169.

9. *Itt.,* fol. 161 r–161 v.

10. See above, p. 55.

11. *Itt.,* fol. 161 v.

12. ASh, vol. 1, pt. 2, pp. 438–439; *Itt.,* fol. 161 v.

13. IW, 1:169.

14. ASh, vol. 1, pt. 2, p. 439.

15. ASh, vol. 1, pt. 2, p. 407; IW, 1:168.

16. For a discussion of the significance of this title, see Ḥasan

al-Bāshā, *al-Alqāb al-Islāmīyah,*
(Cairo, 1957), p. 525 f.

17. *Itt.,* fol. 161 v; IW, 2:455–
462.

18. "The Rise of Saladin," p.
564.

19. ASh, vol. 1, pt. 2, p. 440.

20. ASh, vol. 1, pt. 2, p. 407.

21. ASh, vol. 1, pt. 2, p. 440 f;
Itt., fol. 161 v.

22. ASh, vol. 1, pt. 2, p. 440.

Chapter 5

1. ASh, vol. 1, pt. 2, p. 402.

2. ASh, vol. 1, pt. 2, p. 440; *Itt.,*
fol. 161 v.

3. *Itt.,* fol. 162 r.

4. Supra.

5. ASh, vol. 1, pt. 2, pp. 406, 441;
Itt., fol. 162 r; IS, p. 41.

6. ASh, vol. 1, pt. 2, p. 408.

7. *Itt.,* fol. 162 r.

8. ASh, vol. 1, pt. 2, p. 440; *Itt.,*
fol. 161 v.

9. *Saladin,* p. 100; ASh, vol. 1,
pt. 2, p. 408.

10. ASh, vol. 1, pt. 2, pp. 408,
438.

11. El-Beheiry, *Les institutions
de l'Égypte au temps des Ayyūbīdes,*
(Cairo, 1971), p. 331.

12. Ibid., p. 332.

13. "The Armies of Saladin,"
p. 74.

14. Ibid., p. 76.

15. *Ḥalat,* p. 338.

16. "The Armies of Saladin,"
p. 76.

17. ASh, vol. 1, pt. 2, pp. 402,
438.

18. ASh, vol. 1, pt. 2, p. 450;
Itt., fol. 162 r.

19. IW, 1:174.

20. ASh, vol. 1, pt. 2, p. 451;
Itt., fol. 162 r.

21. Ibid.

22. *Itt.,* fol. 162 r.

23. ASh, vol. 1, pt. 2, p. 452;
Itt., fol. 162 r–162 v.

24. *Itt.,* fol. 162 v.

25. Ibid.

26. *Supra;* BJ, p. 139.

27. ASh, vol. 1, pt. 2, p. 452;
Itt., fol. 162 v.

28. *Itt.,* fol. 162 v.

29. "The Armies of Saladin,"
p. 74.

30. *Itt.,* fol. 162 v; IW, 1:178–179.

31. "The Place of Saladin,"
p. 103.

32. IS, pp. 41–43; ASh, vol. 1,
pt. 2, pp. 456–459; *Itt.,* fol.
162 v–163 r; IW, 1:179–183.

33. ASh, vol. 1, pt. w, p. 457.

34. ASh, vol. 1, pt. 2, p. 460;
IW, 1:183; *Itt.,* fol. 163 r.

35. *BJ,* p. 138.

36. ASh, vol. 1, pt. 2, pp. 466,
487; *Itt.,* fol. 163 r, 163 v.

37. *Saladin,* p. 100.

38. "The Armies of Saladin,"
p. 75.

39. ASh, vol. 1, pt. 2, p. 466.

40. ASh, vol. 1, pt. 2, pp. 486,
489–491; IW, 1:198–199; *Itt.,* fol.
163 v; *Saladin,* p. 106–107.

41. *Itt.,* fol. 163 v.

42. ASh, vol. 1, pt. 2, p. 486; *Itt.,* fol. 163 v.

43. ASh, vol. 1, pt. 2, p. 488; *Itt.,* fol. 163 v.

44. ASh, vol. 1, pt. 2, p. 487; *Itt.,* fol. 163 v.

45. IA, 11:138.

46. *Saladin,* p. 109.

47. "The Rise of Saladin," p. 565.

48. *Saladin,* p. 109. Ḥasan Ibrāhīm Ḥasan, *Ta'rīkh al-Dawlah al-Fāṭimīyah,* (1964), p. 200.

49. Cl. Cahen, "Ayyūbids," *EI,* 1:797; s.v.

50. See above, p. 82.

51. *Itt.,* fol. 163 r.

52. Ibid.

53. Ibid.

54. ASh, vol. 1, pt. 2, p. 486.

55. ASh, vol. 1, pt. 2, p. 487.

56. *Itt.,* fol. 163 v.

57. Ibid.

58. ASh, vol. 1, pt. 2, p. 486. Al-Maqrīzī, *Itt.,* fol. 163 v. lists Friday, 19 *Jumādā* II, as the date of the official appointment.

59. IW, 1:198.

60. *Itt.,* fol. 163 v. The purge of the pro-Fāṭimid elements appears to have been applied even to some judges in the Jewish community of Egypt. (cf., S. D. Goitein "Minority Selfrule and Government Control in Islam," *Studia Islamica* [1970]: 113).

61. Cf., A. H. Helbig, *al-Qāḍī al-Fāḍil, der Wezir Saladins,* (Leipzig, 1908), p. 18.

62. *Itt.,* fol. 163 v–164 r.

63. Ibid., fol 164 r.

64. ASh, vol. 1, pt. 2, pp. 494, 498.

65. IA, 11:138; Ibn Taghrī Birdī, *al-Nujūm al-zāhirah* (Cairo, 1935), 5:357.

66. Ibn Taghrī Birdī, loc cit.

67. IA, 11:138.

68. In A.D. 1174, over two years after the suppression of the Fāṭimid Caliphate, the members of the overthrown establishment managed to set up a dangerous conspiracy which included some of Saladin's commanders, see p. 112 below.

69. IA, loc. cit., 11:138.

70. Cf., IW, 1:55; *Ibn Khallikān's Biogrophical Dictionary,* trans. *MacGuckin De Slane* (Paris and London, 1843–71), 2:368; Ibn Taghrī Birdī, op. cit., 5:367–368.

71. Ibn Khallikān, *op. cit.,* 2:74.

72. IW, 1:54, 12:4; Ibn Khallikān, op. cit., 2:645.

73. Cf. M. Canard, "La procession du Nouvel An chez les Fāṭimides," *Annales de l'Institut des Études Orientales* 10 (1952): 364–398; Ḥasan Ibrāhīm Ḥasan, *Ta'rīkh al-Dawlah al-Fāṭimīyah,* p. 649; Saladin set out on his expedition on Muḥarram 22 (25 September A.D. 1171); ASh, vol. 1, pt. 2, p. 518; Al-Maqrīzī, *Sulūk,* p. 44, gives the date of Muḥarram 19.

74. Ibn Taghrī Birdī, op. cit., 5:357.

75. IA, 11:138.

76. IA, 11:138

77. Cf. H. A. R. Gibb, "Notes on the Arabic Materials for the History of the Early Crusades," *Bulletin of the School of Oriental Studies* 7 (1935): 746; also M. Hilmy M. Ahmad, "Some notes on Arabic Historiography during the Zengid and Ayyūbid Periods (521/1127–648/1250)," in *Historians of the Middle East* (London, 1962), p. 90.

78. IA, 11:138.

79. ʿImād al-Dīn, *apud* ASh, vol. 1, pt. 2, p. 492; ibid., p. 497; Ibn al-Dubaythī, *Taʾrīkh . . . (Al-Mukhtaṣar . . . intiqāʾ al-Dhahabī)*, (Baghdād, 1951), 1:142; Ibn Taghrī Birdī, op. cit., 5:343; Al-Ṣafadī, *Al-Wāfī bi-al-wafayāt*, (Damascus, 1959) 4:390; Ibn Taghrī Birdī also stated that the first to invoke the pro-ʿAbbāsid *khuṭbah* was a Shī ʿite khaṭīb, cf., *al-Nujūm al-zāhirah*, 5:356; Cf., editorial note of Jamāl al-Dīn al-Shayyāl, IW, 1:200, n. 3; Al-Maqrīzī mentions the name of Abū Yaḥyā al-Ghāfiqī al-Andalusī in connection with the first 'khuṭbah incident.' *Itt.,* fol. 164 r.

80. ASh, vol. 1, pt. 2, p. 492. Concerning Abū Shāmah's reliability, see M. Hilmy M. Ahmad, op. cit., p. 94

81. Concerning the reliability of Ibn Abī Ṭayyi, see ibid., p. 91.

82. ASh, vol. 1, pt. 2, p. 499. Ibn Taghrī Birdī recorded that the invocation of the *khuṭbah* on that

day had included the name, *laqab* and *kunyah* of al-Mustaḍī. Cf., *al-Nujūm al-zāhirah,* 5:357.

83. The fact that neither Ibn al-Athīr nor Ibn Abī Ṭayyi (or Abū Shāmah) specified the name of the mosque in question may serve as 'argumentum ex silentio' in favor of identifying *al-jāmiʿ al-ʿatīq* as the site of the incident. This interpretation is corroborated by a pertinent implicit statement found in Ibn Taghrī Birdī, *al-Nujūm al-zāhirah,* 5:356.

84. "The Armies of Saladin," p. 76.

85. ASh, vol. 1, pt. 2, p. 495. According to Ibn Abī Uṣaybiʿah the death occurred on the ninth of Muḥarram; cf. *ʿUyūn al-anbāʾ fī ṭabaqāt al-aṭibbā* (Beirut, 1965), p. 574.

86. IA, 11:138.

87. Ibn Taghrī Birdī, op. cit., 5:357.

88. Sibṭ, p. 292.

89. Ibn Abī Ṭayyi *apud* ASh, vol. 1, pt. 2, p. 499.

90. Sibṭ, p. 290.

91. ASh, vol. 1, pt. 2, p. 499.

92. Ibid., also Sibṭ, loc. cit., also, Ibn Ḥammād, *Akhbār Banī ʿUbayd* (Paris, 1927), p. 63.

93. Ibn Ḥammād, loc. cit. Contemporary Christian authors explicitly accused Saladin of having assassinated al-ʿĀḍid. Cf. William of Tyre, *A History of Deeds Done Beyond the Sea* (New York, 1943), ii:359; also, G. Paris, "Un

poème latin contemporain sur Saladin," *Revue de l'Orient Latin,* 1 (1893): 438; also, *Chronique de Robert de Torigni* (Rouen, 1873), ii:54; Cf. J. Hartmann, *Die Persönlichkeit des Sultans Saladin im Urteil der abendländischen Quellen* (Berlin, 1933), pp. 30, 124.

94. Ibn Taghrī Birdī, *al-Nujūm al-zāhirah,* 5:357.

95. Ibn Abī Uṣaybiʿah, *ʿUyūn al-anbāʾ fī ṭabaqāt al-aṭibbā,* p. 574.

96. ASh, vol. 1, pt. 2, p. 499.

97. IA, 11:138; Abū Shāmah, vol. 1, pt. 2, p. 494, states that in A.H. 628 (A.D. 1231) he talked to al-ʿĀdid's son, Abū al-Futūḥ, chained up in a dungeon of the Cairo citadel. The latter maintained that Saladin had visited the dying caliph who had entrusted his children to the vizier's care. One wonders, however, how much trust one can place in the story or the memory of an unfortunate sexagenarian prisoner claiming to remember an episode that had taken place sixty years earlier.

98. Ibn Taghrī Birdī, *al-Nujūm al-zāhirah,* 5:357.

99. ASh, vol. 1, pt. 2, p. 494.

100. *Itt.,* fol. 169 r.

101. Ibn Ḥammād, *Akhbār, Banī ʿUbayd,* p. 63.

102. Ibid., also, ASh, vol. 1, pt. 2, p. 494.

103. *Itt.,* fol. 169 r.

104. Ibid.

105. *Itt.,* fol. 165 r.

106. *Itt.,* fol. 164 v. Cf. also above, p. 91.

107. ASh, vol. 1, pt. 2, pp. 493–495, 506–507; IA, 11:138.

108. *Sulūk,* p. 44.

109. ASh, vol. 1, pt. 2, p. 455.

110. Ibid., pp. 496, 502.

111. *Sulūk,* p. 45.

112. Ibid., p. 46. In the light of the information of al-Maqrīzī (cf., also note 114 below) the date of 21 of *Rajab* which is listed in ASh, vol. 1, pt. 2, p. 506, appears to be an error.

113. *Sulūk,* p. 47.

Chapter 6

1. See above, p. 43.

2. *Sulūk,* p. 47; "The Armies of Saladin," p. 76.

3. *Sulūk,* p. 45–46; Sibṭ, p. 291.

4. Sibṭ, p. 291.

5. ASh, vol. 1, pt. 2, p. 525.

6. *Sulūk,* p. 52.

7. ASh, vol. 1, pt. 2, pp. 558–560.

8. Elisséeff, 2:647–649.

9. Ibid., pp. 665–666.

10. See below, p. 105.

11. See below, p. 106.

12. IA, 11:139.

13. ASh, vol. 1, pt. 2, p. 522; *al-Nuẓum al-mālīyah,* p. 50.

14. ASh, vol. 1, pt. 2, p. 443.

15. *Sulūk,* p. 46.

16. "The Place of Saladin," p. 106.

17. ASh, vol. 1, pt. 2, p. 522. According to Labib, p. 253, those

were the effective fiscal, even if temporary, concessions made by Saladin. Their value amounted to 66473 *dīnārs*. Their nature was misrepresented by al-Maqrīzī, *Khiṭaṭ*, 1:103–110.

18. Ashtor, p. 141 and *passim*.

19. S. D. Goitein, "Letters and Documents on the India Trade in Medieval Times," *Islamic Culture* 27 (1963): 195.

20. See above, p. 100.

21. Labib, p. 25.

22. Ibid., p. 30.

23. ASh, vol. 1, pt. 2, pp. 621–622.

24. A. S. Ehrenkreutz, "The Crisis of *Dīnār* in the Egypt of Saladin," *Journal of the American Oriental Society* 76 (1956): 182–183.

25. A. S. Ehrenkreutz, "Arabic *Dīnārs* Struck by the Crusaders—A Case of Ignorance or of Economic Subversion," *Journal of the Economic and Social History of the Orient* 7 (1964):167-182.

26. Al-Maqrīzī, *Shudhūr al-ʿuqūd* (Alexandria, 1933), p. 12; *Sulūk*, p. 46.

27. ASh, vol. 1, pt. 2, pp. 495, 506; *Itt.,* fol. 165 v.

28. *Sulūk*, p. 45. The low output is suggested by analysis of available numismatic evidence examined by the present author.

29. *Sulūk*, p. 45.

30. P. Balog, "History of the Dirhem in Egypt from the Fāṭimid Conquest until the Collapse of the Mamlūk Empire," *Revue Numismatique* VI Série, Rome III (1961); 122–129.

31. P. Balog, "The Ayyūbid Glass Jetons and Their Use," *Journal of the Economic and Social History of the Orient* 9 (1966): 242–256.

32. *Sulūk*, p. 47.

33. *al-Nuẓum al-mālīyah*, p. 26.

34. Ibid., p. 41 f.

35. Ibid., p. 52.

36. S. D. Goitein, *A Mediterranean Society*, 1:271.

37. IA, 11:139.

38. Ibid.

39. ASh, vol. 1, pt. 2, p. 518; *Sulūk*, p. 44.

40. *Saladin*, p. 123.

41. ASh, vol. 1, pt. 2, pp. 526–527; Sibṭ, p. 293; IW, 2:475

42. *Sulūk*, p. 45; Elisséeff, 2:694, 3:816 f.

43. See above, p. 100.

44. IA, 11:139; Elisséeff, 2:672.

45. "The Rise of Saladin," p. 565–566.

46. Ibid., p. 47.

47. Ibid., p. 45.

48. Ibid., p. 48.

49. Ibid.

50. ASh, vol. 1, pt. 2, pp. 530–533.

51. ASh, vol. 1, pt. 2, p. 533.

52. IA, 11:146; ASh, vol. 1, pt. 2, p. 548.

53. See below, p. 215.

54. ASh, vol. 1, pt. 2, p. 547.

55. "The Place of Saladin," p. 105.

56. ASh, vol. 1, pt. 2, pp. 507–508.

57. Sibṭ, pp. 303–304.

58. ASh, vol. 1, pt. 2, pp. 551–552.

59. IA, 11:148.

60. ASh, vol. 1, pt. 2, p. 554.

61. ASh, vol. 1, pt. 2, pp. 554–555.

62. ASh, vol. 1, pt. 2, pp. 560–561; IA, 11:149.

63. ASh, vol. 1, pt. 2, p. 560; IW 1:244.

64. ASh, vol. 1, pt. 2, pp. 560–561.

65. Sibṭ, p. 414.

66. ASh, vol. 1, pt. 2, p. 562.

67. "The Armies of Saladin," p. 75.

68. See above, p. 46; also ASh, vol. 1, pt. 2, p. 565.

69. ASh, vol. 1, pt. 2, p. 565; also B. Lewis, *The Assassins* (New York, 1968), p. 114.

70. ASh, vol. 1, pt. 2, p. 561; *BJ*, p. 139.

71. IA, 11:150; IW, 1:236.

72. ASh, vol. 1, pt. 2, pp. 560–561.

73. *Itt.*, fol. 169 r; IW, 1:247.

74. ASh, vol. 1, pt. 2, p. 561; IW, 1:246.

75. ASh, vol. 1, pt. 2, p. 560; IW, 1:246; *Sulūk*, p. 54.

76. ASh, vol. 1, pt. 2, p. 569; *Sulūk*, p. 54.

77. *Sulūk*, p. 54.

78. ASh, vol. 1, pt. 2, p. 561; IW, 1:246; *Sulūk*, p. 54.

79. *Sulūk*, p. 54.

80. *Itt.*, fol. 169 r.

81. *Sulūk*, p. 54.

82. Ibid.

83. Ibid.

84. See above, p. 99.

85. IA, *al-Atābakīyah*, p. 161; ASh, vol. 1, pt. 2, p. 581; IW, 1:259; Elisséeff, 2:692–693.

86. IS, p. 47.

87. Sibṭ, p. 299.

Chapter 7

1. ASh, vol. 1, pt. 2, pp. 585–586; Sibṭ, p. 324; Elisséeff, 2:694–695.

2. ASh, vol. 1, pt. 2, p. 588.

3. ASh, vol. 1, pt. 2, pp. 604–605; *Sulūk*, p. 58.

4. ASh, vol. 1, pt. 2, p. 597.

5. ASh, vol. 1, pt. 2, p. 593.

6. ASh, vol. 1, pt. 2, p. 595; Elisséeff, 2:697.

7. B. Lewis, *The Assassins*, p. 112 f.

8. ASh, vol. 1, pt. 2, p. 586; IW, 2:2.

9. ASh, vol. 1, pt. 2, pp. 589, 594; IW, 2:3.

10. ASh, vol. 1, pt. 2, p. 587; IW, 2:4; Sibṭ, p. 324.

11. IA, 11:152; ASh, vol. 1, pt. 2, p. 590.

12. ASh, vol. 1, pt. 2, p. 588.

13. IA, 11:153; ASh, vol. 1, pt. 2, pp. 590–591; IW, 2:5; Elisséeff, 2:695.

14. IA, 11:153; ASh, vol. 1, pt. 2, p. 589; Sibṭ, p. 324; IW, 2:7.

15. ASh, vol. 1, pt. 2, p. 595.

16. ASh, vol. 1, pt. 2, p. 441.

17. IA, 11:106.

18. ASh, vol. 1, pt. 2, p. 593.

19. ASh, vol. 1, pt. 2, p. 594.

20. ASh, vol. 1, pt. 2, p. 596.

21. See above, p. 55.

22. ASh, vol. 1, pt. 2, p. 596.

23. ASh, vol. 1, pt. 2, p. 441.

24. ASh, vol. 1, pt. 2, p. 590.

25. IA, 11:158; ASh, vol. 1, pt. 2, p. 637; IW, 2:30.

26. IA, 11:152; ASh, vol. 1, pt. 2, p. 590; *Saladin,* p. 135.

27. ASh, vol. 1, pt. 2, p. 363.

28. ASh, vol. 1, pt. 2, p. 595.

29. ASh, vol. 1, pt. 2, p. 597.

30. ASh, vol. 1, pt. 2, pp. 597–598; "The Rise of Saladin," p. 567.

31. ASh, vol. 1, pt. 2, p. 589.

32. "The Place of Saladin," p. 104; H. Wieruszowski, "The Norman Kingdom of Sicily and the Crusades," *A History of the Crusades* (Philadelphia: University of Pennsylvania Press, 1955–62, 2:35–36.

33. IS, p. 47–48; ASh, vol. 1, pt. 2, pp. 600–602; *Sulūk,* p. 57; P. Casanova, "Les Derniers Fāṭimides," *Memoires de la Mission Archéologique Française au Caire,* vol. 6, fasc. 3.

34. IA, 11:156; ASh, vol. 1, pt. 2, p. 592, 604; Elisséeff, 2:698.

35. ASh, vol. 1, pt. 2, pp. 604–605; IW, 2:19.

36. ASh, vol. 1, pt. 2, pp. 604–648.

37. ASh, vol. 1, pt. 2, pp. 602–604; IW, 2:18:19.

38. IW, 2:19.

39. ASh, vol. 1, pt. 2, p. 602; IW, 2:19–20.

40. IS, p. 50; ASh, vol. 1, pt. 2, p. 602.

41. ASh, vol. 1, pt. 2, p. 603.

42. ASh, vol. 1, pt. 2, p. 605; IW, 2:20.

43. ASh, vol. 1, pt. 2, p. 671; Sibṭ, p. 327. According to Sibṭ (p. 340) Saladin wrote to Ibn al-Shahrazūrī, asking him for assistance in seizing Damascus.

44. ASh, vol. 1, pt. 2, p. 602; IW, 2:20.

45. ASh, vol. 1, pt. 2, p. 604; IW, 2:20.

46. See above, p. 72.

47. Sibṭ, pp. 327–38; see above, p. 116.

48. Sibṭ, p. 328.

49. Ibid.

50. ASh, vol. 1, pt. 2, p. 607; IW, 2:21; Sibṭ, p. 328.

51. ASh, vol. 1, pt. 2, p. 607; Sibṭ, p. 328.

52. Sibṭ, loc. cit.

53. Sibṭ, loc. cit.; ASh, loc. cit.

54. ASh, loc. cit.; IW, 2:21.

55. ASh, vol. 1, pt. 2, p. 607.

56. Sibṭ, p. 328.

57. IA, 11:157; ASh, vol. 1, pt. 2, p. 607; IW, 2:22.

58. ASh, loc. cit.; IW, loc. cit.

59. ASh, vol. 1, pt. 2, p. 640; IW, 2:34.

60. See above, p. 122.

61. ASh, vol. 1, pt. 2, pp.

607–608; IW, 2:22–23; IA, 11:157.

62. IA, loc. cit.; ASh, vol. 1, pt. 2, pp. 608–609; IW, 2:23.

63. ASh, vol. 1, pt. 2, p. 612.

64. IA, 11:157–158; ASh, vol. 1, pt. 2, pp. 609–610.

65. ASh, vol. 1, pt. 2, p. 610.

66. IA, 11:158; ASh, vol. 1, pt. 2, pp. 610, 637; IW, 2:24.

67. B. Lewis, "Saladin and the Assassins," *Bulletin of the School of Oriental and African Studies* 15 (1953): 239.

68. William of Tyre *apud* "The Rise of Saladin," p. 568.

69. ASh, vol. 1, pt. 2, p. 614.

70. IA, 11:158; ASh, vol. 1, pt. 2, pp. 627, 631; IW, 2:29.

71. ASh, vol. 1, pt. 2, p. 616; IW, 2:25.

72. ASh, vol. 1, pt. 2, pp. 616–620.

73. ASh, vol. 1, pt. 2, p. 617.

74. ASh, vol. 1, pt. 2, p. 618.

75. ASh, vol. 1, pt. 2, p. 620.

76. ASh, vol. 1, pt. 2, pp. 620–621.

77. ASh, vol. 1, pt. 2, pp. 621–622.

78. ASh, vol. 1, pt. 2, p. 622.

79. ASh, vol. 1, pt. 2, pp. 622–623.

80. IA, 11:158; IW, 2:31.

81. Ibid.

82. IA, 11:159; ASh, vol. 1, pt. 2, p. 637.

83. ASh, vol. 1, pt. 2, p. 637.

84. See above, p. 130.

85. ASh, vol. 1, pt. 2, p. 637; IW, 2:31. According to IA, 11:159,

the initiative to negotiate came from Saladin.

86. ASh, vol. 1, pt. 2, pp. 634, 637; IW, 2:32.

87. IW, 2:32.

88. ASh, vol. 1, pt. 2, pp. 637–638; IW, 2:32.

89. See above, p. 59.

90. ASh, vol. 1, pt. 2, pp. 637–638; IW, 2:32.

91. ASh, loc. cit.

92. IA, 11:159.

93. ASh, vol. 1, pt. 2, p. 635.

94. ASh, vol. 1, pt. 2, pp. 638–639. Slightly different version given by IA, 11:159.

95. IA, loc. cit.; ASh, vol. 1, pt. 2, pp. 639, 640; IW, 2:33; Sibṭ, p. 329; "The Rise of Saladin," p. 568

96. IA, 11:159; ASh, vol. 1, pt. 2, pp. 639–640; IW, 2:34.

97. IA, loc. cit.; *Saladin*, p. 141; also, ʿAbd al-Raḥmān Fahmī, "al-Sikkah al-Ayyūbīyah al-Miṣrīyah bi-Mathaf al-Fann al-Islāmī, bi-al-Qāhirah," in Ibn Baʿrah, *Kitāb Kashf al-Asrār al-ʿIlmīyah,* (Cairo, 1966), p. 98.

98. A subsequent treaty, concluded in 1176 (see below, p. 151), called for the release of the Awlād al-Dayah.

99. See above, p. 130.

100. "The Place of Saladin," p. 104.

101. ASh, vol. 1, pt. 2, p. 643; IW, 2:36.

102. IA, 11:59; ASh, vol. 1, pt. 2., p. 640; IW, 2:34.

103. Sibṭ, p. 329. Bernard Lewis

suggests that this raid might have taken place while Saladin's army was moving northwards to Aleppo (cf. Lewis, *The Assassins,* p. 114.)

104. ASh, vol. 1, pt. 2, p. 669.

105. See above, p. 123.

106. See above, pp. 133–34.

107. ASh, vol. 1, pt. 2, p. 643; IW, 2:35.

108. ASh, vol. 1, pt. 2, p. 643.

109. ASh, loc. cit.; Sibṭ, pp. 329–330.

110. ASh, vol. 1, pt. 2, p. 643; *Sulūk,* p. 60.

111. ASh, vol. 1, pt. 2, p. 665–666.

112. ASh, vol. 1, pt. 2, p. 643; *Sulūk,* p. 60.

113. ASh, vol. 1, pt. 2, p. 644.

114. ASh, vol. 1, pt. 2, pp. 647–648; IW, 2:37; Sibṭ, p. 332.

115. ASh, vol. 1, pt. 2, p. 648; IW, 2:37.

116. IA, 11:161; IS, p. 51; IW, 2:37.

117. ASh, vol. 1, pt. 2, p. 651; IW, 2:38; Marshall W. Baldwin, "The Decline and Fall of Jerusalem, 1174–1189," *A History of the Crusades* (Philadelphia: University of Pennsylvania Press, 1958–62), 2:593, n. 2.

118. See below, p. 179.

119. See below, p. 199.

120. IS, p. 51; ASh, vol. 1, pt. 2, p. 649.

121. ASh, vol. 1, pt. 2, p. 650; IW, 2:38.

122. IS, p. 51; IA, 11:161; ASh, vol. 1, pt. 2, p. 650; IW, 2:38.

123. *Sulūk,* p. 61.

124. IS, p. 52; ASh, vol. 1, pt. 2, pp. 650–651.

125. Sibṭ, p. 333.

126. IA, 11:161; IW, 2:39. According to Sibṭ, p. 333, Saladin was approached by the ambassadors of the opposing camp who tried in vain to talk him into returning to Egypt.

127. IS, p. 52; ASh, vol. 1, pt. 2, pp. 651–652; IW, 2:39.

128. IA, 11:162; IW, 2:40–41.

129. ASh, vol. 1, pt. 2, p. 652; "The Rise of Saladin," p. 570.

130. ASh, vol. 1, pt. 2, p. 651.

131. Ibid.

132. ASh, vol. 1, pt. 2, p. 652; IW, 2:40; Sibṭ, p. 334.

133. IA, 11:160; ASh, vol. 1, pt. 2, pp. 652, 655; IW, 2:40.

134. ASh, vol. 1, pt. 2, p. 655.

135. IS, 11:160; ASh, vol. 1, pt. 2, p. 655; Sibṭ, p. 334.

136. ASh, vol. 1, pt. 2, p. 656.

137. ASh, vol. 1, pt. 2, p. 661.

138. ASh, vol. 1, pt. 2, pp. 657, 661.

139. ASh, vol. 1, pt. 2, p. 656.

140. B. Lewis, "Saladin and the Assassins," *BSOAS,* 15 (1953): 240; also, idem, *The Assassins,* pp. 113–114.

141. Ibid.; ASh, vol. 1, pt. 2, pp. 658–660.

142. B. Lewis, *The Assassins,* p. 114.

143. ASh, vol. 1, pt. 2, p. 661.

144. Ibid.; IW, 2:46.

145. ASh, vol. 1, pt. 2, p. 661.

146. ASh, vol. 1, pt. 2, p. 661.

147. ASh, vol. 1, pt. 2, p. 662.

148. Ibid.

149. *Sulūk,* p. 62.

150. IA, 11:163.

151. ASh, vol. 1, pt. 2, pp. 668–669; IW, 2:46.

152. ASh, vol. 1, pt. 2, p. 669.

153. *Saladin,* p. 146.

154. Only Gertrude Slaughter, in her *Saladin,* (New York, 1955), p. 90, offered a sober comment on that incident.

155. ASh, vol. 1, pt. 2, p. 669.

156. ASh, loc. cit.; IA, 11:165.

157. IA, loc. cit.; ASh, vol. 1, pt. 2, p. 670; *BJ,* p. 142.

158. B. Lewis, op. cit., p. 115.

159. ASh, vol. 1, pt. 2, p. 670.

160. Ibid., p. 675.

161. Ibid., p. 671.

162. Ibid., pp. 671–672.

163. Ibid., pp. 675–676.

164. Ibid., pp. 709–710; IW, 2:423–426.

165. ASh, vol. 1, pt. 2, p. 676.

166. ASh, vol. 1, pt. 2, p. 129; Elisséeff, 2:403.

167. ASh, vol. 1, pt. 2, p. 676; also above, p. 127.

168. ASh, vol. 1, pt. 2, pp. 679, 683.

Chapter 8

1. Steven Runciman, "The First Crusade: Antioch to Ascalon," *A History of the Crusades* (Philadelphia, 1958–62), 1:315; idem, *A History of the Crusades* (New York, Harper & Row, 1964), 1:229.

2. ASh, vol. 1, pt. 2, p. 691.

3. See above, p. 84.

4. ASh, vol. 1, pt. 2, p. 687; IW, 2:52.

5. ASh, vol. 1, pt. 2, pp. 689–690; "The Place of Saladin," p. 105.

6. ASh, vol. 1, pt. 2, p. 692.

7. Ibid.

8. ASh, vol. 1, pt. 2, pp. 692–693.

9. ASh, vol. 1, pt. 2, p. 688.

10. *Sulūk,* p. 63.

11. Ibid., p. 64.

12. W. Hinz, *Islamische Masse und Gewichte* (Leiden, 1955), p. 39.

13. "The Place of Saladin," p. 105.

14. "The Rise of Saladin," p. 571.

15. "The Place of Saladin," pp. 105–106; M. W. Baldwin, "The Decline and Fall of Jerusalem, 1174–1187," *A History of the Crusades* (Philadelphia, 1958–62), 1:595.

16. ASh, vol. 1, pt. 2, p. 697.

17. Ibid.; "The Armies of Saladin," p. 84.

18. IA, 11:168; ASh, vol. 1, pt. 2, p. 706.

19. IA, loc. cit.; ASh, vol. 1, pt. 2, p. 705; IW, 2:64; Sibṭ, p. 343.

20. IA, 11:167; ASh, vol. 1, pt. 2, p. 700; IW, 2:59.

21. IA, loc. cit.; ASh, vol. 1, pt. 2, pp. 700–702; IW, 2:59–62.

22. *Sulūk,* p. 65; "The Armies of Saladin," p. 86, n. 16.

23. ASh, vol. 1, pt. 2, p. 704.

24. B. Lewis, *The Assassins,* p. 117.

25. IA, 11:168; ASh, vol. 1, pt. 2, p. 705; IW, 2:63.

26. ASh, vol. 1, pt. 2, p. 706; Sibṭ, 344; *TD,* fol. 3 v.

27. See above, p. 111.

28. IA, 11:168; ASh, vol. 1, pt. 2, p. 706; "The Place of Saladin," p. 53.

29. IA, 11:170; IW, 2:70.

30. IA, loc. cit.; IW, 2:71.

31. "The Rise of Saladin," p. 572.

32. IA, 11:170; IW, 2:71; Sibṭ, p. 351.

33. Ibn Abī Ṭayyi *apud* IW, 2:79, n. 4.

34. Ibid.

35. IA, 11:173; IW, 2:79.

36. ASh, vol. 1, pt. 2, p. 708; *Sulūk,* p. 66.

37. IW, 2:72; *Sulūk,* p. 66.

38. IW, 2:74.

39. IW, 2:86.

40. Ibid., 2:73.

41. ASh, *RHC, HO,* 4:198.

42. IW, 2:86.

43. IA, 11:171; IW, 2:72; "The Rise of Saladin," p. 572.

44. IW, 2:74.

45. IA, 11:172; IW, 2:75–77.

46. *Saladin,* p. 159.

47. "The Place of Saladin," p. 106.

48. IW, 2:82.

49. IA, 11:176; IW, 2:80–85.

50. IW, 2:83.

51. "The Place of Saladin," p. 106.

52. E. Ashtor, "Le Cout de la vie dans la Syrie Médiévale," *Arabica,* 8 (1961): 60–61.

53. 2:92.

54. IW, 2:93–94.

55. IW, 2:94–95; Sibṭ, p. 365; "The Rise of Saladin," p. 575.

56. IA, 11:177; Sibṭ, p. 362.

57. IA, 11:175; IW, 2:97; M. W. Baldwin, "The Decline and Fall of Jerusalem, 1174–1189," in *A History of the Crusades* (Philadelphia, 1955–62), 1:595.

58. "The Place of Saladin," pp. 107–108; M. W. Baldwin, art. cit., 1:595.

59. IA, 11:175; IW, 2:96–97.

60. IA, 11:175–176; IS, p. 54; IW, 2:97–98; "The Rise of Saladin," p. 575.

61. IA, 11:176; IW, 2:98–100.

62. IS, p. 54; IW, 2:108; "The Rise of Saladin," p. 575.

63. *Sulūk,* p. 72.

64. IW, 2:95, 101.

65. Salāḥ Elbeheiry, *Les institutions de l'Égypte au temps des Ayyūbīdes* (Paris, 1971), 1:331.

66. "The Place of Saladin," p. 108.

67. *Sulūk,* p. 71; "The Armies of Saladin," p. 82.

68. IA, 11:177; IW, 2:101–102; *Sulūk,* p. 72.

69. IA, loc. cit.; IW, 2:102.

70. *Sulūk,* pp. 72, 74.

71. IA, 11:177–178; IW, 2:103–104; *Sulūk,* p. 75–76.

72. IA, 11:178; IW, 2:105; *Sulūk,* p. 76.

73. IW, 2:112; *Sulūk,* p. 72.

74. IW, 2:113.
75. *Sulūk*, p. 76.
76. Ibid.
77. *Sulūk*, pp. 72–73.
78. Ibid., p. 74.
79. Ibid., p. 72.
80. IW, 2:101; *Sulūk*, p. 71, 76.
81. *Sulūk*, p. 76.
82. IA, 11:178; IW, 2:109; IS, p. 55.
83. IA, loc. cit.; IW, 2:108.
84. Ibid.
85. IA, 11:179; IW, 2:109–110; IS, pp. 55–56.

Chapter 9

1. "The Rise of Saladin," pp. 575–576.
2. Sibṭ, p. 367; IW, 2:110–112; "The Rise of Saladin," p. 576.
3. IA, 11:180; IW, 2:113.
4. See above, p. 167.
5. M. W. Baldwin, art. cit., p. 590; Prawer, 1:586–592.
6. Grousset, 2:692, 829.
7. M. W. Baldwin, art. cit., p. 596.
8. "The Armies of Saladin," pp. 78–79.
9. "The Place of Saladin," pp. 108–109.
10. Ibid., p. 109.
11. Ibid.
12. IS, p. 56; IW, 2:116.
13. IS, pp. 56–57; IA, 11:181; IW, 2:116.
14. IW, 2:117.
15. IW, 2:117–118.

16. IW, 2:118–119.
17. IW, 2:119.
18. IW, 2:124.
19. IA, 11:182; IW, 2:119; "The Rise of Saladin," pp. 581–582.
20. IA, 11:182–183; IW, 2:119–120.
21. IS, p. 57; IW, 2:122.
22. IW, 2:122.
23. Ibid.
24. IA, 11:183; IW, 2:123.
25. IS, p. 57; IA, 11:183–184; IW, 2:123–124.
26. IA, 11:184.
27. IS, p. 58; IA, 11:184; IW, 2:132–133.
28. IW, 2:134.
29. "The Place of Saladin," pp. 109–110.
30. IW, 2:130–131; Sibṭ, pp. 369–370; Ibn Jubayr, *The Travels of Ibn Jubayr,* transl. by R. J. C. Broadhurst (London, 1952), pp. 51–53.
31. "The Rise of Saladin," p. 582.
32. Subhi Labib, "Egyptian Commercial Policy in the Middle Ages," *Studies in the Economic History of the Middle East.* (London, 1970), pp. 66–67.
33. IW, 2:134.
34. IA, 11:185–186; IW, 2:135.
35. IW, 2:138; "The Rise of Saladin," p. 578.
36. IW, 2:139.
37. IS, p. 59; IA, 11:186.
38. IW, 2:141.
39. IA, 11:187; IW, 2:143.
40. IS, p. 59; IW, 2:142.
41. IS, p. 59; IA, 11:187; IW, 2:141–143.

42. *Al-Barq al-Shāmī, MS.*
Bodleian, Marsh., 425, fol. 95 r.

43. IS, p. 60; IA, 11:187; IW,
2:146.

44. "The Armies of Saladin,"
pp. 78–80.

45. "The Place of Saladin," p.
110.

46. IW, 2:140; *Sulūk,* p. 80.

47. IW, 2:147.

48. IW, 2:147; "The Rise of
Saladin," p. 579.

49. See above, p. 173.

50. "The Rise of Saladin," p.
579.

51. Ibid.

52. IA, 11:188; IW, 2:147.

53. IA, 11:188; IW, 2:148.

54. IS, p. 61.

55. IW, 2:148; M. W. Baldwin,
"The Decline and Fall of Jerusalem,
1174–1189," *A History of the
Crusades* (Philadelphia, 1955–62),
1:599; Prawer, 1:621.

56. M. W. Baldwin, art. cit.;
Saladin, p. 178.

57. IS, p. 62–63; IW, 2:148–151.

58. IS, p. 63; IA, 11:189.

59. IS, p. 64; IA, loc. cit.; IW,
2:152.

60. IA, 11:190; *Sulūk,* p. 87.

61. IS, p. 66; "The Rise of
Saladin," p. 579.

62. IS, p. 66–67; IA, 11:190–191;
IW, 2:157–159.

63. See above, p. 107.

64. IA, 11:188; IW, 2:153–154.

65. IS, p. 64; IA, loc. cit., IW,
2:155.

66. IW, 2:154.

67. IS, p. 65.

68. Sibṭ, p. 378.

69. IW, 2:162.

70. IS, p. 67; "The Rise of
Saladin," p. 580.

71. M. W. Baldwin, art. cit.,
p. 604.

72. See above, p. 113.

73. Sibṭ, pp. 380–381.

74. *Sulūk,* pp. 86–88.

75. Andrew S. Ehrenkreutz,
"The Crisis of Dīnār in the Egypt
of Saladin," *Journal of the
American Oriental Society* 76
(1956): 181, 183.

76. *Sulūk,* p. 88.

77. Ibid.

78. Ibid.

79. *Sulūk,* pp. 88, 90; Ibn
Jubayr, op. cit., p. 31–32.

80. *Sulūk,* p. 87.

81. Sibṭ, pp. 381–382.

82. The problem of al-Qāḍī
al-Fāḍil's relations with Saladin has
been studied by Mrs. H. R. Dajani
Shakeel who has graciously allowed
me to utilize materials contained in
her doctoral dissertation presented
at The University of Michigan,
1972.

83. *ʿUyūn al-Rasāʾil al-Fāḍilīyah,
MS,* British Museum, *Add.,* 25756,
fol. 63.

84. Ibid., fol. 21.

85. *Dīwān al-Qāḍī al-Fāḍil,*
(Cairo, Matbaʿat al-Risālah), 1:38.

86. *Kitāb al-Mukhtar, MS,*
British Museum, *Add.,* 7307, fol.
71.

87. *ʿUyūn al-Rasāʾil al-Fāḍilīyah,*
fol. 21.

88. Al-Nuwayrī, *Nihayat*

al-ʿArab fī Funūn al-Adab (Cairo, 1933–1949) 8:10.

89. IS, p. 68; IW, 2:165.

90. IS, loc. cit.; IA, 11:192; IW, 2:165.

91. IS, p. 68; IA, 11:192; IW, 2:165.

92. IW, 2:166–167.

93. IW, 2:167.

94. IS, p. 69; IA, 11:193; IW, 2:168.

95. IS, loc. cit.; IA, 11:193; IW, 2:169.

96. IS, p. 69; IA, 11:194.

97. IW, 2:171.

98. IA, 11:194; IW, 2:171–173.

99. IA, 11:195; IW, 2:174; Sibṭ, p. 386.

100. IS, pp. 70–71; IA, 11:194; IW, 2:172.

101. IS, p. 71; IW, 2:174.

102. Sibṭ, p. 386. IA, 11:195.

103. *Saladin,* p. 194.

104. IS, loc. cit., p. 71.

105. *Kitāb al-Muk̲htar,* fol. 20.

106. IW, 2:180–182; *Sulūk,* p. 91.

Chapter 10

1. *Saladin,* pp. 198, 199.

2. "The Achievement of Saladin," pp. 99–100.

3. Prawer, 1:637; M. W. Baldwin, art. cit., p. 605.

4. Ch. M. Brand, "The Byzantines and Saladin, 1185–1192: Opponents of the Third Crusade," *Speculum* 37 (1962): 168–169.

5. Ibid., p. 169.

6. Ibid., p. 168.

7. Ibid., p. 169.

8. Ibid., pp. 169–170.

9. M. W. Baldwin, art. cit., p. 606.

10. Prawer, 1:638–639.

11. IS, p. 75.

12. IS, p. 78.

13. "The Armies of Saladin," p. 81; "The Rise of Saladin," p. 585.

14. Ch. M. Brand, art. cit., p. 170.

15. IS, p. 75; IW, 2:187.

16. For an analysis of the tactical movements of the two opposing armies, see Prawer, 1:643–653; also idem, "La bataille de Hattin," *Israel Exploration Journal* 14 (1964): 160–179.

17. M. W. Baldwin, art. cit., p. 610.

18. *Saladin,* p. 213.

19. IS, p. 78.

20. Ibid.

21. IS, p. 79.

22. IW, 2:196.

23. Cf. ʿImād al-Dīn, *al Fatḥ al-Quds,* in Francesco Gabrieli, *Arab Historians of the Crusades* (1969), p. 138.

24. Ch. M. Brand, art. cit., p. 170.

25. "The Rise of Saladin," p. 586.

26. E. Sivan, *L'Islam et la Croisade,* (Paris, 1968), p. 115 f.; idem, "Le caractère sacré de Jérusalem dans l'Islam aux XIIe–XIIIe siècles," *Studia Islamica* 27 (1967): 160 f.

27. IW, 2:238.

28. Ch. M. Brand, art. cit., p. 170.

29. Saladin, p. 237.

30. IW, 2:242.

31. *Saladin*, p. 239.

32. "The Place of Saladin," p. 111.

33. *Saladin*, p. 241.

34. "The Place of Saladin," p. 111.

35. IW, 2:246.

36. *Saladin*, p. 241.

37. Ibid., p. 243.

38. IW, 2:248. *TD*, fol. 20 r; IW, 2:248–249.

39. IW, 2:248–49.

40. In reality that title was given to Saladin by al-ʿĀdid, cf., above, p. 67.

41. *TD*, fol. 20 v.

42. IA, 11:212; IW, 2:250–252.

43. See above, pp. 191–93.

44. IA, 11:196; *Sulūk*, p. 99.

45. Ch. M. Brand, art. cit., p. 171.

46. Ibid., pp. 171–172.

47. Ibid., p. 172.

48. IS, p. 94; IA, 12:8.

49. IW, 2:253; *Sulūk*, p. 99.

50. *Saladin*, p. 266.

51. IS, p. 146; IW, 2:346.

52. *Saladin*, p. 266.

53. Ibid., p. 277.

54. IW, 2:354.

55. IS, p. 168; *Saladin*, p. 296.

56. IS, loc. cit.; *Saladin*, p. 297.

57. *Saladin*, p. 297.

58. IW, 2:306.

59. *Supra*.

60. ASh, *RHC, HO,* 4:497–505.

61. IW, 2:314; Sibṭ, p. 401.

62. "The Place of Saladin," p. 114.

63. IW, 2:306.

64. IW, 2:371.

65. IS, pp. 213–215; S. Painter, "The Third Crusade: Richard the Lionhearted and Philip Augustus," *A History of the Crusades* (Philadelphia, 1955–62), 2:82.

66. S. Painter, art. cit., p. 85.

67. IW, 2:375–376.

68. Ibid., 2:376.

69. Ibid., 2:378–379.

70. ASh, *RHC, HO,* 5:43.

71. IS, p. 216; IW, 2:387.

72. *Saladin*, pp. 344–347.

73. IS, p. 229; *Saladin*, pp. 352–354.

74. IS, loc. cit.; *Saladin*, p. 354.

75. IS, p. 230.

76. Sibṭ, p. 411.

77. IS, p. 10; H. Corbin, *Suhrawardî d'Alep (+1191) fondateur de la doctrine illuminative (ishrâqî)* (Paris, 1939) pp. 3, 9.

78. "The Place of Saladin," p. 115.

79. Ibid., p. 114.

80. *Saladin*, p. 326.

81. Ibid., pp. 338–339.

82. "The Place of Saladin," p. 115.

83. Ibid.

84. *Sulūk*, p. 99.

85. The low output is suggested by analysis of available numismatic evidence examined by the present

author. For a recent treatment
of the outflow of gold from the
East, see H. L. Misbach, "Genoese
commerce and the alleged flow of
gold to the East, 1154–1253,"
*Revue internationale d'Histoire
de la Banque* 3 (1970): 67–87.

86. Fr. A. Cazel, Jr., "The Tax
of 1185 in Aid of the Holy Land."
Speculum 30 (1955): 385–392;
J. H. Round, "The Saladin Tithe,"
English Historical Review 31
(1916): 447–450.

87. Al-Nābulusī, *Kitāb lumaʿ
al-qawānīn,* ed. by Cl. Cahen, in
Bulletin d'Études Orientales 16
(1958–1960): 12.

88. *Al-Nuẓum al-māliyah,* p. 46.

89. *Sulūk,* p. 110.

90. IA, 12:9–10.

91. *Sulūk,* pp. 110–111.

92. René Grousset, *Les Croisades*
(Paris, 1848), p. 59.

Chapter 11

1. IS, p. 240.

2. IW, 2:407.

3. IS, p. 239; IW, 2:408.

4. IW, loc. cit.

5. See above, p. 210.

6. IS, pp. 237–238.

7. ASh, *RHC, HO,* 5:86–87;
IW, 2:408.

8. ASh, op. cit., p. 87; IW, loc.
cit.

9. ASh, op. cit., p. 84.

10. IW, 2:410.

11. IS, p. 148; IW, 2:368.

12. IW, 2:409.

13. IW, 2:413.

14. IS, p. 241; IW, 2:414.

15. IS, pp. 241–242.

16. IS, p. 242.

17. IS, pp. 242–243.

18. IS, p. 243 f.

19. Sibṭ, p. 430.

20. IS, p. 243.

21. Ibid., p. 245.

22. Ibid., p. 246.

Chapter 12

1. *Saladin,* p. 73.

2. Franz Rosenthal, *A History of
Muslim Historiography* (Leiden,
1952), p. 150.

3. *Sīrat Ṣalāḥ al-Dīn* (Cairo,
1964).

4. C. E. Bosworth, "An Early
Arabic Mirror for Princes: Ṭāhir
Dhū l-Yaminain's Epistle to his son
ʿAbdallāh (206/821)," *Journal of
Near Eastern Studies* 29 (1970): 31.

5. IS, p. 7. Cf. Francesca Gabrieli,
Arab Historians of the Crusades
(Berkeley and Los Angeles, 1969),
p. 88.

6. C. E. Bosworth, loc. cit.

7. IS, p. 10; Gabrieli, op. cit., p.
90.

8. C. E. Bosworth, op. cit., p. 34.

9. IS, p. 17; Gabrieli, op. cit.

Bibliography

Recent Monographs and Articles (1946–71)

ABYĀRĪ, IBRĀHĪM AL-. *Al-Baṭal al-Khālid.* Cairo [1962].

ALTOMA (AL-TUʿMAH), ṢĀLIḤ JAWĀD. "Salāḥ al-Dīn al-Ayyūbī fī al-shiʿr al-ʿarabī al-muʿāṣir," *Al-Ādab* 16 (1970): 17–22; 73–78.

ASHTOR, ELIAHU. "Saladin and the Jews." *Hebrew Union College Annual* 27 (1956): 305–326.

ʿĀSHŪR SAʿĪD ʿABD AL-FATTĀḤ. *Al-Nāṣir Ṣalāḥ al-Dīn.* [Cairo, 1965.]

BANNĀ, ʿARD AL-RAḤMĀN AL-. *Ṣalāḥ al-Dīn al-Ayyūbī, Munqidh Filisṭīn.* Cairo, 1952.

BRAND, CHARLES N. "The Byzantines and Saladin, 1185–1192: Opponents of the Third Crusade." *Speculum* 37 (1962): 167–181.

CAHEN, CLAUDE. "Une traité d'armourerie composé pour Saladin." *Bulletin d'Études Orientales de l'Institut Français de Damas* 12 (1947–48): 103–163.

CHAMPDOR, A. *Saladin, le plus pur héros de l'Islam.* Paris [1956].

DŪMĪ, AḤMAD ʿABD AL-JAWĀD AL-. *Ṣalāḥ al-Dīn al-Ayyūbī.* Baghdad, n.d.

EHRENKREUTZ, ANDREW S. "The Crisis of *Dīnār* in the Egypt of Saladin." *Journal of the American Oriental Society* 76 (1956): 178–184.

———. "The Place of Saladin in the Naval History of the Mediterranean Sea in the Middle Ages." *Journal of the American Oriental Society* 75 (1955): 100–116.

GABRIELI, FRANCESCO. *Il Saladino.* Florence, 1948.

GIBB, HAMILTON A. R. "The Achievement of Saladin." In H. A. R. Gibb, *Studies on the Civilization of Islam,* pp. 91–107. Boston, 1962.

———. "The Armies of Saladin." In H. A. R. Gibb, *Studies on the Civilization of Islam,* pp. 74–90. Boston, 1962.

———. "Al-Barq al-Shāmī: The History of Saladin by the Kātib ʿImād al-Dīn al-Iṣfahānī." *Wiener Zeitschrift für die Kunde des Morgenlandes* 52 (1953–55): 93–115.

———. "The Rise of Saladin, 1169–1189." In Marshall W. Baldwin, ed., *A History of the Crusades,* 1:563–589. Philadelphia, 1958.

———. "The Arabic Sources for the Life of Saladin." *Speculum* 25 (1950): 58–72.

JĀMĀTĪ, ḤABĪB. *Al-Nāṣir Ṣalāḥ al Dīn.* (Cairo, 1962).

JARRĀR, FARŪQ A. "Usṭūl Ṣalāḥ al-Dīn al-Ayyūbī." *Al-Abḥāth* 13 (1960): 70–95.

KAHLE, P. "Eine wichtige Quelle zur Geschichte des Sultans Saladin." *Die Welt des Orients* 1 (1947–52): 299–301.

KEMÂL, NAMIK. *Selâhaddini Eyyûbî.* Istanbul, 1964.

KHULUSI, S. A. "Saladin—the Man of Destiny." *Islamic Review* (July 1950): 19–25.

KRAEMER, J. *Der Sturz des Königreichs Jerusalem (583/1187) in der Darstellung des ʿImād al-Dīn Al-Kātib al-Iṣfahānī.* Wiesbaden, 1952.

LEWIS, BERNARD. "Maimonides, Lionheart, and Saladin." *Eretz-Israel* 7 (1963): 70–75.

———. "Saladin and the Assassins," *Bulletin of the School of Oriental and African Studies* 15 (1953): 239–245.

MĀJID, ʿABD AL-MUNʿIM. *Al-Nāṣir Ṣalāḥ al-Dīn Yūsuf al-Ayyūbī.* (Cairo), 1958.

MAYER, H. E. "Der Brief Kaiser Friedrichs I. Barbarossas an Saladin vom Jahre 1188." *Deutsches Archiv für Erforschung des Mittelalters* 14 (1958): 488–494.

MINORSKY, VLADIMIR. "Prehistory of Saladin." In Vladimir Minorsky, *Studies in Caucasian History,* pp. 107–157. London, 1953.

NAJJĀR, MUḤAMMAD AL-ṬAYYIB. *Al-Ṣalībīyūn wa Ṣalāḥ al-Dīn.* (Cairo, 1962).

PRAWER, J. "La bataille de Hattin." *Israel Exploration Journal* 14 (1964): 160–179.

QALʿAJĪ, QADRĪ. *Ṣalāḥ al-Dīn al-Ayyūbī.* Beirut, 1966.

RICHARD J. "An Account of the Battle of Hattin Referring to the Frankish Mercenaries in Oriental Moslem States." *Speculum* 27 (1952): 168–177.

———. "La Chanson de Syracon et la Légende de Saladin." *Journal Asiatique* 237 (1949): 155–158.

RUNCIMAN, STEVEN. "Saladin: A Great Leader of Islam." *Listener,* 15 April 1954, pp. 648–649.

saʿDāwī, naẓīr ḥassān. *Al-Taʾrīkh al-Ḥarbī al-Miṣrī fī ʿahd Ṣalāḥ al-Dīn al-Ayyūbī.* Cairo, 1957.

semenova, l.a. *Salakh ad-Din i Mamliûki v Egipte.* Moscow, 1966.

slaughter, gertrude. *Saladin.* New York [1955].

tāmir, ʿārif. *Sinān wa Ṣalāḥ al-Dīn.* Beirut, 1952.

sayyīd al-ahl, ʿabd al-ʿazīz. *Ayyām Ṣalāḥ al-Dīn.* Beirut, 1961.

General

ʿabd al-munʿim mājid. *Zuhūr Khilāfat al-Fāṭimiyyin wa-suqūṭuhā.* Cairo, 1968.

abū al-fidāʾ. *Al-Mukhtaṣar fī akhbār al-bashar.* Cairo, [1914].

abū shāmah. *Kitāb al-Rawḍatayn,* vol. 1, pts. 1, 2. Cairo, 1956–62.

———. *Kitāb al-Rawḍatayn.* In *Recueil des Historiens des Croisades, Historiens Orientaux* 4 (1898), 5 (1906).

ahmed zéki pacha. "Notice sur les couleurs nationales de l'Egypte Musulmane." *Bulletin de l'Institut d'Egypte* 2 (1920): 61–95.

ashtor, eliahu. "Le cout de la vie dans la Syrie médiévale." *Arabica* 8 (1961): 59–73.

———. *Histoire des Prix et des Salaires dans l'Orient Médiéval.* Paris, 1969.

atiya, aziz s. *The Crusade, Historiography and Bibliography.* Bloomington: Indiana University Press, 1962.

avalon, david. "L'Esclavage du Mamelouk." *The Israel Oriental Society* (Oriental Notes and Studies). Jerusalem, 1951.

———. "Studies on the Structure of the Mamluk Army." *Bulletin of the School of Oriental and African Studies* 15 (1953): 204, 448–476.

baldwin, m. w. "The Decline and Fall of Jerusalem, 1174–1189." In Marshall W. Baldwin, ed., *A History of the Crusades,* 1:590–621. Philadelphia, 1958.

———. "The Latin States under Baldwin III and Amalric I, 1143–1174." In Marshall W. Baldwin, ed., *A History of the Crusades,* 1:528–561. Philadelphia, 1958.

balog, p. "The Ayyūbid Glass Jetons and Their Use." *Journal of the Economic and Social History of the Orient* 9 (1966): 242–256.

barrāwī, rāshid al-. *Ḥālat Miṣr al-iqtiṣādīyah fī ʿahd al-Fāṭimīyin,* Cairo, 1948.

BARTHOUX, J. "Description d'une fortresse de Saladin découverte au Sinaï."
Syria 3 (1922): 44–57.

BECKER, C. H. "Egypt." S. v. in *The Encyclopaedia of Islam,* 1st ed., 2:4–23.
Leiden, 1927.

BOSWORTH, CLIFFORD E. "The Early Arabic Mirror for Princes: Ṭāhir Dhū-
l'Yaminain's Epistle to His Son ʿAbdallāh (206/821)." *Journal of
Near Eastern Studies* 29 (1970): 25–41.

BRIGGS, M. S. "The Architecture of Saladin and the Influence of the
Crusades (A.D. 1171-1250)." *Burlington Magazine* 38 (1921):
16–20.

BRUNDAGE, J. A. *The Crusades: A Documentary Survey.* Milwaukee,
1962.

CAHEN, CLAUDE. "L'Alun avant Phocée: Un chapitre d'histoire économique
islamo-chrétienne au temps des Croisades." *Revue d'histoire
économique et sociale* 41 (1963): 433–447.

————. "Ayyūbids." S.v. in *The Encyclopaedia of Islam,* 2d ed., 1:796–807.
Leiden, 1960.

————. "Bustān al-Jāmiʿ." *Bulletin d'Études Orientales* 7–8 (1937–38):
113–158.

————. "La 'Chronique des Ayyoubides' d'al-Makīn b. al-ʿAmīd." *Bulletin
d'Études Orientales* 15 (1955–57): 109–184.

————. "Une Chronique Chiite au temps des Croisades." In *C. R. de
l'Académie des Inscriptions de Belles Lettres,* pp. 258-269. Paris,
1935.

————. Les chroniques arabes concernant la Syrie, l'Égypte et la
Mésopotamie de la conquête arabe à la conquête ottomane, dans
les bibliothèques d'Istanbul." *Revue des Études Islamiques* 10
(1936): 333–362.

————. "La correspondance de Ḍiyā al-Dīn ibn al-Athīr: Liste de lettres
et textes de diplômes." *Bulletin of the School of Oriental and
African Studies* 14 (1952): 34–43.

————. "Indigènes et Croisés: Quelques mots à propos d'un medecin
d'Amaury et de Saladin." *Syria* 15 (1934): 351–360.

————. *Pre-Ottoman Turkey: A General Survey of the Material and
Spiritual Culture c. 1071–1330.* Translated by J. Jones-Williams.
New York, 1968.

————. *La Syrie du Nord à l'époque des Croisades, et la principauté
franque d'Antioche.* Paris, 1940.

CANARD, M. "Fāṭimids." S.v. in *The Encyclopaedia of Islam,* 2d ed.,
2:850–862. Leiden; 1964.

————. "Notes sur les Arméniens en Égypte à l'époque fâṭimite." *Annales de l'Institut d'Études Orientales de la faculté des Lettres d'Alger* 13 (1955): 143–157.

————. "Un vizir chrétien à l'époque fâṭimite: L'Arménien Bahrâm." *Annales de l'Institut d'Études Orientales de la faculté des Lettres de Alger* 12 (1954): 84–113.

————. "La procession du nouvel an chez les Fatimides." *Annales de l'Institut d'Études Orientales de la faculté des Lettres de Alger* 10 (1952): 364–398.

CASANOVA, P. "Les derniers Fatimides." *Mémoires de la mission. archéologique française au Caire*, vol. 6, fasc. 3.

CAZEL, FR. A., JR. "The Tax of 1185 in Aid of the Holy Land." *Speculum* 30 (1955): 385–392.

CONDER, C. R. "Saladin and King Richard: the Eastern Question in the Twelfth Century." *Blackwood's* 161 (March 1897): 389–397.

CORBIN, HENRY. *Suhrawardî d'Alep (+1191) fondateur de la doctrine illuminative (ishrâqî)*. Paris, 1939.

CRESSWELL, K. A. C. *The Muslim Architecture of Egypt*, 2 vols. Vol. 2, *Ayyūbids and the Early Baḥrite Mamlūks, A.D. 1171–1326.* Oxford: Clarendon Press, 1952–59.

DERENBOURG, HARTWIG. *ʿOumâra du Yemen*. Paris, 1897.

DHAHABĪ, AL-. *Duwal al-Islām*. Hydarabad, 1918–19.

ELBEḤEIRY, ṢALĀḤ. *Les institutions de l'Égypte au temps des Ayyūbides.* Vol. 1 *L'organisation de l'armée et des institutions militaires.* Paris, 1971.

EHRENKREUTZ, ANDREW S. "Arabic dīnārs struck by the Crusaders—a case of ignorance or of economic subversion." *Journal of the Economic and Social History of the Orient* 7 (1964): 167–182.

————. "Contributions to the Knowledge of the Fiscal Administration of Egypt in the Middle Ages." *Bulletin of the School of Oriental and African Studies* 16 (1954): 502–514.

ELISSÉEFF, N. *La description de Damas d'Ibn ʿAsākir*. Damascus, 1959.

————. *Nūr al-Dīn*. 3 vols. Damascus, 1967.

Encyclopaedia of Islam, The. Prepared by a number of leading orientalists. 1st ed., 4 vols. Leiden: E. J. Brill, 1913–38. 2d ed., 5 vols. Leiden: E. J. Brill, 1954 London: Luzac & Co., 1956–.

FAHMĪ, ʿABD AL-RAḤMĀN. "Al-Sikkah al-Ayyūbīyah al-Miṣrīyah bi-Mathaf al-Fann al-Islāmī bi-al-Qāhirah." In Ibn Baʿrah, *Kitāb Kashf al-Asrār al-ʿIlmīyah*, edited by ʿAbd al-Raḥmān Fahmī, pp. 95–133. Cairo, 1966.

FEDDEN, ROBIN, and THOMSON, JOHN. *Crusader Castles*. Rev. ed. London, 1957.

FÜRST, A. "Der Kreuzzugsbrief Kaiser Friedrichs I. an Saladin." In *Programm des Königlichen Gymnasium zu Regensburg, 1908.*

GABRIELI, FRANCESCO, comp. *Arab Historians of the Crusades.* Translated by E. J. Costello. Berkeley and Los Angeles, 1969.

GAUDEFROY-DEMOMBYNES, MAURICE. "Une lettre de Saladin au Calife Almohade." *Mélanges René Basset* 2 (1925): 279–304.

GAYET, A. "Les monuments de Damiette et Mansourah contemporains de l'époque des Croisades." *Revue de l'Art Ancien et Moderne* 6 (1899): 71–78.

GIBB, HAMILTON A. R. "The Caliphate and the Arab States." In Marshall W. Baldwin, ed., *A History of the Crusades*, 1:81–98. Philadelphia, 1958.

———. "The Career of Nūr al-Dīn." In Marshall W. Baldwin, ed., *A History of the Crusades*, 1:513–527.

———. "Notes on the Arabic Materials for the History of the Early Crusades." *Bulletin of the School of Oriental Studies* 7 (1935): 739–754.

GOERKENS, E. P. *Arabische Quellenbeiträge zur Geschichte der Kreuzzüge.* Vol. 1, *Zur Geschichte Salāḥ ad-Dīns.* Berlin, 1879.

GOITEIN, S. D. "Letters and documents on the India Trade in Medieval Times." *Islamic Culture* 27 (1963): 188–205.

———. "The Main Industries of the Mediterranean Area as Reflected in the Records of the Cairo Genizah." *Journal of the Economic and Social History of the Orient* 4 (1961): 168–197.

———. *A Mediterranean Society: The Jewish Communities of the Arab World as Portrayed in the Documents of the Cairo Geniza.* 2 vols. to date. Vol. 1, *Economic Foundations.* Berkeley and Los Angeles, 1968–.

———. "Minority Selfrule and Government Control in Islam." *Studia Islamica* (1970): 101–116.

GROUSSET, RENÉ. *Histoire des Croisades et du royaume franc de Jerusalem.* Paris, 1934–36.

ḤABASHĪ, ḤASAN. *Miḍmār al-ḥaqāʾiq li-ṣāḥibi Ḥāmah Muḥammad ibn Tāqī al-Dīn ʿUmar ibn Shāhinshāh al-Ayyūbī.* Cairo, [1968].

HAMZAH, ʿABD AL-LAṬĪF. *Al-Ḥarah al-fikrīyah fī Miṣr fī al-ʿaṣrayn al-Ayyūbī wa al-Mamlūkī al-Awwal.* Cairo, 1947.

———. *Salāḥ al-Dīn.* Cairo, 1944.

HAQ, M. ABDUL. "Al-Qadi-ul-Fadil and his diary." In *Proceedings of the 10th All India Orientalist Conference, 1940,* pp. 724–725.

HARTMANN, J. *Die Persönlichkeit des Sultans Saladin im Urteil der abendländischen Quellen*. Berlin, 1933.

ḤASAN ʿABD AL-WAHHĀB. "Al-ʿAṣr al-Ayyūbī." *Al-ʿImārah* 2 (1940): 394–407.

ḤASAN, AL-BĀSHĀ. *Al-Alqāb al-Islāmīyah*. Cairo, 1957.

ḤASAN IBRĀHĪM ḤASAN. *Taʾrīkh al-Dawlah al-Fāṭimīyah*. Cairo, 1964.

HELBIG, A. H. *Al-Qāḍi al-Fāḍil, der Wezir Saladins*. Leipzig, 1908.

HEYD, W. *Histoire du commerce du Levant*. Leipzig, 1923.

M. HILMY M. AHMAD. "Some Notes on Arab Historiography during the Zengid and Ayyubid Periods (521/1127–648/1250)." In *Historians of the Middle East*, pp. 79–97. London, 1962.

HINZ, W. *Islamische Masse und Gewichte, Handbuch der Orientalistik*, suppl. 1, no. 1, 1955.

HOUTSMA, M. TH. *Recueil de Textes relatifs à l'histoire des Seldjoucides*, vol. 2. Leiden, 1889.

HUSSEY, J. M. "Byzantium and the Crusades." in Robert Lee Wolff and Henry W. Hazard, eds., *A History of the Crusades*, 2:123–151. Philadelphia, 1962.

IBN ABĪ UṢAYBIʿAH. *ʿUyūn al-anbāʾ fī ṭabaqāt al-aṭibba*. Beirut, 1965.

IBN AL-ATHĪR, ḌIYĀ AL-DĪN. *Al-Mathal al-sāʾir*. Cairo, 1959–60.

IBN AL-ATHĪR, ʿIZZ AL-DĪN. *Al-Kāmil fī al-taʾrīkh*. Cairo, 1884.

———. *Al-Kāmil fī al-taʾrīkh*, 13 vols. Edited by C. J. Tornberg. Leiden, 1851–83.

———. *Al-Kāmil fī al-taʾrīkh*. Beirut, 1965–66.

———. *Al-Taʾrīkh al-bāhir fī al-Duwlah al-Atābakīyuh*. [Cairo, 1963.]

———. *Al-Taʾrīkh al-bāhir fī al-Dawlah al-Atābakīyah*. In *Recueil des historiens des Croisades*, vol. 2. Paris, 1876.

IBN AL-DUBAYTHĪ. *Al-Mukhtaṣar*. Baghdad, 1951.

IBN AL-FURĀT. *Ayyubids, Mamlukes and Crusades. Selections from the Tārīkh al-Duwal waʾl-Mulūk*. Trans. by U. and M. C. Lyons. Introduction and notes by J. S. C. Riley-Smith. 2 vols. Cambridge, 1971.

IBN ḤAMMĀD. *Histoire des Rois Obaidides (Les Califes Fatimides)*. Algiers and Paris, 1927.

IBN AL-JUBAYR, ABŪ AL-ḤUSAYN MUḤAMMAD IBN AḤMAD. *The Travels of Ibn Jubayr, Being a Chronicle of a Mediaeval Spanish Moor Concerning His Journey to the Egypt of Saladin, the Holy Cities of Arabia. Baghdad the City of the Caliphs, the Latin Kingdom of Jerusalem, and the Norman Kingdom of Sicily*. Translated by R. J. C. Broadhurst. London: Cape, 1952.

IBN KHALLIKĀN, SHAMS AL-DĪN AḤMED IBN MUḤAMMAD. *Ibn Khallikān's*

Biographical Dictionary, 4 vols. Translated by Baron MacGuckin de Slane. Paris and London, 1843–71.

IBN AL-KHAZRAJĪ. *Ta'rīkh Dawlat al-Akrād aw'l-Atrāk.* MS. Hekimoğlu Alī Paša 695, Istanbul.

IBN MAMMĀTĪ. *Kitāb qawānīn al-dawāwīn.* Edited by Aziz S. Atiya. Cairo, 1943.

IBN AL-QALĀNISĪ. *Dhayl ta'rīkh Dimashq.* Leiden, 1908.

IBN ṢAṢRĀ, MUḤAMMAD IBN MUḤAMMAD. *A Chronicle of Damascus 1389–1397.* Edited by William M. Brinner. Berkeley and Los Angeles, 1963.

IBN SHADDĀD, BAHĀ' AL-DĪN. *Sīrat Ṣalāḥ al-Dīn.* Edited by Gamal El-Din El-Shayyal. [Cairo], 1964.

IBN TAGHRĪ BIRDĪ, ABŪ AL-MAḤĀSIN YŪSUF. *Al-Nujūm al Zāhirah.* 11 vols. Cairo, 1929–50.

IBN WĀṢIL. *Mufarrij al-kurūb.* Edited by Gamal El-Din El-Shayyal. Cairo, 1953–60.

ʿIMĀD AL-DĪN AL-IṢFAHĀNĪ. *Al-Barq al-Shāmī,* vol. 3. MS. March. 425, Bodleian Library.

——. *Al-Fath al-Qussī fī'l-Fath al-Qudsī.* Edited by C. Landberg. Leiden, 1888.

——. *Al-Fath al-Qussī fī'l-Fath al-Qudsī.* Edited by Muḥammad Maḥmūd Ṣubḥ. [Cairo, 1965.]

JOHNSON, E. N. "The Crusades of Frederick Barbarossa and Henry VI." In Robert Lee Wolff and Henry W. Hazard, eds., *A History of the Crusades,* 2:87–122. Philadelphia, 1962.

LABIB, SUBHI YANNI. *Handelsgeschichte Ägyptens im Spätmittelalter (1171–1517).* Wiesbaden, 1965.

——. "Egyptian Commercial Policy in the Middle Ages." In *Studies in the Economic History of the Middle East,* pp. 52–63.

LANE-POOLE, STANLEY. "Age of Saladin." *Quarterly Review* 183 (1896): 163–187.

——. *Egypt in the Middle Ages.* London, 1925.

——. *Saladin and the Fall of the Kingdom of Jerusalem.* London, 1898.

——. "Unpublished Inscription of Saladin." *Athenaeum* 112 (1898): 200.

LEWIS, ARCHIBALD R. *Naval Power and Trade in the Mediterranean, A.D. 500–1100.* Princeton, 1951.

LEWIS, BERNARD. *The Assassins: A Radical Sect in Islam.* New York, 1968.

——. "The Fāṭimids and the Route to India." *Revue de la faculté des sciences économiques de l'Université d'Istanbul* 11 (1949–50): 50–54.

————. "The Ismāʿīlites and the Assassins." In Marshall W. Baldwin, ed., *A History of the Crusades*, 1:131. Philadelphia, 1958.

————. "Kamāl al-Dīn's biography of Rāšid al-Dīn Sinān." *Arabica* 13 (1966): 225–267.

MAQRIZĪ, AḤMAD IBN ʿALĪ AL-. *Ighāthat al-ummah*. Cairo, 1940.

————. *Ittiʿāẓ al-ḥunafāʾ*. MS. AS 3013, Topkapu Palace Archives, Istanbul.

————. *Itti ʿāẓ al-ḥunafāʾ*. Cairo, 1948.

————. *Ittiʿāẓ al-ḥunafāʾ*, vol. 1. Cairo, 1967.

————. *Kitāb al-mawāʾ iẓ wa-l-i ʿtibār*. Cairo, 1853.

————. *Kitāb al-mawāʾ iẓ wa-l-i ʿtibār*. Beirut, 1959.

————. *Kitāb al-sulūk*, vol. 1, pt. 1. Cairo, 1956.

————. *Shudhūr al-ʿuqūd fī dhikr al-nuqūd*. Najaf, 1967.

MARIN, L. F. C. *Histoire de Saladin, Sulthan d'Egypte et de Syrie*. Paris, 1758.

MASSÉ, H. "Remarques sur le Fatḥ-el Qossi d'Imad-ed-Din el-Isfahani (Summary)." In *Proceedings of the Twenty-second Congress of Orientalists, 1951*. Vol. 2, *Communications*, 1957, p. 196.

MILLER, J. INNES. *The Spice Trade of the Roman Empire*. Oxford: 1969.

MINORSKY, VLADIMIR. *Studies in Caucasian History*. London, 1953.

MINOST, E. "Au sujet du Traité des Monnaies Musulmanes de Makrizi." *Bulletin de l'Institut d'Égypte* 19 (1936–37): 45–61.

MISBACH, H. L. "Genoese Commerce and the Alleged Flow of Gold to the East, 1154–1253." *Revue Internationale d'Histoire de la Banque* 3 (1970): 67–87.

MUSHARRAFAH, ʿATĪYAH MUṢṬAFĀ. *Naẓm al-ḥukm fī Miṣr al-Fāṭimīyin, al-ṭabʿah al-thānīyah* [Cairo, n.d.]

MUNIER, H., and WIET, GASTON. "L'Égypte byzantine et musulmane." In *Précis de l'histoire d'Égypte*, vol. 2. Cairo, 1932.

NĀBULUSĪ, AL-. "Kitāb lumaʿ al-qawānīn al-mudīyya fī dawāwīn al-diyār al-miṣrīyya." Edited by Claude Cahen. In *Bulletin d'Études Orientales* 16 (1958–60): 1–78, 119–134.

NASSER, GAMAL ABDEL. *Egypt's Liberation: The Philosophy of the Revolution*. Washington, D.C.: Public Affairs Press, 1956.

NUWAYRĪ, AL-. *Nihāyat al-ʿArab*, vol. 8. Cairo, 1949.

OLDENBOURG, ZOE. *Les Croisades*. Paris, 1965.

OMAR TOUSSOUN. "*Les finances de l'Égypte.*" In *Mémoires presentés à l'Institut d'Égypte*, vol. 6. Cairo, 1924.

PAINTER, S. "The Third Crusade: Richard the Lionhearted and Philip Augustus." In Robert Lee Wolff and Henry W. Hazard, eds., *A History of the Crusades*, 2:45–86. Philadelphia, 1962.

PARIS, G. "La legende de Saladin." *Le Journal des Savants* (1893): 284–299, 354–365, 428–438, 486–498.

POLIAK, A. N. "The Ayyūbid Feudalism." *Journal of the Royal Asiatic Society* (1939): 428–432.

PRAWER, J. *Histoire du Royaume Latin de Jérusalem.* Paris, 1969–70.

QĀḌĪ AL-FĀḌIL, AL-. *Dīwān.* Cairo, 1961.

———. *Kitāb al-Mukhtar.* MS. Add. 7307, British Museum.

———. *ʿUyūn al-Rasāʾil al-Fāḍilīyah.* MS. Add. 25, 756, British Museum.

RABIE, HASSANEIN. *Al-nuẓum al-mālīyah fī Miṣr zaman al-Ayyūbīyin.* Cairo, 1964.

———. "Size and Value of the Iqṭāʿ in Egypt 564–741 A.H./1169–1341 A.D." In *Studies in the Economic History of the Middle East,* pp. 129–138. London, 1970.

RÖHRICHT, R. *Beiträge zur Geschichte der Kreuzzüge,* vol. 2. Berlin, 1874.

———. *Regesta regni Hierosolimitani (1097–1291).* Oeniponti, 1893.

———. "Die Rüstungen des Abendlandes zum dritten grossen Kreuzzüge." *Historische Zeitschrift* 34 (1875): 1–73.

———. Zur Geschichte der Kreuzzüge." *Neues Archiv der Gesellschaft fur ältere deutsche Geschichtskunde* 11 (1885): 571–579.

ROSEBAULT, CH. J. *Saladin Prince of Chivalry.* New York, 1930.

ROSENTHAL, FRANZ. *A History of Muslim Historiography.* Leiden, 1952.

ROUND, J.H. "The Saladin Tithe," *English Historical Review* 31 (1916): 447–450.

RUNCIMAN, STEVEN. *A History of the Crusades,* 3 vols. Cambridge, 1951–54.

SADEK, HASSAN. "Salah-El-Din's fort on Ras el-Gindi in Sinai." *Bulletin l'Institut d'Égypte* 2 (1920): 111–119.

ṢAFADĪ, AL-. *Al-Wāfi bi-al-wafayāt,* vol. 4. Damascus, 1959.

SAUNDERS, JOHN J. *Aspects of the Crusades.* Christchurch, New Zealand, 1962.

SCHAUBE, A. *Handelsgeschichte der romanischen Völker des Mittelmeergebiets bis zum Ende der Kreuzzüge.* Münich, 1906.

SCHLUMBERGER, G. *Campagnes du roi Amaury Ier en Égypte.* Paris, 1906.

SETTON, K. M., ed. *A History of the Crusades.* Philadelphia, 1958.

SHAYYĀL, GAMAL EL-DĪN EL-. *Aʿlām al-Iskandarīyah fī ʿaṣr al-Islām.* Cairo, 1965.

———. *Majmūʿat al-wathāʾiq al-fāṭimīyah.* Cairo, 1958.

SIBṬ IBN AL-JAWZĪ. *Mirʾat al-Zamān,* vol. 8, pt. 1. Hyderabad, 1951.

SIVAN, EMANUEL. "The Beginnings of the Faḍāʾil al-Quds Literature." *Israel Oriental Studies* 1 (1971): 263–271.

———. "Le caractère sacré de Jérusalem dans l'Islam aux XIIe–XIIIe siècles." *Studia Islamica* 27 (1967): 149–182.
———. "Notes sur la situation des chrétiens à l'époque ayyūbide." *Revue de l'Histoire des Religions* (1967): 117–130.
———. *L'Islam et la Croisade.* Paris, 1968.
SLAUGHTER, GERTRUDE. *Saladin (1138–1193).* New York, 1955.
SOBERNHEIM, M. "Saladin." S.v. in *The Encyclopaedia of Islam,* 1st ed., 4:84–89. Leiden: E. J. Brill, 1934.
STERN, S. M. "Petitions from the Ayyūbid Period." *Bulletin of the School of Oriental and African Studies* 27 (1964): 1–39.
TRITTON, ARTHUR S. "Sidelights on Muslim History." *Bulletin of the School of Oriental and African Studies* 21 (1958): 464–471.
USĀMAH IBN MUNQIDH. *Usāmah's memoirs entitled Kitāb al-Iʿtibār.* Edited by Philip K. Hitti. Princeton, 1930.
VATIKIOTIS, P. J. "The Rise of Extremist Sects and the Dissolution of the Fāṭimid Empire in Egypt." *Islamic Culture* 31 (1957): 17–26.
WAAS, A. *Geschichte der Kreuzzüge.* Freiburg, 1956.
WIERUSZOWSKI, H. "The Norman Kingdom of Sicily and the Crusades." In Robert Lee Wolff and Henry W. Hazard, eds., *A History of the Crusades,* 2:3–42. Philadelphia, 1962.
WIET, GASTON. "Al-ʿĀdid li-Dīn Allāh." S.v. in *The Encyclopaedia of Islam,* 2d ed., 1:196–197. Leiden, 1960.
———. "Les inscriptions de la Qalʿah Guindi." *Syria* 3 (1922): 58–65, 145–152.
———. "Les inscriptions de Saladin." *Syria* 3 (1922): 307–328.
———. *L'Égypte Arabe.* In Gabriel Hanotaux, *Histoire de la nation égyptienne,* vol. 4. Paris, 1937.
WOLFF, ROBERT LEE, BALDWIN, MARSHALL W., and HAZARD, HENRY W., eds. *A History of the Crusades,* 2 vols. Philadelphia, 1958–62.
YAQŪT AL-RŪMĪ. *Jacut's Geographisches Wörterbuch.* Edited by F. Wüstenfeld. Leipzig, 1866–73.

Index